Making the Market

Corporate capitalism was invented in nineteenth-century Britain; most of the market institutions that we take for granted today – limited companies, shares, stock markets, accountants, financial newspapers – were Victorian creations. So were the moral codes, the behavioural assumptions, the rules of thumb and the unspoken agreements that made this market structure work. This innovative study provides the first integrated analysis of the origin of these formative capitalist institutions, and reveals why they were conceived and how they were constructed. It explores the moral, economic and legal assumptions that supported this formal institutional structure, and which continue to shape the corporate economy of today. Tracing the institutional growth of the corporate economy in Victorian Britain and demonstrating that many of the perceived problems of modern capitalism – financial fraud, reckless speculation, excessive remuneration – have clear historical precedents, this is a major contribution to the economic history of modern Britain.

PAUL JOHNSON is Vice-Chancellor and President of La Trobe University, Melbourne. His previous publications include the three-volume *Cambridge Economic History of Modern Britain* (edited with Roderick Floud, 2004), *Old Age: From Antiquity to Postmodernity* (edited with Pat Thane, 1998) and *Twentieth-Century Britain: Economic, Social and Cultural Change* (1994).

Cambridge Studies in Economic History

Editorial Board

Cambridge Studies in Economic History comprises stimulating and accessible economic history which actively builds bridges to other disciplines. Books in the series will illuminate why the issues they address are important and interesting, place their findings in a comparative context, and relate their research to wider debates and controversies. The series will combine innovative and exciting new research by younger researchers with new approaches to major issues by senior scholars. It will publish distinguished work regardless of chronological period or geographical location

Titles in the series include:

ROBERT MILLWARD *Private and Public Enterprise in Europe: Energy, Telecommunications and Transport, 1830–1990*
S. D. SMITH *Slavery, Family and Gentry Capitalism in the British Atlantic: The World of the Lascelles, 1648–1834*
STEPHEN BROADBERRY *Market Services and the Productivity Race, 1850–2000: British Performance in International Perspective*
CHRISTINE MACLEOD *Heroes of Invention: Technology, Liberalism and British Identity, 1750–1914*
JOYCE BURNETTE *Gender, Work and Wages in Industrial Revolution Britain*
GERBEN BAKKER *Entertainment Industrialised: The Emergence of the International Film Industry, 1890–1940*
ANNE L. MURPHY *The Origins of English Financial Markets: Investment and Speculation before the South Sea Bubble*
NICHOLAS DRAPER *The Price of Emancipation: Slave-Ownership, Compensation and British Society at the End of Slavery*

Making the Market

Victorian Origins of Corporate Capitalism

Paul Johnson

La Trobe University, Melbourne

CAMBRIDGE
UNIVERSITY PRESS

CAMBRIDGE UNIVERSITY PRESS
Cambridge, New York, Melbourne, Madrid, Cape Town,
Singapore, São Paulo, Delhi, Mexico City

Cambridge University Press
The Edinburgh Building, Cambridge CB2 8RU, UK

Published in the United States of America by Cambridge University Press, New York

www.cambridge.org
Information on this title: www.cambridge.org/9781107679887

First published 2010
Reprinted 2011
First paperback edition 2013

A catalogue record for this publication is available from the British Library

Library of Congress Cataloguing in Publication data
Johnson, Paul.
Making the market : Victorian origins of corporate capitalism / Paul Johnson.
p. cm. – (Cambridge studies in economic history – second series)
ISBN 978-0-521-85783-3 (hardback)
1. Corporations–Great Britain–History–19th century. 2. Capitalism–Great
Britain–History–19th century. I. Title. II. Series.
HD2845.J64   2010
338.70941'09034–dc22   2009049665

ISBN 978-0-521-85783-3 Hardback
ISBN 978-1-107-67988-7 Paperback

For Susannah, Oriana and Orlando

Contents

Figures

Tables

Acknowledgements

I wish to thank the President and Fellows of the British Academy for the award of a research readership for 1997–9 which allowed me to commence the research for this book. During this period I enjoyed the benefits of a visiting fellowship at All Soul's College, Oxford, and an academic visitorship at Nuffield College, Oxford, and I wish to thank the Wardens and Fellows of both colleges for their generosity. Progress on the book then slowed as academic administration, first as head of the department of economic history, and then as deputy director of the London School of Economics, consumed the lion's share of my time. I am hugely indebted to my former colleagues and graduate students at the LSE who, over many years, have helped me explore the origins of corporate capitalism in Victorian Britain. I also wish to acknowledge the assistance of the many librarians – the unsung heroes of historical research – whose services I have drawn on throughout this project, particularly at the Bodleian Library, Oxford, the British Library, the LSE library and, latterly, at La Trobe University library. My move to the Vice-Chancellorship of La Trobe University in 2007 came close to scuttling this project – running an academic institution allows little space for engagement in academic activity. I could not have found the energy to finish this work without the encouragement, love and support of my wife, Susannah. It is to her, and to our two beautiful children, that I dedicate this book.

1 Mammon's cradle

> True, it must be owned, we for the present, with our Mammon-Gospel, have come to strange conclusions. We call it Society; and go about professing openly the totalest separation, isolation. Our life is not a mutual helpfulness; but rather, cloaked under due laws-of-war, named 'fair competition' and so forth, it is mutual hostility. We have profoundly forgotten everywhere that *Cash-payment* is not the sole relation of human beings; we think, nothing doubting, that it absolves and liquidates all engagements of man. 'My starving workers?' answers the rich mill-owner: 'Did I not hire them fairly in the market? Did I not pay them, to the last sixpence, the sum covenanted for? What have I to do with them more?' – Verily Mammon worship is a melancholy creed.
>
> Thomas Carlyle, *Past and Present* (1843)

When the citadels of capitalism started to quake and crumble in September 2008, the race began to find someone or something to blame. The venal investment bankers who put personal gain before financial prudence, the complacent regulators who ceded to markets their fundamental responsibilities, the conceited hedge-fund managers who thought they could diversify all risk to the nth degree and beyond, the reckless traders whose short selling corroded value and rendered fragile that which should be secure – these were the characters who populated the dystopia of global financial crisis. A new lexicon emerged – of sub-primes and naked short selling, of CDOs and CDSs, though few beyond the financial markets understood the nature of collateralised debt obligations or credit default swaps, or could tell whether short selling was demurely covered or impudently exposed.

As the quest for agency came up against a cacophony of denial – not me, not me – from bankers, brokers and broken Icelandic bankers, the market became increasingly anthropomorphised. The problem was not the various actors, either individually or collectively, but the market itself. The market was over-confident or depressed, the market was strong or weak, the market was ailing or recovering. But above all, the market was unpredictable. Like a two-year old with tantrums, the market could switch from beatific calmness to screaming fury in the blink of an eye. If the market chose to misbehave, there was little the responsible carers – the bankers, regulators, hedge-fund managers and traders – could do except avert their gaze, cover their ears and wait for a return to equanimity.

How did the market come to be so febrile, so precarious, so incapable of providing the transparency and efficiency that are supposed to be its hallmarks? Ever since the publication of Adam Smith's *Wealth of Nations* in 1776, the dominant idea in economics has been that welfare will be maximised when markets are free and competition is intense. In the nineteenth century the British Empire grew on the back of a free-trade doctrine; in the twentieth century the *Pax Americana* spread across the globe, carried by faith in the greenback, and a commitment to deregulation. Yet after more than two centuries in which economists have analysed market relationships and practitioners have developed sophisticated market instruments and strategies, the market has been revealed as a much less familiar or predictable entity than almost anyone had thought.

The capacity of markets to flip from stability to collapse in a matter of days, though unexpectedly cruel to modern eyes, was disarmingly familiar to people in Victorian Britain. The nineteenth century witnessed the creation of many of the key institutions of the modern market economy, and Victorian society bore the cost of experimentation and failure as different forms of capitalist organisation and activity staked their claim for market domination. The most important institution of the modern market – the joint-stock limited liability company – was a disputed, legally suspect and morally dubious organisational form at the beginning of Victoria's reign, yet by the 1880s it had become the primary form of business organisation in Britain. In 1801, when the London Stock Exchange was founded, it was widely viewed as a locus for morally indefensible gambling, but by the end of the nineteenth century it had become the hub of a global investment market.[1] The process of institutional innovation and development was far from orderly; many by-ways were pursued, many dead-ends encountered. The market institutions that existed at the end of the nineteenth century, and which continue to underpin the structures of modern capitalism, were the result of a specific set of historical conjunctures rather than the outcome of an orderly process of optimal institutional selection.

The institutional structure of corporate capitalism in the early twenty-first century reflects both the winnowing effects of competitive evolution over many decades, and the formative impact of those

---

[1] Ranald Michie, *The London Stock Exchange* (Oxford, 1999), 45.

commercial and political interests that became embedded in nineteenth century corporate legislation and practice. The historical legacy is profound, and the historical parallels striking. The hand-wringing that has accompanied the global financial crisis of 2008 would have been familiar to Victorians who lived through the 'Railway Mania' of 1845, or the credit crunch following the collapse of the finance house of Overend Gurney and Co. in 1866, or any one of the crises that punctuated the equilibrium of financial markets at least once a decade throughout the nineteenth century. Also familiar would have been the call for legislative intervention and tougher regulation to bring wayward market operators to heel and to prevent any future market frenzy. The historical experience is not encouraging. Each set of nineteenth-century market regulations produced new constraints but also a new array of opportunities for businessmen and financiers to develop innovative ways to operate and prosper. With unerring inevitability, innovation trumped regulation, and new ways of doing business promoted further rounds of boom and bust.

This book investigates the legislative, organisational and behavioural foundations of corporate capitalism which were laid in nineteenth-century Britain, and which continue to exercise a profound influence on the manner in which modern markets operate. Despite the huge analytical effort of many generations of economists and historians, the ways in which market structures were consciously constructed in Victorian Britain is only indistinctly glimpsed in the literature. As will be shown below, economists have tended to reify and simplify the market, assuming away many of the contestible and conditional characteristics of exchange, thereby creating an orderly analytical model out of what is, in reality, a complex web of competing economic, legal, political and moral claims. Historians have largely ignored the institutional processes by which market structures were created in nineteenth-century Britain, satisfied perhaps that a general commitment to minimal regulation and free trade was enough to underpin a century of economic growth. This lack of historical and economic understanding of how markets have been constructed results in surprise and fury when markets fail to produce orderly and anticipated results. In truth, we have been there before; the historical parallels are legion, and disconcertingly familiar.

M & M

They could have been brothers, perhaps even twins. In looks and speech, in origins and actions, they were almost as one. They were the most famous capitalists of their time, they rose from obscure beginnings to giddy heights of wealth and power, and when their business empires failed, the fall was calamitous. Even their names were similar, and similarly invented. Yet they lived – if that is the right word – a century apart, one in the mind's eye of an author, the other in the public gaze of the media. For, in a bizarre example of life imitating art, they were Augustus Melmotte, financier and railway promoter, the central character of Anthony Trollope's 1875 novel *The Way We Live Now*, and Robert Maxwell, multi-millionaire and media mogul, whose body was found floating in the Atlantic in November 1991.[2]

Melmotte was 'a large man with ... rough thick hair, with heavy eyebrows, and a wonderful look of power about his mouth and chin'.[3] Maxwell was much the same, but larger. Quite where Melmotte hailed from was never discovered, though he certainly had central European, and possibly Jewish, origins, perhaps not dissimilar to those of Jan Lodvik Hoch, the son of an agricultural labourer from the Ruthenian village of Slatina-Selo on the Czech-Bulgarian border. Whether Melmotte was a family name or an acquired moniker is unclear, but when Jan Hoch arrived in Liverpool in June 1940 as a 17-year-old Free Czech soldier he quickly decided to reinvent himself, first as Leslie du Maurier, and by 1944 as (Ian) Robert Maxwell.[4] They were both superb linguists, though Melmotte never quite lost a touch of his middle-European accent, which always undermined his claim to be a trueborn Englishman. Maxwell, on the other hand, morphed – in speech and demeanour – into an upper-middle-class English persona.

Perhaps there was some element in these personal histories of geographical, nominal and linguistic mutation that accounted for the domineering personalities and overpowering sense of self-belief that characterised these two great men. Descriptions of their behaviour are interchangeable:

[2] All details of Augustus Melmotte's life, and all direct quotations from Anthony Trollope, *The Way We Live Now* (London, 1875) are taken from the Penguin Classics edition published in 1994. Further references appear as *TWWLN*. Details of Robert Maxwell's life and business dealings are taken from critical biographies by Tom Bower, *Maxwell: The Outsider* (London, 1988), by Peter Thompson and Anthony Delano, *Maxwell: A Portrait of Power* (London, 1991), and from the despicably toadyish 'official' biography by Joe Haines, *Maxwell* (London, 1988). Additional details of the financial manoeuvres and misdemeanours which led to the final collapse of the Maxwell empire come from Tom Bower, *Maxwell: The Final Verdict* (London, 1995).
[3] *TWWLN*, 31.   [4] Haines, *Maxwell*, 73.

[He] intimidated visitors as much by his gestures as his words, his gargantuan performance humbling those physically and financially less well endowed. The theatricality, the egocentricity and the vanity of the man were unsurpassed.[5]

[He] was becoming greater and greater in every direction – mightier and mightier every day. He was learning to despise mere lords, and to feel that he might almost domineer over a duke.[6]

The immutable sense of self-worth of both Melmotte and Maxwell was sustained and reinforced by the ostentatious and idolatrous residences they established for themselves in the heart of London, in Holborn and in Grosvenor Square:

The atmosphere in the citadel of his empire ... was suffocatingly imperious. Polished, double doors led across marble floors into a high-ceilinged hall supported by brown marble Doric columns and lit by glass chandeliers. Beyond, the spectacle of a huge living area decked out with expensive mock-Renaissance tapestry covered furniture and with carpets patterned in a vast 'M' design cautioned any visitor who might be contemplating criticism or challenge.[7]

There was the house. There was the furniture. There were the carriages, the horses, the servants with the livery coats and powdered heads, and the servants with the black coats and unpowdered heads. There were the gems, and the presents, and all the nice things that money can buy.[8]

Their homes were theatres for extravagant performance where the worlds of royalty, aristocracy, diplomacy, politics, finance and commerce could sit in attendance and pay homage.

Yet neither man was content with the trappings of wealth gained from commercial activity; they both sought, and achieved, political position. Neither of them had a deep emotional or intellectual commitment to any particular party or political ideology. For them, politics was a way to get closer to the centre of power, rather than to advance a nobler cause. Maxwell appears to have dallied with the Conservative party before becoming a Labour party member and candidate for the constituency of Buckingham at the 1959 election.[9] Melmotte was courted by both Liberals and Tories to stand for the vacant parliamentary seat of Westminster, and finally deigned to offer his commercial expertise to the latter. As busy men of finance and commerce, they had little time for the quaint customs and manners of the House of Commons. Maxwell had been advised by his friend Richard Crossman to 'lie low for six months' before subjecting his parliamentary colleagues to his oratorical skills but patience was as much a Maxwellian trait as humility. Immediately after the Queen's speech which opened the new session

[5] Bower, *Maxwell: The Final Verdict*, 17.
[6] *TWWLN*, 267.   [7] Bower, *Maxwell: The Final Verdict*, 16.
[8] *TWWLN*, 33.   [9] *Ibid.*, 106.

of Parliament in 1964, Maxwell stood up and delivered an over-long peroration, thus becoming the first backbencher to address the new parliament, and the first new member to make a maiden speech.[10] It was as if he was acting out a script penned by Trollope. In the House of Commons of the 1870s 'it was probably not in the remembrance of any gentleman there that a member had got up to make a speech within two or three hours of his first entry into the House', but that did not deter Melmotte from delivering to the House his opinion on commercial affairs. The House was not appreciative, but nor was Melmotte of his reception: 'It seems to me to be a stupid sort of place.'[11] Richard Crossman's judgement might equally well apply to either performance: 'It was absolutely disastrous. There he was trying to bash his way to fame in the first twenty-four hours.'[12]

The political campaigns and the conspicuous consumption of both Melmotte and Maxwell were paid for from the proceeds of large and complex businesses. Complexity and opacity was an ever-present element – almost an organising principle – of their commercial ventures. They pushed the flexibility of accounting practices to the limit and beyond, and they linked their personal financial affairs to those of the public companies they headed in such obscure and multifarious ways that it was practically impossible to determine what was owned by whom and what was owed to whom. It took the receivers years to untangle the links between the public companies chaired by Maxwell and the more than 400 private companies with which they were associated.

Maxwell had laid snares for any auditor in pursuit of financial revelation. The cross-cutting ownership network of his private companies was baroque in structure, and positively rococo in terms of the profusion of near-identical names which he bestowed on these businesses and then incrementally amended. Blessed with a photographic memory, Maxwell had no need to commit the details of this spider's web to paper. For Melmotte also 'it was one of his gifts to remember with accuracy all money transactions, whether great or small, and to keep an account book in his head, which was always totted up and balanced with accuracy'.[13]

But where, exactly, did the wealth come from? Melmotte was a financier and company promoter, Maxwell a publisher, but they both had an extensive range of other business interests. Just how extensive was impossible to determine, because their private business empires were

---

[10] Bower, *Maxwell: The Outsider*, 100.   [11] *TWWLN*, 530, 532.
[12] Bower, *Maxwell: The Outsider*, 100.   [13] *TWWLN*, 404.

never exposed to public view or accountability. Thus the public perception of these empires might expand or contract as the public standing of their proprietor rose or fell. It was said of Melmotte that:

He was the head and front of the railway which was to regenerate Mexico. It was presumed that the contemplated line from ocean to ocean across British America would become fact in his hands. It was he who was to enter into terms with the Emperor of China for farming the tea-fields of that vast country. He was already in treaty with Russia for a railway from Moscow to Khiva. He had a fleet – or soon would have a fleet of emigrant ships – ready to carry every discontented Irishman out of Ireland ... It was known that he had already floated a company for laying down a submarine wire from Penzance ... round the Cape of Good Hope – so that, in the event of general wars, England need be dependent on no other country for its communication with India ... It may have been the case that some of these things were as yet only matters of conversation – speculations as to which Mr Melmotte's mind and imagination had been at work, rather than his pocket or even his credit; but they were all sufficiently matured to find their way into the public press.[14]

Maxwell, through his privately-owned publishing company, Pergamon Press, also had extensive dealings with Russia and other East European countries, a business which involved both serious scientific publishing and the production of extremely profitable and unreadable hagiographies of various communist political leaders. Maxwell's fluency in Russian, Hungarian, Czech and German, as well as French and Yiddish, eased his path into these East European and Soviet trades, as did connections he had made in Berlin in 1946 when, as a captain in the British army, he was involved in intelligence work. Rumours of an MI5/6 connection followed Maxwell to his grave.

Yet despite the grandeur and global outreach of their business ventures, there was always a shadow hanging over the names of Melmotte and Maxwell. Were they really credit-worthy? Could they really be trusted? With their wealth went rumour of how that wealth had been made. Melmotte apparently had made his money in France through company promotion – indeed it was said that he could 'make or mar any company by buying or selling stock, and could make money dear or cheap as he pleased.' Yet it was also said that he was 'regarded in Paris as the most gigantic swindler that had ever lived; that he had made that city too hot to hold him; that he had endeavoured to establish himself in Vienna, but had been warned away by the police'. According to Trollope's notes, Melmotte had been in prison in Hamburg, though as with so many other aspects of Melmotte's career, this point of detail

---

[14] *TWWLN*, 337–8.

remained unconfirmed.[15] What was apparent, however, was Melmotte's way of operating companies. He packed the board with ineffectual directors who were indebted to him, in awe of him, or content to remain passive in exchange for their remuneration, he modified board minutes to reflect his own wishes rather than the true course of discussion, and he raced through business to prevent proper consideration of commercial developments. In effect he ran the public companies of which he was chairman as extensions of his private financial affairs.[16]

The origins of Maxwell's fortune lay in book wholesaling. He was a born salesman, with a phenomenal ability to convince sceptical purchasers that they had a burning desire for whatever book, encyclopaedia, business, bond or share he happened to want to dispose of at the time. But, as with Melmotte, his career was littered with cases of financial irregularity. As early as 1954 he had been censured by the official receiver for trading as a book wholesaler while insolvent, but it was not until an investigation by the Department of Trade and Industry in 1971 that the manner and scale of his commercial impropriety was revealed. In 1969 he sold the scientific publisher Pergamon Press to a US company. Within weeks of the takeover the new owners claimed that Pergamon's accounts had been contrived to project high profits and conceal losses; that they were, in short, fraudulent.[17] The opaque management processes within the Maxwell corporate empire meant that no charges of wrongdoing could be laid against Robert Maxwell in person. Nevertheless, the DTI report on him was damning:

He is a man of great energy, drive and imagination, but unfortunately an apparent fixation as to his own abilities causes him to ignore the views of others if these are not compatible ... The concept of a Board being responsible for policy was alien to him ... We regret having to conclude that, notwithstanding Mr Maxwell's acknowledged abilities and energy, his is not in our opinion a person who can be relied upon to exercise proper stewardship of a publicly quoted company.[18]

Since so much was known, and so much more rumoured, about the financial probity of Melmotte and Maxwell, it seems scarcely credible that people would choose to invest resources in companies that they controlled. Yet they repeatedly managed to launder their commercial reputations through further speculative ventures which made money, and made profits for those who invested in them. When a potential investor, speaking to Melmotte's co-promoter of the South Central

[15] Richard Mullen, *Anthony Trollope: A Victorian and His World* (London, 1990), 558.
[16] *TWWLN*, 280–3.   [17] Thompson and Delano, *Maxwell*, 124.
[18] DTI report quoted in Bower, *Maxwell: The Final Verdict*, 21–2.

Pacific and Mexican Railway, noted that 'many people speak very badly of Mr Melmotte's honesty', he was told that 'There is always a want of charity when a man is successful.'[19] When the sobriquet 'the bouncing Czech' was applied to Robert Maxwell, he could respond by showing how, within two years of taking over the near-bankrupt British Printing Corporation in 1980, he had transformed it into a profitable and efficient enterprise which laid the foundation for his purchase of the Mirror newspaper group in 1984. In fact, so credulous or craven were City investors that in 1987 they provided £630 million to purchase a huge issue of shares in the (now slightly renamed) British Printing and Communication Corporation, which Maxwell used to embark on a spree of acquisitions in an attempt to construct a multi-billion-pound global media empire. The brokerage house of Alexanders, Laing and Cruickshank was well rewarded for placing such a huge rights issue.[20]

Yet Maxwell was still dogged by the damning DTI report, and needed to strengthen his personal credibility in commercial and financial circles, prior to his planned change of name of BPCC into Maxwell Communication Corporation. Who better to assist in this than the literary-minded Henry Poole, a partner in Alexanders, Laing and Cruickshank, who produced a glowing 48-page analysis of BPCC's business prospects entitled 'Unravelling the Melmotte Skein.' Poole argued that BPCC's stock was undervalued for a number of reasons, one of which was 'a feeling of unease, even hostility, towards the Group's chairman' which was akin to the sentiment surrounding Melmotte. Poole quoted from Trollope: 'But still there was a feeling of doubt and a consciousness that Melmotte, though a tower of strength, was thought by many to have been built upon the sands,' but went on to state that 'it is clear that in contrast to Mr Melmotte, Robert Maxwell has built on secure foundations'.[21]

Just four years after this encomium to commercial rectitude, Maxwell Communication Corporation had collapsed. In a desperate attempt to save his corporate empire from sinking in a quagmire of debt, Maxwell plundered hundreds of millions of pounds from the pension funds of the companies he owned and ran, using his sons Kevin and Ian to participate in and cover up the fraud. He died, possibly by his own hand, through falling off his yacht in seas near the Canary Islands. The foundations of his empire were revealed as being just as insubstantial as those of Augustus Melmotte who, as his money and credit ran out, first attempted to persuade his daughter to assign her property to him;

---

[19] *TWWLN*, 67.   [20] Bower, *Maxwell: The Outsider*, 344.
[21] Thompson and Delano, *Maxwell*, 31.

then, when this failed, forged her signature on title deeds; and, when this action was about to be made public, took his own life by drinking a dose of prussic acid.

This comparison of the careers and lives of Augustus Melmotte and Robert Maxwell is, at one level, nothing more than an exercise in coincidence between literature and life. They were both such exceptional characters that at first sight it seems impossible to infer anything from their personal histories about the general nature and tenor of the commercial worlds in which they operated. In fact it would be wrong to read *The Way We Live Now* as a work of social realism.[22] It was a satire on – or in the opinion of many contemporary reviewers, an overblown caricature of – the commercial morality of the 1870s. *The Times* was almost alone among the journals of the day in complimenting the novel for presenting 'only too faithful a portraiture' of modern manners.[23] On the other hand, Trollope had no shortage of models for the character of Melmotte. There was George Hudson (1800–71), the 'railway king', a banker turned railway promoter, MP for Sunderland, and reputedly one of the richest men in England until the revelation of accounting fraud in his railway empire led to the collapse of share prices and his financial and reputational ruin. There was 'Baron' Albert Grant (1830–99). Both the Grant and the Baron were acquired: he was born Albert Gottheimer, and received the title 'Baron' from Leopold 13th of Italy. Grant made a fortune for himself, and lost a fortune for shareholders, by promoting speculative mining companies. He served as an MP, but was ejected from his seat for electoral malpractice, spent much of his money building a palatial mansion in Kensington which was used only once, for a society ball, and he was eventually reduced to relative poverty after being forced by his creditors into bankruptcy. And there was John Sadleir (1814–56), solicitor, railway speculator, MP and director of the Tipperary Bank, from which he embezzled huge sums by forging title deeds as collateral for loans. He committed suicide on Hampstead Heath by drinking prussic acid.

These and other Victorian financiers and businessmen pushed their speculations to the limits of legality and beyond. For a time they reaped the rewards, and then they bore the personal costs of their deception and deceit. Yet no multi-millionaire businessman, whether a scion of moral rectitude or a duplicitous cheat, could operate a complex commercial

---

[22] J. A. Banks, 'The way they lived then: Anthony Trollope and the 1870s', *Victorian Studies*, 12 (1968), 177–200.
[23] N. John Hall, *Trollope: A Biography* (Oxford, 1991), 388.

empire on his own, no matter how good his memory and his mental accounts. They relied on a wide range of institutional and professional services provided by bankers and brokers, accountants and auditors, lawyers, agents and advisors. And they conducted their business operations within a framework formed by the commercial laws and customs of their time. It is these institutions and frameworks of the Victorian market economy that form the subject of this book.

Many of the key institutions of the modern market economy, or of capitalism itself, were created, or assumed their present form, during the nineteenth century: the joint-stock company; limited liability; formal systems of company registration, accounting and auditing; modern conceptions of freedom of contract; the process of bankruptcy and insolvency; the existence of a financial services industry, a financial press, and an active capital market for savings and investments – today these are taken for granted as necessary and important elements of modern society. No newspaper or TV news bulletin is complete without reportage of latest movements in the exchange rate or the stock market, though many readers and viewers may feel like Captain Cuttle from Charles Dickens' *Dombey and Son* who 'felt bound to read the quotations of the Funds every day, though he was unable to make out, on any principle of navigation, what the figures meant'.[24] Hand in hand with the formal institutions and the commercial and financial information that constitute the modern marketplace go the informal institutions that make this market structure work – the moral codes, the behavioural assumptions, the rules of thumb, the unspoken agreements. At the beginning of the nineteenth century these institutions and frameworks were largely unformed; they were at best embryonic, and in many cases entirely absent. By the 1890s they existed in palpably modern guise, and more than a century later they still disport their Victorian origins. In this sense, therefore, it would be true to say that modern capitalism has been built on a largely Victorian institutional foundation. Thus if we wish to seek structural – rather than personal – reasons for the events surrounding Maxwell Communication Corporation, or the sub-prime mortgage calamity, or the collapse in 2008 of most of the Wall Street investment banks, we need to delve into the origins of these formative capitalist institutions, to examine by whom and for what purpose they were conceived and constructed, and what moral, behavioural, economic, legal or other assumptions lie embedded within them.

[24] Charles Dickens, *Dombey and Son* (London, 1848), ch. 25.

It might be thought that the nineteenth-century foundations of modern capitalism have already been comprehensively studied and analysed by historians. The causes and course of the British 'industrial revolution', and the country's subsequent economic development, have been the focus of a huge outpouring of scholarly inquiry and analysis since Arnold Toynbee invented the term 'industrial revolution' in 1884. Economic historians have traced the growth of productive activity, income and wealth, business historians have mapped the scale and scope of commercial activity and organisation, labour historians have revealed the individual and collective impact of economic change on workers, political historians have chronicled the passage of key pieces of legislation, and historians of political economy have shown how the ideas of leading economists influenced, and simultaneously reflected, the development of economic institutions in the world in which they lived. Yet the legal and cultural institutions that constituted the markets of Victorian Britain have only a shadowy and piecemeal presence in this library of scholarship.

A primary explanation for this lacuna can be found in the intellectual history of these various sub-disciplines of history. It might be expected that economic historians would have most to say about the institutional foundations of the capitalist economy; it is, after all, a truism that economic history is the study of economic actors and their actions in past times. Furthermore, for the past two decades, and especially since 1993 when the economic historian Douglass C. North was joint recipient of the Nobel prize in economics for his research on economic and institutional change, economic history has claimed a particular facility for the analysis of institutional form and performance. In his Nobel lecture North stated that 'institutions form the incentive structure of a society, and the political and economic institutions, in consequence, are the underlying determinants of economic performance'.[25] Yet the dominant characteristic of research and writing in modern British economic history has not been the attention devoted to economic institutions, and even less so to an analysis of the economic impact of political institutions. Instead, the overwhelming focus has been on measurement – at the macro level, measurement of the size, structure and rate of growth of the economy, and at the micro level, measurement of the inputs, outputs and efficiency of production of individuals, firms and sectors.

A revealing record of evolving professional enthusiasms among economic historians can be traced through the content of three

---

[25] Douglass C. North – Nobel lecture 1993. nobelprize.org/nobel_prizes/economics/laureates/1993.

multi-author, multi-volume surveys of the state of research on modern British economic history published by Cambridge University Press in 1981, 1994 and 2004.[26] The 1981 compilation was written by economic historians 'who are experts in the use of models and of statistical methods in history', and whose models were drawn almost exclusively from the tool-box of neo-classical economics.[27] This reflected the confidence of 'new' economic historians that their application of theory and econometrics to historical data could provide answers to enduring questions about how the British (or, more accurately, English) economy came to lead the world along the path towards industrialisation, and why the precocious economic advantage of Britain in the nineteenth century was not sustained through the twentieth century. Neither in method nor in sentiment was there much room here for an analysis of the structure and purpose of the economic and political institutions which formed the framework within which the measured economic activity took place. The 1994 collection gave more space, and the 2004 volumes give more space still, to the role of government, the importance of the law, the effect of habit and custom rather than, or in addition to, rational calculus and profit maximisation, and this reflects developments over time in the specialised academic literature. Yet the prevailing viewpoint remains one in which 'the market' is an unproblematised and unproblematic locus for free exchange between economic actors; in which prices more often than not reflect the underlying allocation of factors of production; in which technology is the hand-maiden of change and economic growth.

One reason for the downplaying by economic historians of the role of institutions is that they tend to study the movement of deracinated economic aggregates; it requires some ingenuity and imagination to draw convincing links between the formal rules and informal norms of a society and, say, long-run trends in the labour share of national income, or in the investment ratio or total factor productivity of the economy. Business historians perhaps stand a better chance of building institutional analysis into their historical enquiry. This is partly because most modern businesses are self-evidently institutions which have a formal legal standing, and which depend for their economic existence on the general acceptance of the laws, norms and customs of trade

---

[26] Roderick Floud and Donald McCloskey (eds.), *The Economic History of Britain since 1700*, 2 vols. (Cambridge, 1981); Roderick Floud and Donald McCloskey (eds.), *The Economic History of Britain since 1700, 2nd Edition*, 3 vols. (Cambridge, 1994); Roderick Floud and Paul Johnson (eds.), *The Cambridge Economic History of Modern Britain*, 3 vols. (Cambridge, 2004).

[27] Floud and McCloskey, *Economic History of Britain since 1700*, 'Introduction'.

and exchange. It is also partly because some of the most convincing application of institutional economic theory has been in relation to the structure and function of the firm, and this has allowed historians to draw upon a well-developed set of models and methods for the analysis of business performance in the past.[28] Yet, as Naomi Lamoreaux has pointed out (with reference to the American literature), business historians all too often ignore the fact that firms are constructed, not natural, entities, and that the way they have been constructed reflects both conceptual processes and specific social and cultural contexts.[29] Historical accounts of British businesses seldom reflect on the way in which the social and cultural context created or constrained opportunities for corporate development. The legal rules and procedural customs of company formation and dissolution, of distribution of profit, of accounting and auditing, of winding-up and insolvency, and the economic, social and cultural influences that led businessmen to make choices between alternative combinations of these laws and customs, if given any attention at all, tend to be treated as an incidental, technical addendum to the main story of organisational efficiency and entrepreneurial success or failure.[30] A revealing indicator of the priorities of modern scholars lies in their analysis of business incorporation. Although it has been noted in a recent survey that the extensive adoption of joint stock status by British firms is 'one of the most important aspects of any discussion relating to late-nineteenth century business finance',[31] the two key works on this topic remain those written in 1936 and 1938.[32]

Labour historians have been equally reticent in engaging with those institutions and norms which framed market relationships in the Victorian period, and which set the parameters of the bargain between capital and labour. This is in part because few of the pioneer labour activists of Victorian Britain consciously challenged the unfolding

---

[28] Two particularly influential contributions are O. Williamson, *The Economic Institutions of Capitalism* (London, 1987), and R. R. Nelson and S. Winter, *An Evolutionary Theory of Economic Change* (Cambridge, MA, 1982).

[29] Naomi R. Lamoreaux, 'Constructing firms: partnerships and alternative contractual arrangements in early nineteenth century American business', *Business and Economic History*, 24 (1995), 43–71.

[30] A recent and rare exception to this generalisation is Tim Alborn, *Conceiving Companies: Joint-Stock Politics in Victorian England* (London, 1998).

[31] John F. Wilson, *British Business History, 1720–1994* (Manchester, 1995), 118.

[32] B. C. Hunt, *The Development of the Business Corporation in England, 1800–1867* (Cambridge, MA, 1936); J. B. Jefferys, Trends in Business Organisation in Great Britain since 1856. University of London PhD, 1938. The only significant modern contributions are P. L. Cottrell, *Industrial Finance, 1830–1914* (London, 1980), and James Taylor, *Creating Capitalism: Joint-Stock Enterprise in British Politics and Culture, 1800–1870* (Woodbridge, 2006).

contemporary conception of how and why markets functioned as they did. It is true that there was a Chartist critique of financial institutions: R.J. Richardson's 1841 'Exposure of the Banking and Funding System' presented the activity of the Bank of England, the tax system, and the national debt not as a neutral mechanism for managing public finances, but as a conspiracy to rob working men and impoverish the nation.[33] But this critique was no more entrenched or long-lasting than Chartism itself. The later Victorian labour movement offered little by way of a coherent ideological analysis of market organisation and of the market's institutional and cultural underpinning. There were clear pragmatic reasons for this. At a time when trade unions were strenuously seeking their own legal legitimation, they were not in a strong position to advance a comprehensive refutation of the legal legitimacy of corporate capitalism. This had changed somewhat by the early twentieth century as a more self-consciously socialist strand of trade unionism developed, but, like Owen the housepainter in Robert Tressell's *The Ragged Trousered Philanthropists*, critics of the institutional and legal foundations of capitalism remained in a minority.[34]

Like their Victorian trade union subjects, labour historians have tended to avoid an explicit analysis of the broad topography of Victorian market institutions. The historiography here owes much to the Webbs, in whose view the institutionalisation and incorporation within capitalist society of trade union activity was achieved at the price of submission to the ideological primacy of the bourgeoisie and the theoretical orthodoxy of political economy.[35] Historians taking their cue more from Gramsci than Marx might have been expected to probe the hegemonic structure of market institutions which support corporate capitalism. However, socialist historians in general have devoted far more effort to analysing and explaining the failure of working-class movements to fulfil their transformative potential than to accounting for the often seemingly effortless production and reproduction of the power and privilege of capital.

---

[33] R. J. Richardson, 'Exposure of the Banking and Funding System', *The English Chartist Circular: The Temperance Record for England and Wales* 1.23 (1841), 90–1. Cited in Mary Poovey, 'Writing about Finance in Victorian England: Disclosure and Secrecy in the Culture of Investment', *Victorian Studies*, 45 (2002), 17–41, at 23.

[34] Robert Tressell, *The Ragged Trousered Philanthropists* (London, 1965 [1914]).

[35] S. and B. Webb, *History of Trade Unionism* (London, 1898). See also E. J. Hobsbawm, *Labouring Men* (London, 1964), 316–43. For a countervailing interpretation, focussed on trade union attitudes to political economy, see R. V. Clements, 'British trade unions and popular political economy, 1850–1875', *Economic History Review*, 14 (1961–2), 93–104; E. F. Biagini, 'British Trade Unions and Popular Political Economy, 1860–1880', *Historical Journal*, 30 (1987), 811–40.

Political and administrative history offers an obvious route into the structure of markets and the working of market institutions. Whether the market transaction involved buying a loaf, renting a house, hiring a worker or building a railway, a successful outcome depended ultimately on agreement between the several parties of their rights and duties with respect to the contract, and of their options for redress if agreement could not be reached. Since the legal basis of these transactions resided in legislative enactments, and enforcement ultimately depended on agents of the state, parliament, politics and public administration were necessarily deeply implicated in the formation of the Victorian market. It has long been recognised that there was a Victorian 'revolution in government', in the sense that agents of the state, through parliament and increasingly through the various branches of the central and local civil service, undertook an increasing amount of investigation of and legislation about social, economic, political and moral activities. Commissioners and inspectors gathered information and opinion about an extremely wide array of subjects, and published it in a huge number of parliamentary reports – the 'blue books'. In parliament there was, from the 1830s, a rising trend of legislation on 'social' subjects as concerned reformers pressed their views about conditions of work, housing, health and nutrition. Yet the impact of this 'revolution in government' on the country is disputed.[36] For all the heat and light generated by public and private enquiries about the state of the nation, most Britons remained untouched and untroubled by the 'State', and most mid-Victorians believed theirs was a world of *laissez-faire* thought and behaviour. This was especially so with respect to economic affairs: there was considerable support for the Gladstonian belief that 'government' and 'economy' should be treated as separate entities in order to maintain fiscal rectitude and economic order.[37]

In a judgement on both the ideology and the practice of the age, Colin Matthew has suggested that 'no industrial economy can have existed in which the State played a smaller role than that of the United Kingdom in the 1860s'.[38] This comment begs the question of how the many formal and informal institutions of the Victorian market economy were created, established and embedded in thought and action. It closes off the possibility that the State was a key actor, whether consciously or

---

[36] O. MacDonagh, 'The Nineteenth Century Revolution in Government: A Reappraisal', *Historical Journal*, 1 (1958), 52–67; H. Parris, 'The Nineteenth Century Revolution in Government: A Reappraisal Reappraised', *Historical Journal*, 3 (1960), 17–37.

[37] K. T. Hoppen, *The Mid-Victorian Generation, 1846–1886* (Oxford, 1998), 118, 121.

[38] H. C. G. Matthew, *Gladstone 1809–1874* (Oxford, 1986), 169.

accidentally, in this process. One of the purposes of the chapters that follow is to challenge this widely held belief that the 'nightwatchman State' of Victorian Britain was content to allow the domestic economy to evolve naturally and with little or no governmental intervention or direction. The 'State' may not have had any formal plan for the way in which the market should develop, and perhaps should be seen as much as a pawn in the hands of various competing interests as a proactive creator of market infrastructures. But it would be wrong to think that the absence of direct state ownership or intervention in industry, finance and transportation signalled impotence or lack of interest. It is now widely recognised among economists and other social scientists that one of the most important economic functions of the State is to establish and monitor credible and effective systems of property rights, contract enforcement and corporate governance. In so far as this was achieved in Victorian Britain, the State was imbricated through all economic relationships.

A final route into the study of the market institutions of industrialising Britain might be by way of the history of political economy. Economists of the day – from Adam Smith in the 1770s to Alfred Marshall in the 1890s – drew inspiration from their personal reflections on contemporary economic activity, and attempted to integrate their economic philosophy with both empirical observation and policy prescription. This gives their writing a temporal specificity which has the potential to offer important insights into the structure and performance of markets in past times. Yet there are a number of reasons why the history of political economy can provide only limited access to an understanding of market activity. One limiting factor is the way in which the history of economic thought has been conceived by many authors as pursuit of the origin, development, refinement and ultimate refutation of a series of theoretical propositions. This approach to the history of economic thought – which is not unlike the 'black letter' tradition in legal history, in which the goal is to determine the historical and rational antecedents of modern legal doctrine – is unambiguously teleological. It maps out a pathway of intellectual improvement as archaic misconceptions and misreadings are incrementally challenged and replaced by more coherent, more modern, more rational propositions. Mark Blaug has described this epistemological stance as 'absolutist', in contrast to a 'relativist' approach which attempts to locate economic ideas within the specific socio-economic context in which they arose.[39] The absolutist

[39] M. Blaug, *Economic Theory in Retrospect* (London, 1964), 20–1.

approach has little to say about the development of market institutions for two reasons. First, by concentrating on the more abstract and theoretical elements of economic ideas – growth, value, distribution – it largely ignores the contemporary empirical observation contained in the writings of political economists. Second, economic science has, until very recently, treated markets as naturally occurring *loci* for the exchange of goods and services and thus part of the assumptive world of economic thought, rather than as phenomena with contested origins which require investigation in their own right.

The relativist or historicist approach to the history of economic ideas avoids the first of these problems by giving full weight to the personal, social and political environment in which each text was composed. However, in so far as political economists implicitly or explicitly accepted the proposition that markets are natural phenomena, a historicist reading of their economic texts will provide few insights into the way in which markets were constituted. Furthermore, as Donald Winch has noted, historicist readings need to be precise in their historical contextualisation to be convincing. He cautions, for example, against 'the substitution of the nineteenth for the eighteenth century as the relevant context within which Smith's writings should be viewed'.[40] On the other hand, many Victorians were perfectly content to use passages from Smith's *Wealth of Nations* in support of their economic enthusiasms, in the belief that his economic theory, or his empirical analysis, or both, had enduring applicability. We will return to the influence of political economy on Victorian conceptions of the market in subsequent chapters. For the moment it is sufficient to note that Adam Smith's somewhat casual reference to the 'higgling and bargaining of the market' as the mechanism by which value is determined, sidelined from economic discourse a more incisive discussion of how the market was constituted, and how it operated, until the publication of John Stuart Mill's *Principles of Political Economy* in 1848.[41]

The major sub-disciplines of history offer little by way of a comprehensive analysis of how Victorian markets were conceived and constructed, but that does not mean historians have nothing to contribute to the subject. As the following chapters will show, historical analysis of specific topics – for example workers' wages, company promotion, and financial journalism – though usually not addressed to the wider

---

[40] D. Winch, *Adam Smith's Politics* (Cambridge, 1978), 4.

[41] A. Smith, *An Inquiry into the Nature and Causes of the Wealth of Nations* [1776]. Glasgow Edition, edited by R.H. Campbell and A.S. Skinner (Oxford, 1976) [hereafter cited as Smith, *WoN*]. Book I, ch. 5, 49.

question of how the market was conceived and constructed in Victorian Britain, can nevertheless provide a great deal of highly relevant information. This is especially true of two specialised areas of historical enquiry, each of which has its own learned societies and journals, its own research conventions, and an institutional location outside most history departments. These specialised areas are the history of accounting, and the history of law.

Accounting historians are more likely to be based in university departments of accountancy, finance or management than in history departments, and likewise legal historians are more often than not found in law rather than history faculties. Location matters, because accountancy and law education in universities is focussed to some considerable extent on professional training, and historians located in these departments face strong pressures to integrate their research with that of their non-historian colleagues, rather than with historians in general. In consequence, much research in legal and accounting history is directed towards the internal interests of these two professions. For example, accounting historians have studied in some detail the nineteenth-century evolution of systems of accounting and auditing, and the shifting norms of company reporting and disclosure, but often with the primary purpose of revealing the complex and ambiguous origins of modern accounting conventions.[42] This is an essentially teleological project to map the course of professional development and improvement. In so far as the historical specificity of the Victorian period has been invoked to support these research objectives, it has typically been in relation to the over-arching explanatory context provided by the idea of the rise of *laissez-faire*.[43] Victorian ideas and ideology therefore may be seen to provide a framework within which specific professional development took place, but this relationship is conceived as being uni-directional, with the influence running from the general context to the specific technical or professional issue. There is, in the main, little sense that accounting and auditing systems might themselves be constitutive components of this historical context.[44]

---

[42] For example, J. R. Edwards, 'Companies, Corporations and Accounting Change, 1835–1933: A Comparative Study', *Accounting and Business Research*, 23 (1992), 59–73; A.C. Storrar and K.C. Pratt, 'Accountability v. privacy, 1844–1907: the coming of the private company', *Accounting, Business and Financial History*, 10 (2000), 259–91.

[43] S. Jones and M. Aiken, 'British companies legislation and social and political evolution during the nineteenth century', *British Accounting Review*, 27 (1995), 61–82; S. P. Walker, 'Laissez-faire, collectivism and companies legislation in nineteenth century Britain', *British Accounting Review*, 28 (1996), 305–324.

[44] For a rare but brief discussion of the constitutive power of accounting standards in the nineteenth century, see C. Gilmore and H. Willmott, 'Company law and

Much the same can be said of legal history. The dominant discourse throughout most of the twentieth century has been in the 'black letter' tradition, in which the law is conceived of as an internally coherent and unified body of rules derived from a small number of general principles. From this viewpoint, change in the law is best explained by reference to the intellectual development of an autonomous legal rationalism, as articulated through the decisions of judges.[45] There is little scope here for any significant interaction between the closed world of the law and any other economic, political, social or cultural influences. This rarefied position has been challenged by the 'law and society' strand of legal history scholarship which has produced a number of extremely important works, including Cornish and Clark's *Law and Society in England*, and Atiyah's *The Rise and Fall of Freedom of Contract*.[46] Both these books locate the development of law and legal practice within the context of the surrounding economic, political, social and intellectual climate, and both give prominence to Dicey's influential proposition that the mid-nineteenth century was dominated by an intellectual and emotional commitment to the principles of *laissez-faire*, a commitment which by the early twentieth century had been weakened, and in places undermined, by a new liberal collectivist philosophy.[47]

Writings in this 'law and society' tradition take history seriously, but in doing so they enforce epistemological closure. By 'taking' a context from history and historical scholarship, they reject the idea that the law is an autonomous and neutral set of rules. However, by viewing legal developments as a largely functional (if somewhat laggardly) response to economic, political and ideological change, they implicitly reject the idea that the law, and the infrastructure of legal institutions, has a power of agency which itself contributes to a framing of this context. A further development in legal history has come with the 'critical legal studies' movement which, while often accepting the functionality of legal change, views the legal system as a contested arena in which different groups compete for legitimation and for control over a nexus of economic, political and juridical power. Marxism, radicalism and

financial reporting: a sociological history of the UK experience', in M. Bromwich and A. Hopwood (eds.), *Accounting and the Law* (London, 1992), 159–190.

[45] D. Sugarman, 'A hatred of disorder: legal science, liberalism and imperialism', in P. Fitzpatrick (ed.), *Dangerous Supplements: Resistance and Renewal in Jurisprudence* (London, 1991), 34–67.

[46] W. R. Cornish and G. de N. Clark, *Law and Society in England, 1750–1950* (London, 1989); P. S. Atiyah, *The Rise and Fall of Freedom of Contract* (Oxford, 1979).

[47] A. V. Dicey, *Lectures on the Relation between Law and Public Opinion in England During the Nineteenth Century* (London, 1905).

early post-modernist ideas – drawing heavily of Foucault's conception of power relationships – have all influenced this strand of legal history, but it has had surprisingly little impact on the way in which other historians view law and the legal system.[48] Despite the anticipation in 1984 by David Sugarman and Gerry Rubin that scholarship was moving 'Towards a New History of Law and Material Society in England, 1750–1914', progress so far has been limited, and that which has occurred is due in large measure to the work of scholars based outside the UK.[49] Ron Harris has recently noted that the last fifty years of research in economic history and in legal history appears to be a sorry tale of failed communication and missed opportunities.[50] And, from a slightly different disciplinary perspective, Margot Finn has lamented that scholars of Victorian law, literature and history 'too often navigate shared waters only to pass silently at a measured distance, like three ships sailing into the night'.[51]

Much of the work of legal and accounting historians is directly relevant to students of economic, political, social and cultural history, but institutional separation and different discursive and analytical traditions have served to diminish what could and should have been a fruitful dialogue. This book makes extensive use of the work of these and other historians who, from their own intellectual perspectives, and following their own enthusiasms, have begun to open up the history of market institutions in Victorian Britain. What follows, therefore, is in part an exercise in synthesis, in part an essay in interpretation, and in part a speculation about how Victorian market institutions were fashioned, and in some cases re-fashioned, by contemporaries.

[48] For a review of the impact of critical legal studies on legal history see Robert Gordon, 'Critical legal histories', *Stanford Law Review*, 36 (1984), 57–125. For a brief account of Foucault's conceptualisation of law and legal institutions see Gerald Turkel, 'Michel Foucault: Law, power, knowledge', *Journal of Law and Society*, 17 (1990), 170–193.

[49] David Sugarman and G.R. Rubin, 'Towards a new history of law and material society in England, 1750–1914, in G.R. Rubin and David Sugarman (eds.), *Law, Economy and Society, 1750–1914: Essays in the History of English Law* (Abingdon, 1984) 1–123. Three major studies of the relationship between law and material society in England over this period have been published since the mid-1990s: R.W. Kostal, *Law and English Railway Capitalism, 1825–1875* (Oxford, 1994); Ron Harris, *Industrializing English Law: Entrepreneurship and Business Organization 1720–1844* (Cambridge, 2000); Robert J. Steinfeld, *Coercion, Contract, and Free Labor in the Nineteenth Century* (Cambridge, 2001). These authors are based, respectively, in the USA, Israel, and Canada.

[50] Ron Harris, 'The encounters of economic history and legal history', *Law and History Review*, 21 (2003), 297–346.

[51] M. Finn, 'Victorian law, literature and history: three ships passing in the night', *Journal of Victorian Culture*, 7 (2002), 134–46, at 134.

In undertaking this synthesis, interpretation and speculation I have faced a number of practical and conceptual problems. At a practical level I have had to decide how to unravel the role of institutions, laws and customs in the making of the Victorian market economy. On the one hand, the ubiquity of market exchange makes the subject almost boundless. On the other hand, the fact that most market activity occurred without any explicit comment on or challenge to the prevailing norms, values and institutions of the day makes the subject strangely elusive. There were, of course, a number of specialised markets with their own formal rules of membership – the Stock Exchange, for example. However, there were no rules of membership for that broader 'market' of Victorian Britain in which the economic exchanges of daily life took place, other than an ability to find someone else willing to enter into trade. Thus there are no tidy sets of institutional archives to which the historian can turn when seeking to explore this past behaviour, no neatly ordered records that can provide a chronology and a lexicography of the Victorian market. Furthermore, in so far as the market embraced not just formal organisations but also internalised norms of behaviour, it existed as much in the mindset and imagination of individuals as in explicit rules and organisational structures.

How Victorians thought about the market is therefore an important part of my story, and in the following chapters I will spend some time examining the explicit statements and implicit beliefs about market exchange emanating from groups of political economists, politicians, lawyers, clerics, businessmen, journalists and workers. But I do not take for granted any direct or consistent relationship between beliefs and actions. What people said about the market, and how they believed it operated, did not necessarily condition or reflect their behaviour as market actors. Judges may have espoused a doctrine of legal neutrality and equality before the law, yet in their judgments they may have acted consistently in favour of some groups rather than others. Businessmen may have been staunch opponents of combination and collective action by workers, but active associationists among themselves. Politicians may have argued about the higher principles of market relationships, but may also have legislated in favour of their privileged self-interest. My ambition, therefore, is to provide an introduction not just to what Victorians thought about the operation of the market, but also to how Victorian markets actually worked, and to highlight any apparent dissonance between thought and action.

In working towards this ambition I have chosen to make use of a number of stories about the way in which different market institutions operated in Victorian England. Narrative accounts of particular events are, by their very nature, not representative of the broader totality of market experience. In fact they are doubly non-representative. Not only are the idiosyncrasies of any particular story unlikely to be repeated in any other case, but the very fact that accounts of these idiosyncrasies have been bequeathed to the twenty-first century historian tells us that in their essence or in their mode of production they were sufficiently unusual to be retained for posterity. Very often these stories received contemporary attention and achieved longevity because they revealed a disturbing tension between the way the market institutions actually operated and the way in which many people thought they *should* operate. This tension between beliefs and action in specific cases can provide insights into the nature of the Victorian market that cannot be seen, or which can be glimpsed only indistinctly, from broader, more representative, and more conventional accounts of market activity. This does not mean that I eschew completely the economic historian's more usual use of representative data, of quantification, and of statistical inference. In looking at processes of wage determination in the labour market, and at the choice of institutional form in the insurance market, I make use of some of these more social scientific ways of analysing evidence. However even here I use the representative data to question, rather than to confirm, both Victorian and modern-day assumptions about the operation of market institutions.

Before moving on to the substantive historical analysis, I will briefly provide a sketch of what I take to be the essence of these Victorian and modern assumptions about the market that I wish to question. Adam Smith's well-known description of the natural human propensity 'to truck, barter and exchange', and his extended critique of mercantilist institutions that interfered with the free working of the 'invisible hand' of the market, had a profound impact on Victorian conceptions of how the economy works, and continue to influence modern heuristics about market activity. Smith's insights were developed and used by nineteenth-century political economists – particularly Mill and Marshall – and they motivated, directly or indirectly, an extensive discussion among Victorian writers and thinkers about the character of market activity. Much of this discussion was characterised by a belief about the inherent ordering of economic activity that springs directly from the 'natural law' tradition of Smith's own writing. Smith's invocation of economic exchange as natural, and his condemnation of monopolies and other mercantilist institutions as impediments to efficient market operation, led him – and more so many of his more casual nineteenth-century disciples – implicitly to view also the *locus* of the exchange activity, the market, as natural, and thus as unworthy of extended analysis or discussion.

The Wealth of Nations presents a sustained discussion of 'the market' only in one five-page chapter entitled 'That the division of labour is limited by the extent of the market', and the focus of Smith's attention here is the process of division of labour, not the institutional form of market relationships. Elsewhere in the *Wealth of Nations* 'the market' appears as a reified locus for exchange in which buyers and sellers seek each other out and higgle to establish the price at which they will trade. This abstract conception of 'the market' was bequeathed by Smith to practically all nineteenth-century political economists. In 1890 Alfred Marshall approvingly quoted Cournot's 1838 statement that 'Economists understand by the term *Market*, not any particular market place in which things are bought and sold, but the whole of any region in which buyers and sellers are in such free intercourse with one another that the prices of the same goods tend to equality easily and quickly.'[52]

For economists from Smith to Marshall, the 'market' was characterised not by its specific form, but rather by an absence of institutional structures, and it was this very absence – of monopolies, bounties, apprenticeships, and all other restrictions – that created the environment for beneficent exchange. It is revealing, though not surprising, that in Joseph Schumpeter's massive *History of Economic Analysis* (1954) there is no section on 'the market' in its 1200 pages, nor any entry on 'the market' in its thirty-page index.[53] The market was, and to a large extent continues to be, part of the assumptive world of formal economics, a natural and neutral trading-ground in which competitive pressure produces efficiency, and evolution permits the efficient to dominate, and eventually supplant, the inefficient.

In fact, the market of Victorian England was a deliberate, and thus far from natural, construction of ideas, conventions, beliefs, customs, laws and enforcement mechanisms. As with any construction, the building blocks were assembled not randomly, but in accordance with the design of key actors, and thus reflected both their interests and their political power. Once assembled, contemporaries found sometimes unexpected ways of making use of the market construct, and also made efforts to remodel parts of the edifice better to accommodate their changing needs. Thus the Victorian market was neither natural, nor neutral, nor, I will suggest, was it in any conventional sense socially or economically optimal.

---

[52] Alfred Marshall, *Principles of Economics* (London, 1890), Book V, ch. 1, s. 2.
[53] Bernard Barber, 'Absolutization of the market: some notes on how we got from here to there' in Gerald Dworkin, Gordon Bermant and Peter G. Brown (eds.), *Markets and Morals* (Washington, DC, 1977), 15–31.

To be sure, the market did not always appear immediately to produce optimal outcomes. In the Railway Mania of 1845 the market seemed to be over-active, producing too many speculative companies that could not deliver on their promises of profit and growth. In the Irish potato famine of 1846 the market seemed to be under-active, incapable of meeting the needs of starving Irish peasants even though ample food stocks were available in England. Yet within a few years of these events the self-correcting forces of supply and demand had re-established order: within six years of the Railway Mania the revenue of the railway network had trebled; by 1850 living standards in Ireland were rising, in part because more than a million Irish men, women and children had emigrated in search of a better life.[54]

There was also recognition in mid-century that in a small number of very specific circumstances the market might systematically fail to produce the optimal outcomes that so often featured in the texts of political economy. John Stuart Mill explicitly identified three aspects of what today's economists call 'market failure' – the cases of natural monopoly, public goods and externalities. The issue of natural monopoly was already widely (if usually informally) recognised, and had received explicit attention from government.[55] Mill noted that in most circumstances gas and water companies, and owners of roads, canals and railways, were monopolists, because it was not economically feasible for multiple suppliers to construct exactly parallel networks. Water and gas were essential commodities and 'the charge made for services which cannot be dispensed with, is, in substance, quite as much compulsory taxation as if imposed by law'. In these circumstances, he thought, provision could best be undertaken by municipal authorities, with expenses covered by a local rate (property tax). Transport services, particularly those provided for by canal and railway companies which had been granted a monopoly over a particular route by act of parliament, should be regulated by government, or the companies should be granted their operating right for a fixed term only, after which the business should revert to the state.[56]

Here Mill was both drawing on, and systematising, contemporary activity. As early as 1843 Mancunians were receiving their gas from a sole municipal supplier, and from 1847 Liverpudlians received their

---

[54] For a more extensive discussion see Paul Johnson, 'Market discipline' in P. Mandler (ed.), *Liberty and Authority in Victorian England* (Oxford, 2006), 203–23.

[55] James Foreman-Peck and Robert Millward, *Public and Private Ownership of British Industry, 1820–1990* (Oxford, 1994), ch. 2.

[56] John Stuart Mill, *Principles of Political Economy* (London, 1848), Book V, ch. 11, s. 11.

water from a similar source.[57] And in 1844 Gladstone, who is generally (and correctly) thought of as an advocate of free trade and minimal state involvement in the economy introduced, in the Railway Act, one of the most interventionist pieces of economic legislation of Victoria's reign. He argued that the normally beneficent outcomes of competition did not apply to railways; rather than reduce prices, competition would produce 'a mere multiplication of monopoly'.[58] To remedy this wrong, his Railway Act introduced compulsory price reductions on lines that consistently returned a profit of over ten per cent, compulsory workmen's trains at low fares, and, most radical of all, the option for the government to purchase any new railway line after twenty-one years of operation. Mill provided a consistent rationale for these market interventions by local and national government, thereby setting clear and logical limits to these deviations from the competitive ideal.

The same was true in the second area of market failure – the provision of public goods. These were cases 'in which important public services are to be performed, while yet there is no individual specially interested in performing them, nor would any adequate remuneration naturally or spontaneously attend their performance'. Scientific exploration and research, and the provision of lighthouses and navigational aids were two examples he gave in which government already intervened by means of subsidy and direct provision, but he was clear that such instances were strictly circumscribed, and that, 'before making the work their own, governments ought always to consider if there be any rational probability of its being done on what is called the voluntary principle'.[59]

Mill's third case of market failure related to what modern economists call externalities, when 'acts done by individuals, though intended solely for their own benefit, involve consequences extending indefinitely beyond them, to interests of the nation or of posterity, for which society in its collective capacity is alone able, and alone bound, to provide'.[60] Mill had in mind the positive benefits for 'the future and permanent interests of civilisation itself' that could emerge from a process of colonisation, but equally important, and equally deserving of public intervention, were the negative effects of individual action where one person, through infection or pollution, might adversely affect the health of a multitude.

---

[57] John Sheldrake, *Municipal Socialism* (Aldershot, 1989), ch. 3.

[58] *House of Commons Debates* [hereafter *HCDeb*] 5 February 1844, col. 237.

[59] Mill, *Principles*, Book V, ch. 11, s. 15. On lighthouses see James Taylor, 'Private property, public interest, and the role of the state in nineteenth-century Britain: the case of the lighthouses', *Historical Journal*, 44 (2001), 749–771.

[60] Mill, *Principles*, Book V, ch. 11, s. 14.

Mill's analysis of market failures provided powerful intellectual support for the idea that harmonious equilibrium was the natural state of any market. He constructed a clear set of principles which identified deviation from this equilibrium, and which justified limited national or local government intervention – as facilitator, regulator or provider.[61] In all other cases, he argued, the market provided, regulated and facilitated far more effectively than could the government.

Not all economic commentators agreed. In the first half of the nineteenth century a robust critique of market relations developed among High Tories. They used organicist metaphors of the economy as a palsied body to counter classical economic ideas of a natural, self-regulating market system.[62] And they argued that the manifest ailments and weaknesses of the economic system could be ameliorated only through positive action by the government to secure an unreformed, propertied constitution that would provide the foundation for a stable economic system.[63] This challenge to classical political economy, which found its most significant and contentious manifestation in the debate over agricultural protection and free trade in the 1840s, finally lost out within the Tory party to a liberal Peelite approach to tariff reform. This did not mean that conceptual and practical alternatives to free market capitalism disappeared. Christian political economists, romantic conservatives, working-class radicals, co-operators and socialists continued to develop their own distinct critiques of *laissez-faire* ideas and policies.[64] Despite these several oppositional strands of economic ideology, the idea of a generally beneficent free market continued to dominate public discourse in the mid-Victorian period.

The following chapters interrogate the belief that the Victorian market was free, fair, neutral and natural. The first section of this book looks at how individuals – mainly working-class individuals – interacted with Victorian market institutions. Chapter 2 examines the institutions of contract and recovery of debt which daily impinged on everyone who bought, sold or borrowed. These institutions operated via a

---

[61] Similar ideas about the merits of regulation were presented, using very different terminology, by Edwin Chadwick, who suggested that regulated monopolies should be sold to the highest bidder. See his 'Results of different principles of legislation and administration in Europe, of competition for the field, as compared with competition within the field, of service', *Journal of the Statistical Society of London*, 22 (1859), 381–420.

[62] David Eastwood, 'Tories and Markets, 1800–1850', in Mark Bevir and Frank Trentmann (eds.), *Markets in Historical Contexts* (Cambridge, 2004), 70–89.

[63] For a detailed discussion of Tory economic ideas see Anna Gambles, *Protection and Politics: Conservative Economic Discourse, 1815–1852* (Woodbridge, 1999).

[64] G. R. Searle, *Morality and the Market in Victorian Britain* (Oxford, 1998).

far-from-neutral legal system in a manner which seemed to construct and reinforce contemporary attitudes about class-specific social and economic morality. Chapter 3 turns to the labour market, and shows that it was characterised as much by coercion and entrenched customary practices as by the free play of supply and demand. Together these two chapters reveal Victorian conceptions of freedom of contract and free labour to have been idealistic, rather than realistic, representations of market structures.

The next section shifts attention from individuals to institutions, particularly the corporate institutions that came to exemplify the most innovative and dynamic elements of Victorian capitalism. Over the course of the nineteenth century the business corporation evolved from being an unusual and slightly disreputable form of economic enterprise to being the core institution of the market economy. This section examines the key nineteenth-century developments in company law that established the parameters of corporate capitalism, many of which still exist today. Chapter 4 investigates the concept of general incorporation, and the economic and moral implications of the division of absolute ownership rights between directors and shareholders which was ushered in by the rise of the joint-stock company. Chapter 5 explores the debate around, and the consequences of, the introduction of limited liability in 1855–6. Chapter 6 then challenges the general argument that incorporation was adopted because it was conducive to economic efficiency through a case study of different organisational forms in the Victorian insurance market. This shows that joint-stock companies did not dominate other forms of insurance company organisation in terms of their internal efficiency or the price and quality of the service they sold, and that organisational choice is better conceived of in terms of the somewhat accidental advantage gained by particular interest groups than in terms of an optimal selection procedure operated by the disinterested competitive pressures of the market.

The final section of the book deals with information, and the way in which individuals and institutions exchanged, shared, and sometimes concealed information in order to engage in market activity. Particular attention is paid to the working of the stock market which had acquired, by the end of the nineteenth century, the iconographic status it still retains as the weathervane of corporate capitalism. Chapter 7 examines the process of company promotion and the institutions developed to float new companies on the Stock Exchange, and explores the extent to which this supposedly competitive market was inherently subject to degrees of internal influence and control.

The book concludes with some reflections on the extent to which the market institutions of the nineteenth century endure in the structures and practices of market activity in the twenty-first century. Although history does not repeat itself, and there are no simple lessons to be drawn from the past, many modern institutions have deep historical roots, and thus previous decisions and past events have a clear legacy in the way in which they help to structure modern market behaviour. The similarity between a fictional Melmotte and a factual Maxwell is coincidental, but the similarity between the market institutions that facilitated or encouraged such extraordinary behaviour is not. If different decisions had been taken by Victorian jurists and legislators, the modern economy might operate in some quite different and distinct ways. My parting shot is to suggest that a number of nineteenth-century institutional dead-ends might, if re-opened and applied to the twenty-first-century market economy, improve the performance and strengthen the moral reputation of modern capitalism.

Part I

Individuals

> Two greyhounds, in running down the same hare, have sometimes
> the appearance of acting in some sort of concert ... This, however,
> is not the effect of any contract, but of the accidental concurrence
> of their passions in the same object at that particular time. Nobody
> ever saw a dog make a fair and deliberate exchange of one bone for
> another with another dog ... But man has almost constant occasion
> for the help of his brethren, and it is in vain for him to expect it
> from their benevolence only. He will be more likely to prevail if he
> can interest their self-love in his favour, and shew them that it is
> for their own advantage to do for him what he requires of them.
> Whoever offers to another a bargain of any kind, proposes to do
> this. Give me that which I want, and you shall have this which you
> want, is the meaning of every such offer; and it is in this manner
> that we obtain from one another the far greater part of those good
> offices which we stand in need of.[1]
>
> Adam Smith, *Wealth of Nations* (1776)

Adam Smith recognised the capacity to 'make a fair and deliberate
exchange' as a unique characteristic of the human species: 'It is common
to all men, and to be found in no other race of animals, which seem to
know neither this nor any other species of contracts.'[2] For Smith it was
this essential human drive of one individual to exchange with another
that motivated all the beneficent outcomes of the economic system –
production, employment, consumption and wealth. Individuals were
not adjuncts to an economic system, but rather the fundamental units,
the building blocks, of that system. Where individual capacity freely to
strike a bargain was constrained – for instance by the laws governing
apprenticeship – the outcomes were sub-optimal, not just for the individuals concerned, but for the entire economic system. The principle
of individual freedom of action was, therefore, fundamental to Smith's
conception of how the economic system should work.

The overwhelming majority of nineteenth-century political
economists enthusiastically embraced Smith's belief that individual
self-interest, expressed through market interactions, was the mainspring of the economy, and that obstacles to the free expression of this

---

[1] Smith, *WoN*, Book I, ch.2.   [2] *Ibid.*

self-interest in the market should be eradicated. This set of views came loosely to be described by the term '*laissez-faire*' – meaning the removal of legislative obstacles to free exchange and the retreat of government from regulation or interference in the economy. Political and public opinion was never as consistent in support of *laissez-faire* as were the voices of political economy, but the repeal of the Corn Laws in 1846 marked the broad ascendancy of the doctrine. Thereafter, the idea that individuals should be free to transact with whomsoever they wished became part of the assumptive world of educated Victorians – something so obvious it required little or no comment. It also came to be widely viewed as not simply a description of how market relationships *should* be structured, but how they *were* structured. Old restrictions controlling the prices of goods and labour were repealed or allowed to lapse, as were those regulating apprenticeship, and the principle for any market transaction became *caveat emptor* – or buyer beware. Everyone entered the market as an equal, trying to better themselves through a process of fair and equal exchange.

This characterisation of the market economy was in many respects accurate. Every day millions of Victorians carried out transactions to buy their daily bread, to sell their daily toil, and they did so in an environment in which they had choice, for they were in company with a multitude of other buyers and sellers. Yet a close look at market processes shows that individuals were often constrained by laws, regulations and customs which established very different capacities to make 'fair and deliberate exchange'. These constraints were seldom recognised by contemporaries, and when they were recognised they were often explained or justified by reference not to economic principles but to moral values. The chapters in this section examine the nature and extent of these constraints in two areas of economic activity – recovery of debt, and sale of labour – which were key determinants of individual and household welfare. Many Victorians, particularly manual workers who had neither the financial nor the social resources to argue and defend their economic position before the law, found that their freedom to make fair and deliberate exchange in the market was severely circumscribed.

2   Contracts, debts and debtors

Contracts are to the market what oil is to an engine. Without contracts, markets would be frozen institutions, structures without actions, frameworks without content. Contracts allow parties in a market to interact, to put their 'propensity to truck, barter and exchange' into effect.[1] As the legal theorist Charles Addison noted in 1845:

There is scarcely an individual of any property or station in the country who does not every week, nor any mercantile man who does not every day of the week, nay every hour of the day, contract obligations, or acquire the rights, of a buyer or seller, or a hirer or letter to hire, of a debtor or creditor, of a borrower or lender, of a depositor or depositary, of a commissioner or employer, of a receiver or agent, or trustee.[2]

The nature of contract law, and its development over the course of the nineteenth century was, therefore, a vital element in the making of the Victorian market economy. As economic exchange multiplied in scale, extent and character with the development of Britain's domestic and colonial economies, so the law of contract – which by 1700 was already a large and complex body of doctrine and precedent – continued to expand and adapt to new circumstances, in part through legislation, in part through judicial interpretation.[3] Many of the details of this expansion and adaptation have been traced by Patrick Atiyah.[4] This chapter looks briefly at Atiyah's argument about the rise of the common law concept of freedom of contract in the nineteenth century, and goes on to examine some of the contemporary assumptions about Victorian markets that lay embedded within the judicial process of enforcement of promises to pay.

[1] Smith, *WoN*, Book I, ch. 2: 25.
[2] C. G. Addison, *A Treatise on the Law of Contracts and Parties to Actions ex contractu* (London, 1845), iii.
[3] A. W. B. Simpson, *A History of the Common Law of Contract* (Oxford, 1975).
[4] Atiyah, *Rise and Fall*.

Of course, resort to law occurs only when the expectations of at least one of the contracting parties are unmet. Thus the view of market exchange derived from legal records is necessarily unrepresentative of the huge number of transactions daily undertaken, to the apparent mutual satisfaction of all parties, in Victorian Britain. Furthermore, formal contracts that are enforceable at law were (and are) only one element of the contractual nexus of a commercial society. Many of the 'contracts' made between buyers and sellers were informal, based upon verbal agreements, customary conventions, and the like. Compliance was often achieved more because of the desire of both parties to undertake repeat transactions, or to avoid the reputational cost associated with contract default, than because of the threat of legal sanction.[5] In other cases, parties to a contract consciously attempted to avoid the costs of resort to law by agreeing to resolve disputes by arbitration, a procedure that saw considerable extension of use from the middle of the nineteenth century.[6] Yet legal records are crucial to an understanding of nineteenth-century contracts; by revealing those activities in which mutual understandings of the market were contested, they allow the historian to look behind the consensual façade of market mentalities.

The formative cases in nineteenth-century contract law – the ones that appeared in contemporary legal treatises, and which live on in the modern canon of contract law precedent – invariably involved relatively wealthy individual or corporate litigants, as well as contentious or complex points of law.[7] Resort to law, especially to the higher courts of record, was time-consuming and expensive, both before and after the Judicature Acts (1873–5) introduced rationalisation of court structure and competence by unifying common law and equitable jurisdictions.[8] But the principles and practice of contract law had enormous and direct impact on working-class individuals – and in far greater numbers than for middle-class litigants – through legal action for recovery of debt in the lower civil courts. Although contract law may have been made by learned judges sitting in Exchequer or Queen's Bench courts, it was

[5] Steve Hedley, 'The "needs of commercial litigants" in nineteenth and twentieth century contract law', *Legal History*, 18 (1997), 85–95.
[6] Robert B. Ferguson, 'The adjudication of commercial disputes and the legal system in modern England', *British Journal of Law and Society*, 7 (1980), 141–57.
[7] See, for example, Sir William R. Anson, *Principles of the English Law of Contract* (Oxford, 1879); Frederick Pollock, *Principles of Contract at Law and in Equity* (London, 1876); A. W. B. Simpson, *Leading Cases in the Common Law* (Oxford, 1995).
[8] A. H. Manchester, *A Modern Legal History of England and Wales* (London, 1980), 144–50.

overwhelmingly dispensed – to hundreds of thousands of working-class men (and a small number of women) each year – by commissioners in the courts of requests, and, after 1846, by judges and registrars in the County Courts.[9] The pages that follow will contrast the treatment of working-class debtors with that of their middle-class counterparts who, though often equally impecunious, were subject to different, usually more lenient, laws and legal processes. The neutral and disinterested market mechanism of classical political economy, when refracted through the lens of legal process, is seen to be biased and structured by class interests. It was not that the law corrupted the natural and elegant objectivity of the market, for the market cannot exist without law. Contract law, and the judicial structure that advanced and enforced that law, were constitutive elements of the Victorian market economy, something that few political economists acknowledged when they expounded their theories of economic activity.

It has already been noted that explicit analyses of markets and market mechanisms were few and far between in the writings of the classical political economists. It should come as no surprise, therefore, to find that the same is true of their attitude to the contractual basis of market exchange. Adam Smith noted that, once division of labour has occurred, 'every man thus lives by exchanging, or becomes in some measure a merchant',[10] but he said almost nothing about how this process of exchange was to be effected or managed. He identified a clear duty of government to protect citizens from oppression, force and fraud, and to administer a system of justice to that end, but his discussion of contract enforcement was confined to one paragraph, the primary focus of which was the overlapping and competitive jurisdictions of the Kings's Bench, Exchequer and Chancery courts.[11]

Smith never gave direct attention to the way in which law might be justly administered in the myriad market transactions of the 1770s, and for the next seven decades political economists followed and developed the somewhat abstract rationale of market exchange proposed by Smith. They continued to criticise legislative restrictions on contract deriving from mercantilist laws relating to monopolies, tariffs and bounties, but they did not construct a positive conception of the enforcement of

---

[9] Debts could be recovered only from those who had the legal authority to contract them in the first place. Thus, throughout the nineteenth century minors aged under 21 were not legally liable for their debts, nor were married women prior to the passage of the Married Women's Property Act in 1882. For details see Margot Finn, *The Character of Credit: Personal Debt in English Culture, 1740–1914* (Cambridge, 2003), 264–73.

[10] Smith, *WoN*, Book I, ch. 4, 37.   [11] *Ibid.*, Book V, ch. 1, part II, 720–1.

contracts: they seemed to regard as 'natural' that which patently was not. As Atiyah has noted, to political economists, freedom of contract meant that all contracts should be *permitted*, whereas to lawyers freedom of contract means not only that exchange should be permitted, but also that executory contracts (i.e. contracts for future performance) should be *enforced*.[12]

It was not until the publications of Mill's *Principles of Political Economy* in 1848 that the issue of contract enforcement was addressed directly as part of a discussion on the legitimate role of the state:

The legitimacy is conceded of repressing violence or treachery; but under which of these heads are we to place the obligation on people to perform their contracts? Non-performance does not necessarily imply fraud; the person who entered into the contract may have sincerely intended to fulfil it; and the term fraud, which can scarcely admit of being extended even to cases of voluntary breach of contract when no deception was practised, is certainly not appropriate when the omission to perform is a case of negligence. Is it not part of the duty of governments to enforce contracts? Here the doctrine of non-interference would no doubt be stretched a little, and it would be said that enforcing contracts is not regulating the affairs of individuals as the pleasure of government but giving effect to their own expressed desire. Let us acquiesce in this enlargement of the restrictive theory, and take it for what it is worth. But governments do not limit their concern with contracts to a simple enforcement. They take upon themselves to determine what contracts are fit to be enforced ... But when once it is admitted that there are any engagements which for reasons of expediency the law ought not to enforce, the same question is necessarily opened with respect to all engagements. Whether, for example, the law should enforce a contract to labour, when the wages are too low or the hours of work too severe; whether it should enforce a contract by which a person binds himself to remain for more than a very limited period, in the service of a given individual; whether a contract of marriage, entered into for life, should continue to be enforced against the deliberate will of the persons, or of either person, who entered into it. Every question which can possibly arise as to the policy of contracts, and of the relations which they establish among human beings, is a question for the legislator.[13]

This brief and inconclusive passage constitutes 'virtually the sum total of classical discussion on the actual enforcement of contracts'.[14] Far from the issue being opened up by Mill, it became further entombed in the abstract reasoning of economic writers. The 'marginalist revolution' of Marshall, Jevons and Pigou took the academic study of economic relations down a formalist pathway in Britain, and further away

[12] Atiyah, *Rise and Fall*, 330.   [13] Mill, *Principles*, Book V, Ch. 1, s. 2.
[14] Atiyah, *Rise and Fall*, 331.

from any explicit analysis of the institutional and legal context in which economic exchange occurred.[15]

Contracts and their enforcement remained part of the assumptive world of economists, both classical and marginalist, but they received direct and explicit attention from a number of legal theorists, notably Sir Henry Maine and Albert Venn Dicey. Maine's *Ancient Law*, published in 1861, was a legal tract for the times, a best-seller that combined anthropology, history, political economy, psychology and jurisprudence in an accessible reflection on the difference between past and present societies.[16] In Maine's reading of history, ancient societies (and many of the less-developed colonial societies of the time) were characterised by status hierarchies. In such societies the law fixed a man's position at birth by reference to his position within a particular caste, clan or family, and thus the citizen had no legal standing other than that acquired through his status within such groups. Modern society, by contrast, 'is mainly distinguished from that of preceding generations by the largeness of the sphere which is occupied in it by Contract'.[17] The widespread influence of Maine's ideas of an historical and progressive transition from status to contract thus brought to prominence the idea that a formal, ordered, predictable law of contract was central to, and a necessary part of, modern society.[18] Indeed, Maine explicitly saw this transition from status to contract as a precursor to the development of an individualistic political economy in which men were left 'to settle rules of conduct for themselves with a liberty never allowed to them till recently'.[19] However, even in Maine's writing, contract exists within an ideal set of economic relationships rather than as a practical set of laws and procedures; for Maine, as for Smith, enforcement of contracts was implicitly assumed to be automatic and uncontentious.

---

[15] In the United States, on the other hand, institutional economists such as Clark, Commons and Veblen carried the debate on the nature of the market well into the twentieth century. See M. Rutherford, 'Predatory practices or reasonable values? American Institutionalists on the nature of market transactions', in Neil De Marchi and Mary Morgan (eds.), *Higgling: Transactors and their Markets in the History of Economics*. Annual Supplement to Volume 26 of *History of Political Economy* (Durham, NC, 1994), 253–75.

[16] R. C. J. Cocks, *Sir Henry Maine* (Cambridge, 1988).

[17] Sir Henry Maine, *Ancient Law* (London, 1861), 304.

[18] For example, Herbert Spencer directly appropriated this idea of a transition from status to contract as being fundamental to the rise of modern commercial society: 'for in proportion as contracts are unhindered and the performance of them certain, the growth is great and the social life active'. Herbert Spencer, *The Man versus The State* (Indianapolis, 1981 [1884]), 155.

[19] Maine, *Ancient Law*, 305.

Dicey's lectures on *Law and Public Opinion in England* (1905) placed great emphasis on the rise of the concept of freedom of contract in nineteenth-century England – for him it was one of the principal practical manifestations of the rise of *laissez-faire*. The utilitarian foundation of freedom of contract he concisely summarised as follows:

Once admit that A, B, or C can each, as a rule, judge more correctly than can anyone else of his own interest, and the conclusion naturally follows that, in the absence of force or fraud, A and B ought to be allowed to bind themselves to one another by any agreement which they each choose to make – i.e., which in the view of each of them promotes his own interest, or, in other words, is conducive to his own happiness.[20]

Dicey dwelt at some length on whether and how the limits to contractual freedom should be fixed, and whether an individual should be permitted to enter into a contract which deprives him of the very freedom of which it is assumed to be the exercise.[21] However, his purpose in pursuing this line was to comment (adversely) on the liberty of individuals to combine together in an association which may itself limit the future actions of its originators or of other parties. Although he devoted some of his lectures to tracing the legislative pathway whereby individualistic freedom of contract was constrained and in places overturned by a collectivist impulse in the latter part of the nineteenth century, he said almost nothing about the practical operation of contract in the Victorian market, or of enforcement of contract in Victorian courts.

Dicey's significance, therefore, derives not from the specifics of what he wrote about the operation of contract law, but for the way that he represented a strong (though not universal) line of thought among Victorian lawyers, who had received their legal education before the political economy of Smith, Ricardo and Mill had been seriously challenged. As Atiyah has noted:

It seems quite likely that Dicey was, by 1905, reflecting a strong legal professional tradition. English lawyers are, as a rule, very conservative people, not merely in their current beliefs, but also in their beliefs about history. Moreover, when lawyers encounter ideas from outside the law, as they do from time to time, they tend to absorb a smattering of these ideas which may then remain with them, handed down from generation to generation until they emerge from their narrow professional interests to look at the same problem perhaps fifty or a hundred years later ... There is some evidence to support the view that the ideas based on laissez-faire principles may well have had more influence on the judges and on judge-made law than on any other organ of the state.[22]

---

[20] Dicey, *Lectures*, 149.   [21] *Ibid.*, 152.
[22] Atiyah, *Rise and Fall*, 235.

Evidence for this proposition can be found in the rulings of many senior judges, especially after the Judicature Acts merged the separate but parallel courts of Common Law and Equity into a unified judicial system. The common law was responsible for determining disputes in relation to ownership and agreements – those which might normally come under the umbrella term of contractual relations. Equity, on the other hand, evolved from principles of good conscience and natural justice and, as administered by the Court of Chancery, had the power to override the common law where a difference arose. Procedures and doctrines in common law and equity were quite different, sometimes in conflict, and there was no clear line of demarcation. By the mid-nineteenth century Chancery had become a byword for expense and delay, and was memorably and mercilessly pilloried by Dickens in *Bleak House* (1853) in the fictional but all too plausible case of *Jarndyce* v. *Jarndyce*. Once Common Law and Equity jurisdictions were merged, equity took a back seat and a common law view of the sanctity of freedom of contract was seen to prevail. As the Master of the Rolls, Sir George Jessel, affirmed in a case in 1875, 'if there is one thing more than another which public policy requires, it is that men of full age and competent understanding shall have the utmost liberty of contracting and that their contracts, when entered into freely and voluntarily, shall be held sacred and shall be enforced by courts of justice'.[23] Jessel viewed it as a matter of 'paramount public policy' that judges 'are not lightly to interfere with the freedom of contract'.[24]

There is some dispute among legal scholars about the pace and timing of this doctrinal move towards freedom of contract. Atiyah sees this as an abrupt, almost wholly nineteenth-century development, coincident with the rise of an individualistic political economy, and reactive to the functional needs of a newly industrialising society. Others dispute the precipitous development of doctrine and practice implied by Atiyah's account.[25] In fact, Cornish and Clark have speculated, and Finn has demonstrated, that there was a prolonged tension, from at least the 1750s to the 1850s, between an increasingly individualist view of contracts and bargains within the common law, and an enduringly

---

[23] Jessel M. R. in *Printing and Numerical Registering Co. v. Sampson.* (1875) 19 LR Eq 462, quoted in Manchester, *Legal History*, 262.

[24] *Ibid.*, quoted in Anson, *Principles*, 175.

[25] Simpson, *Common Law*; J. L. Barton, 'The enforcement of hard bargains', *Law Quarterly Review*, 103 (1987); Michael Lobban, *The Common Law and English Jurisprudence, 1760–1850* (Oxford, 1991), ch. 9; David Lieberman, 'Contract before "Freedom of contract"', in Harry N. Scheiber (ed.), *The State and Freedom of Contract* (Stanford, 1998), 89–121.

protective jurisdiction of conscience within the parallel legal structure of equity.[26] This tension was played out most overtly in the lower
courts, particularly in relation to recovery of debts, and it was a tension
which exposed the moral assumptions which underpinned Victorian
conceptions of contract and the rule of law. It is to these tensions and
assumptions we now turn.

The curious case of the crier who cried

A loud voice and a commanding presence – these are necessary attributes
for a town crier. Thomas Turner had both, and this made him a natural
choice for the post of part-time town crier of Wallingford in Berkshire.
Turner's high-volume broadcasting of local announcements earned him
some scarce and valued pennies to add to the meagre wages he earned
from agricultural labouring. But his physical presence and voice also
cost him dear: he made the mistake of crying out the wrong words, at
the wrong time, in the wrong place, to the wrong person.

In 1853 the granddaughter of the eminent English jurist, Sir William
Blackstone, entered in her local County Court a plaint for damages
against Thomas Turner. Following an earlier County Court case
between Turner's brother, William, and Miss Blackstone over the rent
of allotment gardens, in which the case against Blackstone had been dismissed, Thomas Turner was alleged to have assaulted Miss Blackstone
as she left the court. According to the plaintiff, Turner 'thrust both his
clenched fists' at her over the shoulder of another man, 'and struck at
me three or four times close to my face. He did not touch me but was
very close … He also made use of some very opprobrious expressions
unfit for any woman to hear. He said "D – your b – eyes you have
robbed and swindled me of £30".'[27]

The initial reason for the resort to legal process by William Turner,
and common to the great majority of cases pursued through the new
County Courts established in 1846, was an alleged contractual debt.
Indeed, the legislation establishing this County Court system, which
rapidly came to dominate all other civil courts in terms of the volume
of business conducted, was entitled 'An Act for the more easy Recovery
of Small Debts and Demands in England'.[28] However, these courts also
had jurisdiction in actions founded on tort for damages up to the value
of £50, and it was on this basis that Miss Blackstone brought her case

---

[26] Cornish and Clark, *Law and Society*, 200–26; Finn, *Character of Credit*.
[27] *Berkshire Chronicle*, 16 July 1853.   [28] 9 and 10 Vict. c. 95.

for damages against Thomas Turner. This case of *Blackstone* v. *Turner* is of significance for reasons other than the juridical ancestry of the plaintiff, because it illustrates some of the biases of court procedure and sentencing policy in these lowly civil courts.

Thomas Turner 'conscientiously, strongly and firmly' denied that the alleged offence of constructive assault had been committed, though he agreed his language had been unguarded. Blackstone called forth her maid, her land surveyor, a butcher and a labourer as witnesses to the assault; Turner called a hotelier, two painters, a boot maker and the boot-maker's daughter (who also happened to be, respectively, his brother-in-law and niece), all of whom attested to the fact that they had not seen Turner raise his fists. Judge J. B. Parry, QC, had no doubt about Turner's guilt, since in his view 'if every person in that court had been called and said they did not see the defendant strike the plaintiff, it could not have countervailed the evidence of unimpeached witnesses'.[29]

This unequivocal verdict stood at odds with the evidence. Miss Blackstone had initially attempted a criminal action against Turner, and had taken out a summons for him to appear before the magistrates, but had been forced to abandon that course.[30] This may have been because of the flimsy nature of the case; one anonymous Wallingford JP noted in a letter to the *County Courts Chronicle* that there had been 'a great discrepancy of the evidence produced, and several credible witnesses swore positively that no assault had been committed'.[31] But it may have been due to personal animosity among members of the Wallingford bench. Miss Blackstone's brother, William Seymour Blackstone, with whom she co-resided at Howberry House, had been a magistrate since the early 1830s, but in 1852 had been accused by one of his fellow magistrates of perjury.[32] Quite why Judge Parry took such a one-sided view of the conflicting evidence is unclear, but the social pressures for him to do so must have been great. In addition to Miss Blackstone's brother being a local magistrate, he was also the Deputy Lieutenant for Berkshire, had been the Conservative MP for Wallingford for the twenty years from 1832, the family had the patronage of the Anglican living at Wallingford,[33] and according to Dod's *Electoral Facts* in 1853, 'the territorial and personal influence of Mr Blackstone and his family' remained considerable.[34]

---

[29] *Berkshire Chronicle*, 16 July 1853.   [30] *Ibid.*
[31] *County Courts Chronicle* (hereafter *CCC*) Sept. 1853, 120.
[32] *The Times*, 11 June 1852, 7.
[33] M. Stenton, *Who's Who of British Members of Parliament: Volume I, 1832–1885* (Hassocks, 1976), 36.
[34] C. R. Dod, *Electoral Facts from 1832 to 1853* (London, 1853), 323.

We see in this verdict a clear favouring of the word of a person of standing above that of a labourer. This is perhaps not surprising; similar social biases in the evaluation of witnesses and the assessment of evidence were endemic within both the criminal and civil law in eighteenth-century England, and continued to be a powerful force in the shaping of the Victorian criminal justice system.[35] What is more revealing here is the nature of the sentence passed and the way it was enforced by this minor civil court. Judge Parry awarded damages at the maximum sum of £50, plus full costs, to Miss Blackstone, and quite exceptionally ordered immediate execution of this award – that is, immediate payment. Turner could not pay, and so his personal possessions were seized by the court bailiff; at sale they realised just £3 3s. Turner was then ordered by the court to pay off his debt at the rate of 6s. per month, which, in the words of the trade journal, the *County Courts Chronicle*, had the effect of 'alienating a considerable proportion of his weekly earnings for seventeen years prospectively, and subjecting him, in default of payment, to repeated monthly imprisonments during the whole of his future life'.[36] Turner defaulted on the first instalment, and in November he again appeared before Judge Parry, now owing £63 12s. 9d., a result of additional court charges.

In the previous month Turner had earned an average of 14s. 8d. per week, on which he attempted to maintain his wife and five dependent children aged between 18 months and 15 years. He had spent his savings of over £6 on legal expenses, and since the seizure of his goods the family had no possessions other than clothing and basic household goods. Nevertheless Judge Parry concluded that Turner had had the means to pay his instalment, and had wilfully refused to do so. Turner was sent to Abingdon Gaol for thirty days for deliberate non-payment of a debt; his wife and family sought relief in the local workhouse. When William Church, 'a respectable tradesman of the town' rose in court with an offer to pay the instalment on behalf of Turner, he was 'ordered by the judge to sit down and remain silent'.[37]

The evident vindictiveness of Judge Parry's decision inspired the 'leading inhabitants and tradesmen' of Wallingford to send a deputation

---

[35] For the eighteenth century, see Douglas Hay, 'Property, authority and the criminal law', in Douglas Hay *et al.*, *Albion's Fatal Tree* (Harmondsworth, 1977); E. P. Thompson, *Whigs and Hunters* (London 1975); Joanna Innes, 'Prisons for the poor: English Bridewells, 1555–1800', in Francis Snyder and Douglas Hay (eds.), *Labour, Law and Crime* (London, 1987), 42–122. For the nineteenth century, see Carolyn A. Conley, *The Unwritten Law: Criminal Justice in Victorian Kent* (New York, 1991).

[36] *CCC*, January 1854, 4.   [37] *Berkshire Chronicle*, 19 November 1853.

of protest, led by the mayor, to the Home Secretary, Lord Palmerston. They were perhaps mindful of the commonly held principles of justice before the law that had been so eloquently identified by Miss Blackstone's grandfather, in his *Commentaries on the Laws of England* (1765), as a characteristic of every freeborn Englishman's liberty:

> Of great importance to the public is the preservation of this personal liberty: for if once it were left in the power of any, the highest, magistrate to imprison arbitrarily whomsoever he or his officers thought proper (as it is in France daily practiced by the crown) there would soon be an end to all other rights and immunities.[38]

With similar reasoning the good citizens of Wallingford argued that, regardless of the merits of the verdict in the case of *Blackstone* v. *Turner*, the sentence was unjust in principle:

> People of England with all their boasted privileges, could never live in a state of security if upon any trivial breach of the law, they might be subjected to fines amounting to more than the whole of their property, or, in default of payment, to imprisonment during the whole of their lives.[39]

Palmerston was reported to have taken a *prima facie* view that the case was one of great 'hardship and cruelty'[40], perhaps because of his own considerable experience of being hounded through the courts by his creditors.[41] But Palmerston's personal views were of no consequence; as the *County Courts Chronicle* noted, this was 'a wrong without a remedy'.[42] The judge had acted strictly within the law, there was no right of appeal from the County Court to a higher court, the Secretary of State had no power to interfere with the orders of a judge, and the Royal prerogative did not extend to custody under civil process.[43] Thomas Turner had received a sentence of virtual 'life long imprisonment for himself, and hopeless poverty for his family' because of non-payment of a debt incurred through an alleged minor verbal abuse of a middle-class

---

[38] Sir William Blackstone, *Commentaries on the Laws of England* (Oxford, 1865–9), book 1, chapter 1, 131. The quotation is taken from the online version of the first edition at: www.yale.edu/lawweb/avalon/blackstone/blacksto.htm.

[39] *Berkshire Chronicle*, 17 Dec. 1853.   [40] *Ibid.*

[41] Between 1811 and 1841 Palmerston was sued by creditors on twenty separate occasions. In eighteen cases judgement and full costs were awarded against him, in one case he settled out of court. Dennis Judd, *Palmerston* (London, 1975), 27; Kenneth Bourne, *Palmerston: The Early Years 1784–1841* (London, 1982), 256.

[42] *CCC*, January 1854, 4.

[43] Patrick Polden, 'Judicial Selkirks: the County Court judges and the press, 1847–80', in Christopher W. Brooks and Michael Lobban (eds.), *Communities and Courts in Britain 1150–1900* (London, 1997), 245–62. Some County Court judges became notorious for their erratic behaviour, but there was little sanction that could be applied to them unless they committed breaches of the law.

woman. The only way Turner could escape this fate was through voluntary internal exile to a court district presided over by a judge less vindictive than Parry, since a judgment summons could be issued only from a court of the district within which the defendant resided or carried on business.[44]

The case of Thomas Turner was exceptional in its detail, and also in its final resolution – as we shall see, Turner was ultimately able to exact some sweet revenge. However, the imprisonment of small debtors by County Court judges was common, both before and after the 1869 Act 'for the Abolition of Imprisonment for Debt'.[45] Meanwhile, large-scale debtors – or at least those who had both the financial status and the presence of mind to petition for bankruptcy – could avoid the double jeopardy faced by Turner of a creditor imposing a substantial claim on his future income, and threatening imprisonment in the case of non-payment. Bankruptcy was intended to facilitate a rational distribution of assets to creditors, not saddle the debtor with long-term liabilities. By the 1870s the nature and extent of this legal discrimination was widely recognised. It was not just the radical political economist Leone Levi who was noting the 'incongruity, if not injustice' in this system;[46] a leading article in *The Times* concluded that 'the law is really unfair and unequal. Under an appearance of justice to all classes, it presses hardly on some'.[47]

The differential treatment of what, almost oxymoronically, might be called 'rich' and 'poor' debtors, appears to be at odds with both contemporary and modern interpretations of the rise of contract law in Victorian England. In his *Treatise on the Law of Contracts* (1845) Charles Addison argued that 'the law of contracts may justly indeed be said to be a universal law adapted to all times and races, and all places and circumstances, being founded upon those great and fundamental principles of right and wrong deduced from natural reason which are immutable and eternal'.[48] More recently Atiyah has suggested that 'the period 1770–1870 saw the emergence of general principles of contract law closely associated with the development of the free market and the ideals of the political economists'.[49]

[44] *Ibid.*   [45] 32 & 33 Vict., c.62.
[46] L. Levi, 'On the Abolition of Imprisonment for Debt', *Law Magazine and Review*, 3 (1847), 598.
[47] *The Times*, 27 December 1879, reprinted in *County and Borough Prisons: Correspondence in the 'Times'*, (London, 1880), 6.
[48] Addison, *Treatise*, v.   [49] Atiyah, *Rise and Fall*, 398.

While general principles may characterise some elements of contract law in Victorian England, they do not seem to apply to the legal relationship between creditors and debtors. Despite three official enquiries into the working of the County Courts and the imprisonment of small debtors between 1873 and 1909[50], there was no move towards universalism in the law regulating the recovery of debts in the Victorian and Edwardian period. As well as suffering their poverty, the poor had to suffer an overtly prejudicial class bias in one of the two areas of contract law that had direct and repeated bearing upon their lives. As we will see in the next chapter, similar bias characterised the law regulating labour contracts.

Why was it that small debtors received disproportionately harsh treatment as compared with bankrupts? Why were legal theory and legal practice so consistently and enduringly at odds with each other? There are four possible explanations for this discriminatory treatment: differences in the legislative basis of the separate debt recovery systems relating to bankruptcy and small debts, differences in their practical procedures, differences in the economic circumstances of the debtors, and differences in their social status. But before analysing the causes of this social structuring of contract enforcement it is necessary to outline the development of the law relating to small debts and bankruptcy in Victorian England.

In 1846 a comprehensive system of County Courts was established to supersede the idiosyncratic network of local courts through which civil actions for low value had hitherto been conducted.[51] The County Courts had jurisdiction where the debt, damage, or demand claimed did not exceed £20, a limit raised to £50 in 1850 and to £100 in 1905.[52] This definition of 'small' was relative. In the 1850s few manual workers, even skilled artisans, could have earned more than £1 per week, a figure that may have doubled by the turn of the century,[53] so debts equal to a year's wage income could be pursued through these courts. In practice the sums owing were generally much less. Throughout the period 1847–1914 over 98 per cent of cases were for sums of less than £20, with an average amount owing of around £3,[54] and many claims

<hr />

[50] *Select Committee on Imprisonment for Debt*, PP 1873 XV; *House of Lords Select Committee on the Debtors Act* PP 1893–4 (HL) IX; *Select Committee on Debtors (Imprisonment)* PP 1909 VII.

[51] H. W. Arthurs, '"Without the Law": Courts of Local and Special Jurisdiction in Nineteenth Century England', *Journal of Legal History*, 5 (1984), 130–49.

[52] Sir Thomas Snagge, *The Evolution of the County Court* (London, 1904), 14.

[53] C. H. Feinstein, 'New estimates of average earnings in the United Kingdom, 1880–1913', *Economic History Review*, 43 (1990), 595–632.

[54] Aggregate statistics of court business are derived from the returns of the County Courts, published annually in the Judicial Statistics volume of the Parliamentary

were for less than the equivalent of a week's wages. Court records from both London and an industrial area of north-east England for 1910–11 show that half of all small debt cases were for sums owing of less than £1, and a quarter were for less than 10 shillings.[55]

The County Court system was an immediate success, at least in terms of the amount of business conducted. In the first quinquennium the yearly average number of cases was 433,000, and by 1904 over 1.4 million plaints for recovery of debt were initiated in these courts. This may, in part, have reflected the accessibility of the courts. Despite their name, the County Courts were not organised by administrative county, but instead the country was mapped out into 60 circuits encompassing over 500 court towns, chosen according to the Registrar General of Population's enumeration districts.[56] Court towns within each circuit had an average range of jurisdiction of seven miles, which was considered a reasonable distance for a plaintiff or defendant to walk in order to attend a hearing.[57] Accessibility to the due process of law was a necessary requirement for an effective system of contract law, and in this sense at least, County Courts represented one element of a more general Benthamite process of legal rationalisation.

The local courts system that the County Courts replaced was chaotic. The extensive credit networks which underpinned the expansion of commercial activity in seventeenth- and eighteenth-century England had created a demand for low-cost resolution of contractual disputes.[58] In response, many towns petitioned parliament for the establishment of a local 'court of conscience' or 'court of requests' which could determine claims for recovery of small debts on the basis of summary justice – that is, without the expensive panoply of legal representation, formal pleading and right of appeal which characterised the higher courts.[59]

Papers. See also H. Smith, 'The Resurgent County Court in Victorian Britain', *American Journal of Legal History*, 13 (1969), 126–38, at 128.

[55] West Hartlepool County Court plaint book, 1910; Public Record Office AK 19/9 (these records have now been transferred to the Cleveland County Archives); Wandsworth County Court, ordinary summons book B (1911); Greater London Record Office AK21/1.

[56] Snagge, *Evolution*, 13. There were fifty-nine new County Court circuits, plus the existing City of London court.

[57] J. E. D. Bethune, Report to the Lord Chancellor on the formation of County Court Districts, 19 Dec. 1846. National Archives, Kew, LCO 8/1 137401.

[58] Craig Muldrew, *The Economy of Obligation: The Culture of Credit and Social Relations in Early Modern England* (Basingstoke, 1998); Julian Hoppit, 'The use and abuse of credit in eighteenth-century England' in R. B. Outhwaite and N. McKendrick (eds.), *Business Life and Public Policy* (Cambridge, 1986).

[59] Finn, *Character of Credit*, ch. 5, esp. 202. The terms 'courts of conscience' and 'courts of request' were used with local variation to describe courts with essentially similar

By the 1820s these courts of request were hearing about 200,000 cases each year, which can be contrasted with the 80,000 or so cases handled annually by all of the central courts in London.[60] Yet in the 1830s the Law Reform Commission reported that 'the inadequacy of the present Courts, in causes of action from 40s. to at least £20, amounts almost to a denial of justice'.[61] The geographical coverage of such courts was partial, their financial remit and internal practices lacked any form of standardisation, and – perhaps their greatest weakness in the eyes of the Law Commissioners – their reliance on the services of untrained and unpaid commissioners (usually local worthies) to hear evidence and pass judgment meant that they frequently failed to follow the principles and precedent of the common law.[62] Yet these courts had wide powers to enforce contracts and compel payment, including the compulsory seizure and sale of the defendant's possessions (execution against goods) and the imprisonment of the debtor (execution against the person), powers which they exercised with widely varying enthusiasm and alacrity.[63]

Margot Finn has recently examined the position of these local courts within the evolving culture of credit in eighteenth- and early nineteenth-century English society. It was their growing number, expanding competence, and widespread resort to execution against the body of the debtor that changed the nature of imprisonment for debt in England. In the eighteenth century, she suggests, debt litigation was focused disproportionately on substantial rather than petty debtors. This was a consequence of the high legal costs associated with formal processes of debt recovery, and a custodial tradition of confinement which embraced the particular culture and privileges of the unreformed debtors' prison.[64] Incarceration in these prisons was a negotiable process, with more affluent debtors able to purchase various privileges which included roomier accommodation, better food, access to alcohol, unrestricted visits from persons of both sexes and, in some cases, residence in a clearly defined area outside the prison walls known as 'The Rules'.[65]

---

purpose and remit. Finn suggests that the former term was more common in eighteenth century usage, and the latter in the nineteenth century.

[60] Christopher Brooks, *Lawyers, Litigation and English Society since 1450* (London, 1998), 41–2.

[61] Fifth Report of the Commissioners on the Courts of Common Law. PP 1833 (247) XXII: 17.

[62] Patrick Polden, *A History of the County Court 1846–1971* (Cambridge, 1999), ch. 1.

[63] Finn, *Character of Credit*, 244.   [64] *Ibid.*, 150.

[65] V. Markham Lester, *Victorian Insolvency* (Oxford, 1995), 93–4; Finn, *Character of Credit*, 129–48. In the case of the Fleet prison, The Rules extended to an area within 3 miles of the prison, thus encompassing all of the City and most of Westminster.

These practices survived into the Victorian period more in the imagination of novelists than within the prison walls.[66] By 1857, when Dickens
used *Little Dorrit* to publicise the capricious nature of imprisonment for
debt and the dysfunctional internal culture of the Marshalsea debtors
prison, he was evoking for his readers a world that no longer existed. The
imprisonment of debtors on *mesne* process – that is, before trial – had
been abolished in 1838, and the Marshalsea had been closed down in
1842 as part of a consolidation and reform of London's debtor prisons.
Even before the inception of the County Courts, the growing network of
courts of requests was sending many thousand plebeian debtors to local
prisons and bridewells for their failure to honour their contractual debts,
and these small debtors were increasingly subjected to a punitive penal
regime.[67] Meanwhile, the middle class insolvent debtor, whose sometimes self-indulgent lifestyle provided such fertile characters and plots
for contemporary novelists, was able largely to avoid the risk of incarceration by availing himself of the new process of personal bankruptcy.[68]

Although the County Courts introduced a degree of uniformity to
what had hitherto been a jigsaw of inconsistent local jurisdictions, this
did not produce a unified system of contract enforcement and debt
recovery for all individual debtors in England because of the evolution
of quite separate but parallel legal systems for the administration of personal insolvency and bankruptcy. Bankruptcy law evolved in the sixteenth century in order to facilitate execution against a debtor's goods,
and to circumvent imprisonment; from 1706 it allowed the bankrupt
to be relieved of liability on existing debts that could not be repaid.[69]
This privilege was restricted to traders, a peculiarity explained by Sir
William Blackstone in the following terms:

[The laws] are cautious of encouraging prodigality and extravagance by this
indulgence to debtors; and therefore they allow the benefit of the laws of bankruptcy to none but actual traders; since that set of men are, generally speaking,
the only persons liable to accidental losses, and to an inability of paying their
debts, without any fault of their own.[70]

---

[66] Margot Finn, 'Being in Debt in Dickens' London: Fact, Fictional Representation and
the Nineteenth-century Prison', *Journal of Victorian Culture*, 1 (1996), 203–36.
[67] Debtor prisoners were segregated from criminal inmates in the reformed prisons
of Victorian England, but in 1899 they were deprived of their right to supply their
own food, and became subject to compulsory labour. Lester, *Insolvency*, 119; Finn,
Character of Credit, 187.
[68] For the use of bankruptcy as an element of plot, and as a moral metaphor, in Victorian
novels, see Barbara Weiss, *The Hell of the English* (Lewisburg, 1986).
[69] Julian Hoppit, *Risk and Failure in English Business, 1700–1800* (Cambridge, 1987),
35–7.
[70] Blackstone, *Commentaries*, book 2, ch. 31, 473.

Exactly what constituted a 'trader' was an issue of some legal dispute, and the boundaries were progressively widened to include even someone who had bought and sold goods only once, provided that they had an intention to repeat the transaction in the future.[71] However, innkeepers, labourers, others who sold their services rather than goods, farmers and gentlemen, were, until 1861, excluded from the remit of the bankruptcy legislation. Non-traders whose debts exceeded those that fell within the purview of the courts of requests and County Courts, and traders whose debts did not attain the minimum bankruptcy threshold of £100, were subject to the laws of insolvency.[72] These laws gave the creditor significant power over the person of the debtor, but not over the debtor's assets – hence the use of imprisonment to attempt to force the debtor to make payment. In 1813 a Court for Insolvent Debtors was created to provide incarcerated debtors with an established mechanism to petition for release from prison. The procedure was, in many respects, similar to procedure in bankruptcy, in that the debtor transferred all his property to the court, and an assignee was then appointed to arrange sale of assets and distribution of proceeds to creditors. However, whereas bankruptcy proceedings protected the future income of the discharged bankrupt from compensatory claims in relation to past debts, the Insolvent Debtors Court could, and frequently did, require the debtor to make future income and property available to his creditors.[73]

The indistinct demarcation between bankruptcy and insolvency in the case of debtors who were only occasional (or even hypothetical) traders, together with clear inequity in the treatment of prospective income and wealth, led to a recommendation in 1840 by the Royal Commission on Bankruptcy and Insolvency that bankruptcy should become available against traders and non-traders alike, something that was not achieved until 1861.[74] From that date both traders and non-traders who owed substantial debts could file a petition in bankruptcy. Debtors had to be well resourced in order to go bankrupt, since a £10 fee was levied on bankruptcy petitions, but this could be a sound investment. Bankruptcy status protected the assets of the debtor from summary seizure by creditors, and safeguarded any future earnings from claims arising from previously acquired debts and liabilities.

[71] Jay Cohen, 'The history of imprisonment for debt and its relation to the development of discharge in bankruptcy', *Journal of Legal History*, 3 (1982), 153–71.
[72] David A. Kent, 'Small businessmen and their credit transactions in early nineteenth-century Britain', *Business History*, 36 (1994), 47–64.
[73] Lester, *Insolvency*, 96.
[74] Cornish and Clark, *Law and Society*, 234.

The annual business of the bankruptcy courts was, relative to the County Courts, minuscule in terms of number of cases, but significant in terms of sums owing. Up to 1860 there were between 1,100 and 2,000 bankruptcy cases annually, with losses averaging £4 million to £5 million a year, plus an additional 3–5,000 or so insolvent debtor cases.[75] After the 1883 Bankruptcy Act, there were around 4,000 bankruptcies a year, with losses averaging £5 million – a not dissimilar figure to the more than £4 million of debts annually being pursued through the County Courts in the Edwardian period. It should be noted that formal bankruptcy was not the only way of shedding debts; private arrangements between creditors and debtors appear to have been more numerous than formal bankruptcy proceedings at least until the 1880s, and the growth in the number of limited liability companies (discussed in Chapters 4 and 5 below) meant that by the end of the century company winding-up accounted for annual losses in the order of £20 million.[76]

However, it was not differences between County and bankruptcy courts in the average size of debt or number of cases heard which produced the accusations of unfairness, injustice and class bias in the treatment of debtors. What concerned the critics was the relative viciousness of the County Courts in exacting full payment from small debtors, and in imposing penal sentences on those who could not or would not pay. In the small debt courts, when a case was found for the plaintiff (and the chances of a case being found for the defendant were never better than 1:50, and usually nearer 1:100),[77] the debtor was required to pay 100 per cent of the sum owing. Since, almost by definition, small debtors had few assets, the requirement to pay off the debt in full was effectively a lien on future earnings. This contrasted with bankruptcy proceedings where the object was to distribute the bankrupt's remaining assets proportionately among the creditors on some *pro rata* basis which seldom exceeded a payment of 10s. per £ of debt, and to prevent creditors exercising a claim on the future earnings of the bankrupt. In the case of small debtors, past errors were to be redeemed by future virtue, while for bankrupts, past errors were to be written off.

The degree of financial discrimination against small debtors was striking, but it was not the primary justification for describing the legal

[75] Weiss, *Hell*, 176–81. These data are indicative rather than precise. As Weiss notes, the complexity of the bankruptcy process, together with the unsystematic nature of data collection in the first half of the nineteenth century, makes it impossible to produce anything other than 'a highly imprecise approximation'.

[76] Lester, *Insolvency*, 240–6, 306–13.

[77] Paul Johnson, 'Small debts and economic distress in England and Wales, 1857–1913', *Economic History Review*, 46 (1993), 65–87; Polden, *County Court*, 61.

system of debt recovery as 'class law'.[78] This epithet was used particularly to characterise the quite iniquitous system of imprisoning small debtors who failed to redeem their debt by paying up the sums due, and at the times specified by the court. Arrest on *mesne* process was abolished in 1838, and the Debtors Act of 1869, entitled 'An Act for the Abolition of Imprisonment for Debt' appeared to abolish arrest and imprisonment on final process, but in practice, as Gerry Rubin has demonstrated in his pioneering analysis of this Act, several thousand people each year continued to be incarcerated for non-payment of small debts.[79] The 1869 Act introduced a new legal twist: small debtors who failed to make the instalment payments commanded by the court could be imprisoned for up to six weeks for contempt of court if it could be shown that they had wilfully defaulted. In fact, the law became harsher in 1869, because whereas previously the imprisonment of a defaulting debtor purged the debt, now the imprisonment purged the contempt, but the debt still stood, and if a further instalment payment was missed, a further period of imprisonment could be imposed.

As well as being discriminatory, this retention of the power of committal over small debtors seems to run counter to the more general, rational and market-oriented development of contract law in the Victorian period. If the purpose of a legal system for the recovery of debt is to maximise the payments to creditors, it seems perverse to apply the sanction of imprisonment on the debtor, since this will almost of necessity prevent him acquiring or earning the means to pay. Imprisonment for debt signified the continuation of a pre-modern punitive sanction against the body of the debtor for his economic transgression. Bankruptcy proceedings, on the other hand, sought a rational distribution of economic loss among the creditors, on the principle they had all openly entered into contracts with the defaulting party, and had to accept the downside of market fluctuations and business failure.

Describing the difference in treatment of bankrupts and small debtors is easy; explaining it is more tricky, especially when we know that the prejudice the law expressed towards small debtors was widely

---

[78] Paul Johnson, 'Class Law in Victorian England', *Past and Present*, 141 (1993), 147–69; G. R. Rubin, 'Law, Poverty and Imprisonment for Debt, 1869–1914', in G. R. Rubin and David Sugarman (eds.), *Law, Economy and Society, 1750–1914* (Abingdon, 1984), 241–99, at 275–6.

[79] Arrest on final process had been abolished for debts of less than £20 in 1844, but in 1845 this liberalising measure was reversed by a new Act which designated as fraudulent any debt contracted by an individual lacking any reasonable prospect of being able to pay; a condition which applied to most working-class debtors most of the time. Fraudulent debtors were not exempted from arrest on final process by the 1844 Act. See Rubin, 'Law', 244–9.

recognised by contemporaries. Was the utilitarian pursuit of general legal principles, rational administration and equal treatment nothing more than a rhetorical smoke screen to disguise blatant class prejudice, or should we look for a more complex and more subtle historical explanation? In most respects both the reforms to, and the operation of, the laws of bankruptcy and indebtedness were rational and equitable; that the outcomes should have been so diverse was a consequence of contemporary presumptions about economic psychology and moral worth. In order to demonstrate this, the chapter will look in turn at the legislative basis and the practical procedures of the small debt and bankruptcy systems, at the economic circumstances of the debtors, and at their social status.

The legislative intention of the 1846 Act which established the County Courts was clear – to improve the efficiency of debt collection. Pursuit of debtors through the existing Courts of Request involved a number of hindrances which became increasingly burdensome as the scale and range of commercial activity expanded in the era of the penny post and the railway. The commissioners or judges who decided on cases in these courts were laymen (by the 1830s they had to be substantial property owners) with limited legal knowledge, and limited time to devote to hearings. More important, perhaps, the jurisdiction of each court was limited to a specific local area, so judgments could not be enforced against defendants whose goods or persons lay beyond the court borders.

What the County Courts provided, from 1847, was a comprehensive and standardised network of small-claim courts, with common competences and rules of procedure. There was an official code of rules, forms and scale of costs, judges were trained lawyers with seven years' standing at the Bar (later raised to ten years), and they were assisted by Registrars who required five years' standing as solicitors.[80] This professionalisation of small debt recovery procedure was not restricted to the judiciary; lawyers also enhanced their status by obtaining a formal right to represent litigants, to the exclusion of unqualified 'low attorneys'. The 1846 Act gave courts the power to refuse to hear any but the parties to a suit or their attorney or counsel. In practice this work was conducted by solicitors rather than barristers; there was no acknowledged County Court Bar, even in the largest towns.[81] There remained, however, some

---

[80] Snagge, *Evolution*, 12.
[81] Snagge, *Evolution*, 23–4; David Sugarman, 'Simple images and complex realities: English lawyers and their relationship to business and politics, 1750–1950', *Law and History Review*, 11 (1993), 257–301. See particularly 295.

ambiguity about exactly who could speak on behalf of whom in court. Narrow application of the restrictive conditions of the 1846 Act[82] gave way to a recognition that working men might often be unable to attend a hearing and so should be allowed to be represented by a wife or other family member or even a 'friendly neighbour'.[83] Likewise employers could be represented by someone in their employment, for instance a book-keeper, but judges attempted, not always successfully, to draw the line at 'the class of accountants and debt-collectors' because 'their function is not to represent absent parties'.[84]

H. W. Arthurs has written rather negatively of the way in which the 1846 legislation saw the final demise of local and communal justice and the rise of formalism and professionalism,[85] but in terms of rational administration of the law on general principles, the County Courts represented a positive step. Greater legal formalism was a way of reducing the discretion of the courts and, as far as parties to any contract were concerned, of increasing the certainty of outcome. In economic terms, this contributed to an overall reduction in transaction costs, a factor identified by Douglass North as the key element in the development of the industrial economies in the nineteenth century.[86]

Victorian legislation on bankruptcy was similarly intended to improve efficiency and reduce costs; this has been analysed by Markham Lester. He sees this history as fitting very definitely into Atiyah's model of reform induced by classical economic ideals, even though the creation of the posts of official assignee by the 1831 Bankruptcy Act, and official receiver under the 1883 Act, do not conform to an absolutist interpretation of *laissez-faire* government.[87] The primary intention of these reforms was to promote the most efficient administration of bankrupt estates, and to maximise the dividends paid to creditors. Some legal regulation was required to ensure the rational distribution of assets among a multiplicity

---

[82] *CCC* (4), September 1847, 79.   [83] Finn, *Character of Credit*, 256.

[84] Comments of Judge Snagge in Halifax County Court, on the question of unqualified practitioners. *CCC* (31) April, 1888, 368. The fact that this opinion needed to be reiterated more than forty years after the establishment of the County Courts indicates that the boundaries of professional competence between lawyers and other professionals or quasi-professionals remained contested throughout the Victorian period. See D. Sugarman, 'Who colonised whom? Historical reflections on the intersection between law, lawyers and accountants in England, in Y. Dezalay and D. Sugarman (eds.), *Professional Competition and Professional Power: Lawyers, Accountants and the Social Construction of Markets* (London, 1995), 226–37.

[85] Arthurs, 'Without the Law', 143–4.

[86] D. North, 'Institutions and Economic Performance', in U. Maki, B. Gustafsson and C. Knudson (eds.), *Rationality, Institutions and Economic Methodology* (London, 1993), 242–61.

[87] Lester, *Insolvency*, 301–2.

of competing claims from creditors, and to prevent bankrupts spiriting away any assets in their possession before administration of their estate could begin. There were substantial differences of opinion, within both the commercial and legal communities, about how these goals could best be achieved, but little disagreement about the goals themselves.

Legislative intent is not always readily translated into effective action. How rational, general, open and efficient was the system of debt recovery in practice? Bankruptcy administration faced a particular procedural problem in the case of small estates – it was not worth the while of any individual creditor to expend time and effort administering the bankrupt's estate for a small share of the dividend, and collective supervision of private assignees was also often more trouble than it was worth. The result was erratic, sometimes irresponsible, and sometimes corrupt administration of bankrupt estates, yet consistent bankruptcy administration was a necessary feature of an efficient commercial society. Private interest was not sufficiently motivated to ensure the public good, and it was this failure of both individual and collective action in the case of small estates that motivated Lord Brougham to propose that an official assignee be appointed by the court to administer the bankrupt estate, and to draw appropriate compensation from the estate. This element of officialism was a key component of the 1831 Bankruptcy Act.

The introduction of official administration may have promoted the public good by imposing a more standardised and rational distribution of assets to creditors, but the creditors themselves were far from convinced of the merits of the system. Lester has shown that the business community, although far from unanimous in its attitudes towards bankruptcy reform, was vociferous in its opposition to official administration. The principal complaint related to cost: the expenses of administration on average consumed one-third of the assets available for distribution in a bankrupt's estate.[88] Yet a return to creditor-managed bankruptcy in 1869 did nothing to reduce costs, and the 1883 Act which re-imposed administration by official receivers for bankruptcies with assets under £300 failed to bring administration costs below 40 per cent of gross receipts in these smaller cases.[89]

The small debt courts, by comparison, were models of efficiency. The average debt was around £3, the cost of entering a plaint and issuing a summons for a claim of this sum was 4s., followed by a further charge of 1s. for taking the admission if the case was admitted, or 6s. 9d. for a hearing. No costs were allowed for actions for 40s. or less, and were limited to 10s. on actions not above £5, and to 15s. on higher

[88] *Ibid.*, 133.   [89] *Ibid.*, 295.

amounts – thereby effectively precluding the use of legal representatives in the smallest of cases.[90] For a straightforward case of average value, therefore, costs represented around 8% of the sum owing if settlement was achieved before a court hearing, and 18% if the case came to court. Even if a case was pursued through to the issue and execution of a warrant of commitment, the additional fees amounted to only 1s. 2d. per £ of debt, or a total cost of under 24% of the average debt.[91] In 1852 it was reported that total costs (including allowable fees) represented 26% of the sum for which judgment was given.[92]

Not only was the small debt recovery procedure cheap, it was also quick. The first stage was for the creditor to enter a plaint for recovery of the debt with the registrar of the court. This plaint gave the name and address of the alleged creditor and debtor and the nature and size of the alleged debt. A summons stating the substance of the action was then served on the defendant, giving the date of a court hearing, which was usually within four weeks of a plaint being entered. If the case came to court and a judgment was issued, it was up to the plaintiff to secure the compliance of the debtor. If the debtor could not or would not pay, the creditor could apply for a judgment summons to be issued, which obliged the debtor to attend court to explain why he had not paid as directed. If a defendant failed to attend a judgment summons hearing without notification of good cause, then a warrant for execution against goods owned, or for commitment to prison for up to six weeks, was issued against him. Few cases went this far; on average only 60% of cases came to court, judgment summonses were issued in about 20% of cases, warrants of commitment issued in about 7%, and imprisonment enforced in less than 0.5% of cases.[93]

Universal accessibility to a uniform system of law had been one of the objectives in the establishment of the County Courts, and simplicity of procedure was held to be an important element of accessibility. Particulars of claims were entered in straightforward language in the plaint book, parties were able to be witnesses in their own case, and judges were empowered to admit hearsay evidence about, for instance, a defendant's ability to pay. Compared with the complexity of bankruptcy

---

[90] Polden, *County Court*, 43.
[91] Scale of Court Fees. *CCC* March 1855. See also *Select Committee on Imprisonment for Debt*, P.P. 1873 XV, q. 197 (Evidence of Mr Henry Nicol, superintendent of County Courts in the Treasury).
[92] House of Lords 1852–3 (257) XVIII. *Costs awarded in relation to judgements*, cited in Polden, *History of the County Court*, 52.
[93] A convenient summary of County Court statistics is provided by Polden, *County Court*, 333–58. An analysis of these data in relation to economic fluctuations is provided by Johnson, 'Small debts'.

administration, this was almost a model of plain man's law, although which plain man benefited could depend on the outlook of the particular judge or registrar. In 1905 the President of the County Court Registrars' Association prompted a fervent exchange of opinion in the trade journal, the *County Courts Chronicle*, by stating in his presidential address that:

> In the smaller class of cases, as they knew, they did not insist on the rules of evidence. No registrar who knew his business thought of insisting on the rules of evidence. He asked for the tradesman's books the very first thing, and, if the entries were properly made up and in order of date, that was taken as *prima facie* evidence in many cases to which, very rightly, a great deal of importance was attached.[94]

Yet this flexibility could equally work in the interests of the debtor. Courts had no resources to investigate the means of each defendant, and in determining the size and frequency of repayment instalments they typically took the unsubstantiated word of the defendant or his representative about how much could be afforded each week or month.

In the early days of the County Courts some judges took informality and accessibility too far, at least in the eyes of the *County Courts Chronicle*. At Brentford County Court in 1847, not only did the court sit in the back room of a public house, with large numbers of 'intoxicated and noisy' defendants present, but the judge, clerk and high bailiff all sat at 'at a common lodging table, none of them being distinguished by any badge of office'.[95] The *Chronicle* remarked that Judges should always appear in wig and gown, and clerks in robes, because 'it is a form in the administration of justice to which the public mind has become so familiarised that it will not associate the idea of equal dignity and importance to a Court that shows them not'.[96]

Concern about the public 'face' of justice, as represented by the theatre of court proceedings, recurred throughout the years up to 1914. In 1905 it was reported that Judge Edge had refused audience to an unrobed solicitor in his court, even though robing was a recommendation, not a requirement, of the Law Society; in an echo of the discussion almost fifty years earlier, it was suggested in the *County Courts Chronicle* that robing should be enforced 'to maintain the dignity of the legal profession'.[97] But the stage set was as important as the costumes. After an extension of the jurisdiction of the County Courts in 1903 the editor of the *Chronicle* lamented the 'disgraceful accommodation at

[94] *CCC* July 1905, 175. See also correspondence in *CCC*, August 1905, 203.
[95] *CCC*, September 1847, 77.   [96] *CCC*, October 1847.
[97] *CCC,* May 1905, 123.

the metropolitan County Courts', and argued that their physical facilities should be enhanced to match their increased importance. As in Brentford in 1847, part of the concern was that the propriety of legal proceedings was being compromised by an association with common drinking dens. In Westminster County Court, of all places, it was claimed that:

> The registrars' court is about as large as a railway carriage, and situated in a sort of passage; the robing-room is about the same size, and has no adequate accommodation at all. There are no waiting rooms or proper lavatories for suitors. Consultations must be held in the public street or the public house. In the court, counsel, solicitors, witnesses and judge are all huddled together in a miniature Black Hole of Calcutta.[98]

But if the external status of the courts continued to be a cause for concern, their rising professional status was a matter for some self-congratulatory puffery: fifty years on from the foundation of the County Courts, the *Chronicle* could boast that of the twenty-nine judges appointed in the previous six years, thirteen were QCs.[99]

There was no obvious sign of this growing legal formalism crowding out the layman's direct access to the due process of law. Whilst many traders used solicitors to represent them in court, in around 2 per cent of cases working-class plaintiffs appeared in person to pursue their claims for payment by lodgers or for repayment of small loans.[100] It is unclear how far this use of the County Courts by working-class plaintiffs indicates a general acceptability of the institution and the process of debt recovery. The enormous number of cases annually processed by these courts must mean that the experience of being 'county courted' was common among manual workers, even though defendants failed to attend initial hearings in around half of all cases that came to court. For those who did attend a hearing (or, as was frequently the case, whose wife attended the hearing), the experience of court procedure must have been breathtaking: records of the West Hartlepool court show that cases were heard and judgments dispensed at the rate of one every 85 seconds.[101]

If bankruptcy and small debt procedure are compared in terms of cost, speed and accessibility, then it is small debt recovery in the County Courts that most closely reflects a universal law responding to the novel needs of a commercial society. It seems unlikely, therefore, that the widely perceived discriminatory nature of small debt enforcement can be attributed either to differences in the legislative basis or the

---

[98] *CCC*, January 1905, 3–4.   [99] *CCC*, April 1897, 87.
[100] Johnson, 'Class law', 166, note 61.   [101] Johnson, 'Small debts', 70.

procedural norms of the bankruptcy and small debt courts. Perhaps, then, the explanation lies in substantive differences in the economic circumstances of bankrupts and small debtors.

The majority of defendants in the small debt courts were male manual workers – in the small number of surviving plaint books in which occupation is recorded, over 90 per cent of defendants fall into this category, with around 5 per cent being dealers or traders of some sort; barely 2 per cent were female, and these were predominantly widows.[102] It was not until 1882 that married women could sue and be sued in their own name, and some elements of the legal concept of coverture, by which a married woman's property was subsumed within that of her husband's, lingered on until 1935, when wives at last became liable to the sanction of imprisonment for wilfully unpaid debts.[103] The plaintiffs in the small debt courts were overwhelmingly local traders, with drapers usually heading the list, but with general dealers and grocers following closely behind.[104] In the bankruptcy courts (and prior to 1861 in the Insolvent Debtors' Courts), on the other hand, grocers, publicans, builders and farmers constituted the largest categories of debtors, followed by bootmakers, tailors, drapers, butchers and bankers.[105] In the main, therefore, bankrupts were shopkeepers and dealers who owed other traders, small debtors were working men who owed shopkeepers and dealers.

But this clear distinction by occupation becomes fuzzy when we attempt to distinguish by reference to the financial value of the debts. By the late Victorian and Edwardian period, between 30 and 40 per cent of bankruptcy estates had a gross asset value of under £25, with an average value of around £12.[106] By comparison, in 1911 the average per capita value of working class financial assets held across a broad array of saving and insurance institutions was around £11,[107] and a contemporary estimate put the average value at death of working class estates in the period 1899–1904 at £16.[108] In 1910, 70 per cent of bankrupt estates yielded gross assets of less than £100, which was the maximum threshold for action in the County Courts. But since individual creditors pursued their claims independently in the County Courts, a

---

[102] *Ibid.*, 68

[103] Margot Finn, 'Women, consumption and coverture in England, c. 1760–1960', *Historical Journal*, 39 (1996), 703–22; Lee Holcombe, *Wives and Property: Reform of the Married Women's Property Law in Nineteenth-Century England* (Toronto, 1983).

[104] Johnson, 'Small debts', 68.

[105] Lester, *Insolvency*, 314–5; Kent, 'Small businessmen', 51.

[106] Lester, *Insolvency*, 253.

[107] Paul Johnson, *Saving and Spending: The Working-Class Economy in Britain 1870–1939* (Oxford, 1985), 205.

[108] L. G. Chiozza Money, *Riches and Poverty* (London, 1906), 51.

multiple debtor could face several simultaneous claims for recovery of small debts, and so could be liable for rather more than £100. The crisp distinction of scale between bankruptcy and small debt proceedings, which was established in the title of legislation, was in fact illusory.

What really distinguished the defendants in bankruptcy and small debt proceedings was their social status, and this mattered because of assumptions made by statute and by judges about the economic motivations of people of different social class. The majority of County Court judges presented a consistent view, in both their judgments and their responses to official inquiries, that the majority of working men defaulted on their debts deliberately, that this was an oppressive burden on honest traders, and that the power of imprisonment must be retained in order to extract due payment. A few examples must suffice.

In an open letter to Lord Palmerston, Home Secretary, in 1854, Judge Johnes of the Caernarvon County Court could not have been more explicit in his beliefs about the rights and wrongs of plaintiffs and defendants:

Take a common case – a young man, without family, earning high wages as a miner or mechanic, contracts a debt of a few pounds with a small trades-man, who sues him and obtains judgment. To take out execution against the goods is futile because, though in one sense wealthy, the defendant probably has none worth levying on. His high wages are possibly squandered in taverns or secreted in such a way that they cannot be reached by the creditor ... The defendants who thus evade and defy their creditors, are commonly men who are, in a pecuniary sense, much better off than the great majority of the pro-fessional men of this country – the wages they receive being commonly higher than the average remuneration of professional men, especially when we take into account the less refined mode in which they live ... On the other hand, the creditors, whose confidence they abuse, generally belong to the poorest and most necessitous class of small retail dealers, a class who have no superfluous funds to spend in dubious litigation with knaves, and to whom legal redress, unless it be really cheap and accessible, is a mockery.[109]

Here we see, combined in one short comment, moral judgement about the fecklessness of workers and the integrity of small traders, together with a gross misrepresentation of the economic circumstances of working-class life.

Judge Snagge, one of the more liberal County Court judges, noted in his in Witney Court in 1897 that:

a judgment summons is the only way in which a levy can be made effectually upon the pockets of the labouring man who has obtained credit and wishes to

---

[109] *CCC*, July 1854, 164.

button up his pocket and does not wish to pay. They often say they will not pay, but do so cheerfully when they hear the clang of the prison door behind them.[110]

This sentiment was echoed by Judge Cadman, an enthusiast of custodial sentences, at Dewsbury: 'There was undoubtedly a determination on the part of persons not to pay until the very last moment. Debtors in the past had been given every consideration, and tradesmen and other plaintiffs who had to pay for the goods they sued for in court were worthy of equal consideration.'[111] The fact that 99.5 per cent of defendants paid up before the prison door closed behind them was taken to imply that the initial non-payment was, in many cases, wilful. It was also asserted that many of the initial purchases, particularly from itinerant traders or tallymen, were unnecessary fripperies, so the debtor was doubly unworthy. The fact that in Scotland traders were able to recover debts from working-class customers without the threat of imprisonment, which had been abolished in Scottish law in 1835, seems to have been largely ignored by the majority of County Court judges.[112]

In bankruptcy proceedings, on the other hand, the general presumption was that unpaid debts were an unfortunate consequence of the inevitable uncertainties of the commercial world. Blackstone's rationale for the restriction of bankruptcy status to traders was repeatedly echoed in legislation and commentary on the bankruptcy laws. In 1860 an MP put it thus: a trader may be ruined through circumstances totally out of his control; the non-trader, on the other hand, 'almost necessarily incurred his debts in consequence of his own thoughtlessness and extravagance'.[113] The Bankruptcy Act of 1849 had attempted to monitor the morality of bankrupts by introducing a system to rank discharged bankrupts according to their behaviour. A first-class certificate of discharge was to be awarded to the 'virtuous' debtor whose bankruptcy had been caused by unavoidable misfortune, a second-class certificate to the 'unfortunate' debtor who may have been careless or reckless, but not dishonest, and a third-class certificate to the 'spendthrift, speculating or fraudulent' debtor.[114] However, after just a few year's experience of this system of certification it was being called into question by bankruptcy commissioners who complained about the lack of an agreed 'moral, legal or commercial standard' by which to classify the certificates.[115] Furthermore, the system of classification seemed to

---

[110] *CCC*, June 1897, 155.   [111] *CCC*, February 1897, 35.
[112] *Select Committee on Imprisonment for Debt*, PP 1873 xv, 18–26.
[113] Lester, *Insolvency*, 136.   [114] *Ibid.*, 67–8.
[115] *House of Lords Select Committee on the Bankruptcy Bill*. PP 1852–3 XXII, 51.

have little or no impact on the creditworthiness of bankrupts, or on commercial morality in general, and it was abandoned in 1861.[116] From this date County Courts acquired additional jurisdiction with respect to bankruptcy hearings, so that both bankrupts and small debtors were dealt with in the same arena, but under different laws. As Patrick Polden has noted, this meant that a man could be whitewashed in the County Court of debts of several thousand pounds, irresponsibly incurred, via bankruptcy, while a wretched workman could be relentlessly pursued for a few pounds.[117]

The moral basis of this different treatment was, of course, specious even before bankruptcy proceedings were opened to non-traders. In an age before extensive sickness and unemployment insurance, when most manual workers were hired and paid by the day or the week, it was almost certainly workers rather than traders who had least control of their economic circumstances, and who had least economic opportunity to be extravagant. In one respect this was recognised by County Court judges; they agreed that 'that upon which the labouring classes obtain credit is, beyond all question, not their realised property, but their presumed ability to pay out of future earnings'.[118] However, since future earnings were, in Victorian England, inevitably precarious, especially for those who were driven to contract a debt by a period of under- or unemployment, it was seldom possible for a working-class debtor to demonstrate a reasonable prospect of paying. Since the law conceived as fraudulent any debt contracted without a reasonable prospect of repayment, the courts essentially were driven to infer criminal intent, and to punish with the criminal sanction of imprisonment, what was in fact a structural condition of working-class poverty.[119]

Not all judges were as questioning of working-class intentions as Cadman – there was always a diversity of opinions among the County Court judiciary. Some judges persevered with equitable rather than common law interpretations of the debt recovery process, and used their wide array of discretionary powers to frustrate attempts at contract enforcement by what they held to be avaricious creditors. A favoured method was to order repayment by instalment, but to set the level of each payment so low, and the interval between payments so long, as to render the debt effectively worthless as far as the creditor was concerned. This tension between judges and creditors over their

---

[116] Weiss, *Hell*, 45.   [117] Polden, *County Court*, 72.
[118] *Return of the Questions Addressed by the Committee of County Court Judges to the Judges of Those Courts, on County Court Commitments.* PP 1867 (209), lvii: 52.
[119] Johnson, 'Class law', 161.

interpretation of contractual rights and responsibilities was particularly apparent in the way in which some County Court judges deliberately frustrated the attempts of tallymen and scotch drapers – door-to-door sellers of clothes and fancy goods – to recover payment from husbands for goods sold to housewives on credit.[120] Nevertheless, the majority of judges and registrars adhered to a formal interpretation of contract, and supported the ultimate sanction of imprisonment as a means of forcing working men to honour agreements they had openly entered into with traders. Yet after 1861 these same judges, in the same courts, regularly acquiesced in the shedding of past debts by middle-class bankrupts.

It is clear that in structure and procedure, small debt recovery and bankruptcy administration both became more rational in the nineteenth century; this was particularly so in the recovery of small debts, where costs were low and action swift. But rational reform of both the small debt and bankruptcy systems did not produce similar outcomes. In theory the different financial circumstances of bankrupts and small debtors might explain the divergence in outcomes. In practice, however, the financial standing of most bankrupts was not significantly different from that of many manual workers, so different outcomes cannot easily be explained by reference to objective economic criteria. What led to the harsh and discriminatory treatment of small debtors was a judicial assumption that they ended up in court because of a fundamental lack of desire and intention to honour debts they had willingly entered into. What allowed lower-middle-class bankrupts up to 1861 to shed a large proportion of their debts was a legal presumption that they were worthy but unlucky traders who wished honestly to repay, to the best of their ability, debts often unwittingly incurred because of fluctuations in trading conditions. After 1861 there could not even be the pretence that the vicissitudes of trade justified the shelter of bankruptcy protection; henceforth what was required was simply appropriate legal advice and the £10 needed to file a petition in the bankruptcy court.

Of course the moral presumptions that underpinned these different legal processes were seldom investigated. The primary responsibility of bankruptcy administrators was to distribute assets, not uncover fraudulent intent, and when required to do the latter under the 1849

---

[120] G. R. Rubin, 'The County Courts and the tally trade, 1846–1914', in Rubin and Sugarman (eds.), *Law, Economy and Society* (Abingdon, 1984), 321–48; Margot Finn, 'Scotch drapers and the politics of modernity: gender, class and nationality in the Victorian Tally Trade', in M. Daunton and M. Hilton (eds.), *The Politics of Consumption: Material Culture and Citizenship in Europe and America* (London, 2001), 89–107.

bankruptcy Act they quickly declared their inability so to do. In the County Courts the judges and registrars, dealing with cases in little more than one minute each, had not the time, even if they had the inclination, to enquire into the motives and morals of the debtors. What we see, then, is a considerable social inequality of legal outcomes that derives from a deeply-rooted sense of the moral inferiority of the working class. When applied to the issue of recovery of debt, nineteenth-century contract law in action was hugely different from that model of a 'universal law' founded on immutable and fundamental principles of right and wrong proposed by Addison and other Victorian legal theorists.

It has already been noted that the class bias inherent in this element of contract law was no secret – it was debated in parliament and discussed in the national press – yet it endured throughout the nineteenth century, and for much of the twentieth.[121] This was in part because it conformed with the deeply held beliefs of the majority of the judiciary and the majority of the legislature that working-class borrowers would not honour their debts unless compelled to do so. In part it was because there was no organised working-class response to this legal discrimination. In 1865 the National Association of Trade Protection Societies was formed to press the interests of credit traders in local and national politics, but effective organisation of a countervailing consumer voice did not occur until after the Second World War.[122] Thomas Wright, the journeyman engineer, regarded the discriminatory treatment of bankrupts and debtors as one of the 'things that sting and rankle, that perpetuate and intensify class jealousy and hatred',[123] and there was fleeting interest within the trade union movement. Robert Knight, general secretary of the Boilermakers' Society, spoke several times at the Trades Union Congress in the 1870s and 1880s about the need for law reform, particularly relating to the imprisonment of small debtors.[124] In 1873 the TUC's parliamentary committee raised the issue of the widespread imprisonment of debtors as a possible subject for legislative action, but this was dropped, along with all other non-industrial matters, from the list the TUC subsequently submitted to candidates at the

---

[121] Imprisonment of small debtors who defaulted on a court order to pay was finally abolished in 1970.

[122] Finn, *Character of Credit*, ch.7; Matthew Hilton, *Consumerism in Twentieth-Century Britain* (Cambridge, 2003).

[123] Thomas Wright, *Our New Masters* (London, 1873), 155.

[124] A. J. Reid, 'Old unionism reconsidered: the radicalism of Robert Knight, 1870–1900', in E. F. Biagini and A. J. Reid (eds.), *Currents of Radicalism: Popular Radicalism, Organised Labour and Party Politics in Britain, 1850–1914* (Cambridge, 1991), 214–43.

1874 general election.[125] The priority for organised labour at this time was to secure legal protection for the organisational status and finances of trade unions, and social concerns took a back seat. This was not the case when it came to the impact of contract law on employment – as the next chapter will show, organised labour played an important role in campaigning against the more coercive aspects of nineteenth-century employment law. But as far as debts and debtors were concerned, there was a strong element of autonomy in the development of contract law; Victorian judges were able to preserve a two-tier system of debt recovery with which they felt comfortable. As far as middle-class debtors were concerned, by mid-century they had to be either particularly stupid or particularly venal to end up in prison. William Seymour Blackstone appears to have been both.

On 27 January 1854, just six weeks after Palmerston, as Home Secretary, had declared his inability to intercede in the case of Thomas Turner, an opportunity presented itself to Turner for revenge against the Blackstone family. William Seymour Blackstone had accumulated personal debts to the value of over £24,000 over the previous ten years.[126] Since his election as MP for Wallingford in 1832 his status as a Member of Parliament had given him immunity from arrest as a debtor – a privilege simultaneously enjoyed by the similarly indebted Benjamin Disraeli.[127] But Blackstone's retirement from the House in July 1852 allowed his creditors to initiate actions to recover debts which Blackstone had been 'vexatiously' defending since 1845. Numerous warrants were lodged in the hands of the sheriffs of Oxfordshire and Berkshire for his arrest, and as a counter-measure, Blackstone petitioned the Insolvent Debtor's Court for a protection order against his creditors. However, he failed to attend a hearing in November 1852, thereby exposing himself to the constant risk of arrest.

Yet for the next twelve months Blackstone revelled in his personal liberty. A number of attempts were made to take him into custody, but they were repeatedly thwarted. Blackstone was 'a favourite with the people of Wallingford' who gave him advance notice of the movement of court bailiffs. Furthermore, his house lay on the banks of the river Thames

[125] Ross M. Martin, *TUC: The Growth of a Pressure Group, 1868–1976* (Oxford, 1980), 46.
[126] *The Times*, 16 June 1854, 9.
[127] Judgments against Disraeli in the Queen's Bench, Common Pleas and Exchequer courts, which were revealed in the Shrewsbury election contest of 1841, totalled over £22,000. Stanley Weintraub, *Disraeli: A Biography* (London, 1993), 195–7, 304; Jane Ridley, *The Young Disraeli* (London, 1995), 251, 262.

which divided Oxfordshire and Berkshire. Here he 'kept a punt, which enabled him to make his escape across the river when pursued by the sheriff's officers of one county, and take refuge in another jurisdiction'. Finally, he possessed 'three large formidable dogs' which accompanied him on all his walks 'so that the attempt to arrest him was attended with some danger'.[128]

Frustrated by these repeated failures, in early January 1854 the Sheriff of Oxford decided to appoint a special bailiff with the specific purpose of serving an arrest warrant on Blackstone. What was required was a person of unusual determination who would brave the dangers and obstacles put in his path. Who better to take this role than Thomas Turner, former (and now exiled) town crier of Wallingford. Three weeks after his appointment, Turner seized his opportunity and, with the assistance of two others, took Blackstone into custody. This action was not without personal risk, since four local men, one armed with a shovel, and another with a dung fork, attempted to prevent Blackstone's removal to Oxford gaol, but their efforts were as nothing compared to Turner's determination. Blackstone languished in Oxford prison for 162 days until his case was finally discharged by the Insolvent Debtor's Court. Sweet revenge for Thomas Turner, and something for him to really shout about. But a revenge very much of the moment. Seven years later Blackstone would have needed neither punt nor wild dogs to have preserved his liberty; he could simply have filed a petition in bankruptcy.

[128] *The Times*, 4 March 1854, 11.

3   Coercion, custom and contract at work

The freedom of workers to seek out those employments that best suited their abilities and preferences was seen by classical economists as a necessary element of an efficient economy. Without such freedom, the invisible hand of the market could not nudge workers from less to more productive employments. Hence the antipathy of classical economists to those myriad archaic laws and customs which interfered with the free working of the labour market. Adam Smith complained at length about apprenticeship and restrictions on the movement of workers, even though many of these restrictions were of limited significance by the 1770s.[1] Although the principal restrictions of the 1563 Statute of Artificers relating to the fixing of wages by local justices, and to the seven-year duration of apprenticeship, were not repealed until 1813 and 1814 respectively, they were largely ignored by the end of the eighteenth century.[2] A Tudor statute originally designed to respond to the disruptive economic effects of rural vagrancy had diminished relevance to a more integrated, more urban, more commercial economy which, in some years during the Napoleonic wars, exhibited clear signs of general labour shortage. Although a number of local attempts – successful and unsuccessful – were made in the early 1800s to use the provisions of the statute to obtain an increase in the formal wage rate and to preserve apprenticeship restrictions, they are notable for their rarity.[3] By this date, the more common view, at least among parliamentarians, was that:

No interference of the legislature with the freedom of trade, or with the perfect liberty of every individual to dispose of his time and of his labour in the way and on the terms which he may judge most conducive to his own interest, can

---

[1] Smith, *WoN*, Book I, ch. 10 part 2, 135–59.
[2] The wage-setting provisions were removed in 1813 by 53 Geo. III, c. 40; the apprenticeship clauses in 1814 by 54 Geo. III c. 96. See T. K Derry, 'The repeal of the apprenticeship clauses of the Statute of Apprentices', *Economic History Review*, 3 (1931), 67–87.
[3] Cornish and Clark, *Law and Society*, 292.

take place without violating general principles of the first importance to the prosperity and happiness of the community.[4]

These general principles were those of classical economics, in which the forces of supply and demand were given free rein to find the price which would clear the unregulated market. But this popular interpretation of how the labour market should work, and how wages should be determined, represented a rather narrow interpretation of the complex, and confusing, set of classical economic theorems about wages.

Adam Smith devoted two chapters of the *Wealth of Nations* to the process of wage determination, one dealing with the principles that set the general level of wages within the economic system, the other dealing with the variation of wages between different types of employment. In aggregate, he suggested, wages were paid out of the stock or capital of the employer, in advance of the sale of the product of labour. Thus 'the demand for those who live by wages, it is evident, cannot increase but in proportion to the increase of the funds which are destined for the payment of wages.'[5] This idea that there was a given pool of resources from which wages can be paid – a 'wages fund' – became a central tenet of classical economic ideology until the late 1860s, and lingered on in popular beliefs well beyond that date. Ricardo played an important role, by linking the idea of a given stock of wage goods in the economy to the Malthusian population principle. With a given wages fund, an increase in population would raise labour supply relative to demand, thus forcing wages back down to their 'natural' level (which was commonly held to be a subsistence level which would permit the reproduction of the labour force).[6]

This model of a natural process of aggregate wage determination was adhered to by virtually all political economists from Smith to John Stuart Mill, and was disseminated to a wider public through newspaper articles, parliamentary discussions, and through didactic writings by the popularisers of political economy.[7] Jane Marcet's *Conversation on Political Economy in which Elements of that Science are Familiarly Explained*

---

[4] *Report of the Select Committee on the Weavers' Petition*, PP 1810–11 II, 1. See also *Select Committee on Woollen Manufacture*, PP 1806 III. Cited in Cornish and Clark, *Law and Society*, 292.

[5] Smith, *WoN*, Book I, ch. 8, 86.

[6] Though Hollander insists that Ricardo did not subscribe to the wages fund theory to account for market wage determination. See Samuel Hollander, *The Economics of David Ricardo* (London, 1979), 326–39

[7] F. W. Taussig, *Wages and Capital: An Examination of the Wages Fund Doctrine* (London, 1896); John Vint, *Capital and Wages: A Lakatosian History of the Wages Fund Doctrine* (Aldershot, 1994).

(1816) contained the following exchange between a precocious pupil, Caroline, and her teacher, Mrs B:

CAROLINE: What is it that determines the rate of wages?

MRS B: It depends upon the proportion which capital bears to the labouring part of the population of the country.

CAROLINE: Or, in other words, to the proportion which subsistence bears to the number of people to be maintained by it?

MRS. B: Yes, it is this alone which regulates the rate of wages, when they are left to pursue their natural course.[8]

A logical extension of this wages-fund doctrine was that efforts by workers to force up their rate of pay by collective action were destined to fail in all but the short run. If employers raised wages today in excess of the wages fund, then the capital available to pay labour tomorrow would be diminished by a similar amount, and thus wages, or the size of the workforce, would have to fall to bring the system back into equilibrium. In her *Illustrations of Political Economy* (1832), Harriet Martineau put this idea into the mouth of a sympathetic employer, Wentworth, in his conversation with workers contemplating a strike:

If the masters had more capital than was necessary to pay you all at the rate you have hitherto received, you might gain your point by a strike, not as you sometimes do, just for a little time till the masters can shake themselves free of their engagement, but permanently. But this is not the case. The masters' capital does not return enough to pay you all at the rate you desire. If they are to keep their capital entire, you must take less wages, or fewer of you must take wages at all. If you will all have the wages you desire, the capital which pays them wastes away, and ruin approaches.[9]

Thus workers were trapped by what, in 1863, Ferdinand Lasalle called the 'iron law' of wages – attempts to raise wages through collective action could succeed only in the short run, while in the long run the Malthusian population principle would drive wages down towards the subsistence level.[10]

The wages fund set the (short-run) limit to the demand for labour, and population growth set the (long-run) limit to supply; the wage rate was the market-determined outcome. Yet this was far from being the only theory of wage determination that existed within classical economics.[11] Smith also proposed a productivity theory of wages when he

---

[8] Jane Marcet, *Conversation on Political Economy in which Elements of that Science are Familiarly Explained* (London, 1816), 117–8.

[9] Harriet Martineau, 'The Manchester Strike' in her *Illustrations of Political Economy* (London, 1832), 98–9.

[10] Michael T. Wermel, *The Evolution of Classical Wage Theory* (New York, 1939), 161.

[11] D. P. O'Brien, *The Classical Economists* (Oxford, 1975), 111–118.

stated that 'the produce of labour constitutes the natural recompense or wages of labour',[12] a principle that derived from his residual conception of a labour theory of value, something that was developed and formalised by Ricardo. But more directly relevant to the actual working of the labour market was Smith's bargaining theory of wages. He noted that:

What are the common wages of labour depends every where upon the contract usually made between [masters and workmen], whose interests are by no means the same. The workmen desire to get as much, the masters to give as little as possible. The former are disposed to combine in order to raise, the latter in order to lower the wages of labour.[13]

He went on to note that this bargaining game was not symmetric, for three reasons. First, because there were many fewer masters than workers, masters found it easier to make secret collective agreements, and to monitor and enforce them. Second, the law authorised, or at least permitted, collective agreements among masters, whereas it prohibited them among workmen. Third, the greater resources of masters enabled them to endure a labour dispute for longer than could the majority of wage labourers. Smith did not regard this asymmetry as a problem. He deplored the 'violence and outrage' that sometimes accompanied labour disputes, and noted that 'partly from the interposition of the civil magistrate, partly from the superior steadiness of the masters, partly from the necessity which the greater part of the workmen are under of submitting for the sake of present subsistence', these disputes generally ended in nothing for the workers other than 'the punishment or ruin of the ringleaders'.[14]

This bargaining theory of wage determination is not necessarily at odds with the idea inherent in the wages-fund model that the price of labour is determined by the forces of aggregate demand and aggregate supply. In fact the bargaining process could be viewed as short-run 'noise' around a long-run equilibrium wage. On the other hand, if the causes of the asymmetry identified by Smith were long-standing or structural, there would be no good reason for believing that the market wage achieved by the bargaining process would be identical to the equilibrium wage in a truly free market. In fact, in this situation labour would be mis-priced, resources would be mis-allocated, and the invisible hand of the market would be incapable of re-establishing the optimal conditions of production. This potential difficulty did not unduly trouble the majority of Smith's nineteenth-century followers,

---

[12] Smith, *WoN*, Book I, ch. 8, 82.   [13] *Ibid.*, 83.
[14] *Ibid.*, 85.

who considered the political economy of wages to be encapsulated by the twin ideas of the wages fund and the subsistence principle. Mill, in his *Principles of Political Economy*, reiterated the wages fund theory when stating that 'wages depend mainly upon the demand and supply of labour, or as it is often expressed, on the proportion between population and capital'. He then explicitly ruled out any significant role for bargaining by claiming that 'wages not only depend upon the relative amount of capital and population, but cannot, under the rule of competition, be affected by anything else'.[15]

Although the 'wages fund' of any economy could not be directly identified or measured, this idealistic concept framed the practical analysis of the labour market undertaken by economists and legislators throughout the first half of Victoria's reign.[16] It was not until 1866 that a direct attempt at refutation was attempted, on the grounds that there exists within the economy no special ring-fenced fund solely devoted to the payment of labour.[17] The critique was elaborated and extended by William Thornton in 1869, who pointed out that for a general 'wages fund' of a fixed value to exist, there must be similar smaller funds held by each and every employer, and it was an empirical fact that no such funds existed.[18] In a review of Thornton's book, Mill famously recanted his views:

The doctrine hitherto taught by all or most economists [including myself], which denied it to be possible that trade combinations can raise wages, or which limited their operation in that respect to the somewhat earlier attainment of a rise which the competition of the market would have produced without them – this doctrine is deprived of its scientific foundation, and must be thrown aside. The right and wrong of the proceedings of Trades' Unions becomes a common question of prudence and social duty, not one which is peremptorily decided by unbending necessities of political economy.[19]

This change of mind by Mill – whose name 'stood for political economy'[20] – rendered void the common argument that strike activity by unions was necessarily self-defeating. The contemporaneous publication

[15] Mill, *Principles*, Book II, ch. xi.
[16] Alfred Marshall, 'The doctrine of the wages-fund', appendix J to book VI, ch. 2 of his *Principles of Economics*.
[17] Francis D. Longe, *A Refutation of the Wages Fund Theory of Modern Political Economy, as Enunciated by Mr Mill and Mr Fawcett* (London, 1866).
[18] William Thornton, *On Labour: Its Wrongful Claims and Rightful Dues, Its Actual Present and Possible Future* (London, 1869).
[19] J. S. Mill, 'Thornton on Labour and its Claims', *Fortnightly Review*, May 1869, 517–8.
[20] J. H. Clapham, *An Economic History of Modern Britain, vol II: Free Trade and Steel* (Cambridge, 1926), 390.

of the report of the Royal Commission on Trade Unions, and the subsequent passage in 1871 of the Trade Union Act and the Criminal Law Amendment Act, recognised the legality of trade unions, gave them protection of their funds, and repealed the aggressive combination laws which had been used to criminalise picketing and other collective actions by union members.[21] Henceforth the bias in the law against combinations of workmen was, if not completely eradicated, massively reduced.

The intellectual and legal adjustments of the late 1860s and early 1870s were clearly of great significance to organised labour, but they may have had only a marginal impact on the general working of the labour market. Trade union membership was small – even by 1892 it encompassed only 10 per cent of the labour force[22] – and although Smith appeared to think that employers regularly and repeatedly colluded with each other to keep down wages, the evidence is sparse. As McIvor has shown, before the 1850s employer combinations were 'brief, temporary, ephemeral', and formal employer associations really developed only from the 1880s.[23] In the majority of trades, untouched by trade unionism and the heavy hand of the combination laws, bargaining over wages should have approximated to that ideal process of 'higgling' by which buyers and sellers freely interacted in order to agree a fair market price. But for most of the nineteenth century this model labour market existed only in the minds of those who accepted the assumptions and theories of political economy. For the hundred years following the publication of Smith's *Wealth of Nations*, labour in Britain was constrained, coerced, and at times terrorised, by the semi-feudal provisions of the Master and Servant Acts.

Poor Mary Dawson

Teenagers are wont to express a definite sense of when they have been wronged. Mary Dawson was adamant that she had been traduced by her former employer Mr Hattersley.[24] Mary was born and bred in the

[21] J. V. Orth, *Combination and Conspiracy: a Legal History of Trade Unionism 1721–1906* (Oxford, 1991), chs. 8 and 9; Jonathan Spain, 'Trade unionists, Gladstonian Liberals and the labour law reforms of 1875.' In Eugenio F. Biagini and Alastair J. Reid (eds.), *Currents of Radicalism* (Cambridge, 1991), 109–33.

[22] G. Bain and R. Price, *Profiles of Union Growth* (Oxford, 1980), 37–8.

[23] Arthur J. McIvor, *Organised Capital: Employers' Associations and Industrial Relations in Northern England, 1880–1939* (Cambridge, 1996), 36.

[24] Details of Mary Dawson's case are taken from *HCDeb* 1847 XCIII, cols 947–53, and *The Times* 26 June 1847.

woollen town of Keighley in the West Riding of Yorkshire, and like many of her peer group, she began working life in one of the local woollen mills. In March 1847 she was hired by Hattersley as a weaver, and was put to work at a power loom at which there was a warp partly woven. She finished this piece of cloth, and several others, before being placed at another loom where there were two or three warps. She hired another teenage girl to help her, but found she could not complete the work and make enough to pay her assistant's wages because the condition of the warp was so bad. She therefore left her job to take up work for another mill-owner, Mr Mitchell, who was reputed to offer a higher rate of pay than did Hattersley. An ordinary story of an ordinary worker responding to simple economic incentives – a model of how a free labour market should work.

But the labour market of mid-nineteenth century Britain was anything but free, as Mary Dawson found out on 30 April 1847. On that day, a constable acting under the authority of the Huddersfield magistrates entered Mitchell's mill, arrested Mary for breach of contract and, without giving her time to change her weaving clogs or her mill-dress, hurried her though the crowded streets of Keighley to the railway station, and conveyed her to the Wakefield House of Correction. There she was placed on the treadmill in the company of prostitutes and common criminals. After three weeks of incarceration, by which time she was unable to walk unaided because her feet were so swollen, her father managed to secure her release.

Mary's original sentence was for one month's imprisonment with hard labour, and her early release was due entirely to the assiduous pleading of her father John Dawson. He believed she had been wrongly imprisoned, and asked the committing magistrates to provide him with details of the specific legislation of which she was deemed to be in breach. The magistrates refused, at which point John Dawson approached William Ferrand, MP for Knaresborough and a Conservative paternalist who 'looked upon labour as the source of all wealth, and the well-being of the productive classes as a chief duty of government'.[25] Ferrand raised Mary's case with the Home Secretary, and it was this intervention which led to her release. Did the abrupt termination of Mary's imprisonment mean that her incarceration had been illegal from the outset, as her father and William Ferrand believed? Yes, and no.

The enquiry by the Home Secretary, Sir George Grey, revealed that there was some doubt as to the legality of Mary's conviction. This related

[25] This unattributed contemporary description is quoted in M. Stenton, *Who's Who of British Members of Parliament, vol 1: 1832–1885* (Hassocks, 1976).

not to any uncertainty as to the nature of Mary's action, but rather to a technical issue regarding the specific Act of Parliament under which the committal had taken place. The magistrates had proceeded under the 1843 Worsted Embezzlement Act,[26] whereas they should have proceeded under the 1777 Fraudulent Hatters Act, which was one of several Master and Servant Acts introduced in the eighteenth century.[27] Mr Ferrand was probably correct to argue that the Worsted Embezzlement Act – which he viewed as 'one of the most tyrannical and oppressive acts that was ever passed by the Legislature' – applied only to those who worked at looms in their own dwellings. The 1777 act, however, had a much wider reach. Most of this act related to the theft of materials, but section 8 explicitly dealt with the contract of employment:

If any person, being hired, retained, or employed, to prepare or work up any materials, whether mixed or unmixed, for any master or masters, shall wilfully neglect or refuse the performance thereof for eight days consecutively ... or shall procure or permit himself or herself to be employed or retained in any other occupation or employment whatever sooner than eight days before the completion of the work first taken; then such person ... shall be sent to the house of correction, or other publick prison, there to be kept to hard labour for any length of time not exceeding three months, nor less than one month.

Ferrand presented two distinct arguments to support his claim that Mary had been illegally imprisoned. First, since Mary was a minor under twenty-one years of age, she could not legally commit to a contract, and her father had not entered into a contract with Hattersley for her employment. Second, Mary had committed no offence against the law or against any rule in Hattersley's mill, since, 'there was no general rule at Keighley relating to weavers, with regard to the setting on or turning off hands'. Furthermore, the absence of any local custom of extended employment contracts was demonstrated by the fact that on the very day that Mary decided to leave her work unfinished , Hattersley had apparently turned a weaver off a loom 'without a moment's notice'.

The government denied that the imprisonment was illegal. Mary's actions were in clear breach of the 1777 Act: 'It was shown that twelve pieces had been delivered to her, and that she had woven nine pieces and a half, leaving two and a half unfinished; she then absented herself from her employment and went into the service of another millowner, where she got better wages and better work.' The only legal issue was whether

---

[26] 6&7 Vict. c.40.
[27] 17 Geo. III c. 56. *An Act for amending and rendering more effectual the several laws now in being for the more effectual preventing of frauds and abuses by persons employed in the manufacture of hats, and in the woollen, fustian, cotton, iron, leather, fur, hemp, flax, mohair, and silk manufactures; and also for making provision to prevent frauds by journeymen dyers.*

the committal had been made under the correct Act, and since there was uncertainty about this, Mary was given the benefit of the doubt and released before the expiry of her one-month sentence. It remained open to Mary to seek redress for any improper imprisonment by appealing to a court of law – a suggestion that Ferrand thought 'ridiculous': 'the idea of a girl working for a few shillings a week bringing an action that would cost £100 or £150, against two magistrates, was absurd'.

So ended the case of poor Mary Dawson, put on the treadmill for three weeks for thinking and acting as if the classical economic principles of a free labour market really applied to mid-nineteenth-century Britain. It was exceptional for mill girls to be discussed in the House of Commons, but it was commonplace for the Master and Servant Acts to be used to coerce workers. Just seven weeks after Mary was arrested while working at her loom, the Huddersfield magistrates were again using the 1777 Act to bring workers to heel:

Benjamin Lodge, a weaver in the employ of Mr Norton, of Cumberworth Half, was brought up by that gentleman, for having neglected his work for eight consecutive days. On the 2nd inst. as many as 150 weavers in Mr Norton's employ, turned out (it is said in consequence of an attempted reduction in their wages), and they have not been near their work since. Mr N. therefore brought up Lodge and three others, to be made examples of in order to induce the others to return to finish their work. Lodge was committed for a month.[28]

The survival of coercive elements of the Statute of Artificers into the nineteenth century was not the accidental outcome of legislative inertia. In 1823 parliament added new restrictions to the Master and Servant laws, paying particular attention to the specific issue of contract. From this date, the law explicitly penalised any 'servant' who, having signed a written labour contract, failed to commence work as agreed. Furthermore, it recognised the informal nature of most labour agreements by stating that, once work had commenced, any failure to complete this work according to contract, 'whether such Contract shall be in writing or not' presented employers with grounds for proceeding with criminal action against the worker.[29] In 1843 the Worsted Embezzlement Act explicitly applied criminal sanction to breach of contract by domestic out-workers in seven specified trades, thereby nullifying a King's Bench ruling of 1829 which had effectively placed home piece-workers beyond the reach of the 1823 Act.[30]

---

[28] *Halifax Guardian*, 19 June 1847, 5.   [29] 4 Geo. IV c.34, s.3.
[30] *Hardy* v. *Ryle*, 7 L.J. (mag. Casu) 118 (1829): 118–9, cited in Steinfeld, *Coercion*, 129.

The following year a Bill was introduced which would have extended this criminal sanction to 'all labourers and persons', regardless of whether their trade had been specifically enumerated in any of the preceding Master and Servant Acts, and even when 'the relations of Master and Servant may not actually subsist between such Labourers, or other persons, and their Employers'.[31] The rationale for this extension of the Master and Servant provision to all forms of wage labour was uncertainty created by earlier legal judgments about what activities, in which contexts, were covered by the existing laws. Once the Bill was introduced to Parliament, the Chartist solicitor W. P. Roberts alerted the labour movement to the threat posed by the Bill, and the Potters' Union was particularly active in organising opposition throughout the Midlands. Over 200 petitions, said to represent over two million workmen, were received by the House of Commons. With forceful opposition from radical reformers, the Bill was defeated.[32] This did not mean, however, that the provisions of the Master and Servant Acts remained confined to narrowly specified trades. Over the next twenty years a series of court judgments developed an expansive reading of the 1823 Act to cover an extremely broad range of waged work, regardless of whether the engagement was for a specified term or for a specified task. Thus, by mid-century, time-work and piece-work were held equally to fall under the remit of the Master and Servant Acts.[33]

The mid-Victorian labour market came to be regulated by an increasingly anachronistic reading of a sixteenth-century statute. The section of the 1563 Statute of Artificers which related to leaving work unfinished was framed in terms of the specific tasks undertaken and duties discharged by artificers and servants. This made sense in an economy in which virtually all production was 'bespoke', in the sense of individual workers manufacturing unique products. The nineteenth-century legislation preserved this language, yet the organisation of production was by then very different. By the 1840s many working men and women in the textile, metal and engineering trades literally never finished their work, because for them, as for the stylised worker in Adam Smith's pin factory, their daily labour involved not the complete making and finishing of a good or object, but the performance of an intermediate process. Although the continuous production line was not to emerge until the 1920s, the application of the principle of division of labour

---

[31] Steinfeld, *Coercion*, 135–41.
[32] Webb, *History of Trade Unionism*, 167.
[33] Steinfeld, *Coercion*, 142–53.

fundamentally changed many nineteenth-century manufacturing jobs from craft to process work.

It is by no means always the case that archaic laws have significant effects; many ancient laws linger on the statute book without ever being used in a court of law. Most historical accounts of labour in nineteenth-century Britain pay little or no attention to the Master and Servant Acts. The Webbs, for instance, mention them just twice in their classic *History of Trade Unionism*, and Daphne Simon's marxist account of the waning of the Master and Servant laws represents them as a largely dysfunctional inheritance from feudal times, with little relevance to nineteenth-century work except in those few sections of the economy where pre-modern relations of production between small masters and workmen endured.[34] In fact, criminal prosecution of workers for breach of contract in mid-Victorian England appears to have been widely used across a wide range of employments, including coalmining, the iron industry, building, printing, transport, engineering, tool and cutlery making, glass and pottery manufacture, coach building, boiler-making and common labouring.[35] This resort to law was not the preserve of small employers. Among the cotton spinners of Preston and Blackburn, the prosecution of workers for leaving work without notice was 'an almost weekly occurrence' in mid century.[36] In the case of the Preston firm of Horrockses, the largest integrated cotton firm in the world in the first half of the nineteenth century, prosecution of absent workers was part and parcel of an aggressive approach to labour management that included periodic pay cuts.[37] In that part of south Staffordshire known as the Black Country, an area with a particularly high rate of prosecution which Simon explained by reference to the concentration of pre-modern workshop production, at least one-third of cases were brought by large-scale iron and coal masters.[38]

---

[34] Webb, *History of Trade Unionism*, 232–6, 275; Daphne Simon, 'Master and Servant' in J. Saville (ed.), *Democracy and the Labour Movement: Essays in Honour of Dona Torr* (London, 1954), 160–200. There is no mention of Master and Servant legislation in Neville Kirk's two volume study of *Labour and Society in Britain and America* (Aldershot, 1994) and only two mentions in E. H. Hunt, *British Labour History, 1815–1914* (London, 1981).

[35] See evidence to the *Select Committee on the State of the Laws as Regards Contracts of Service between Master and Servant*. PP 1865 viii (370) and 1866 xiii (449), and Simon, 'Master and Servant', 190–5. See also Simon Deakin and Frank Wilkinson, *The Law of the Labour Market* (Oxford, 2005), 61–85.

[36] H. I. Dutton and J. E. King, 'The limits of paternalism: the cotton tyrants of North Lancashire, 1836–54', *Social History*, 7 (1982), 59–74.

[37] Michael Huberman, *Escape from the Market* (Cambridge, 1996), 53–4.

[38] Simon, 'Master and Servant', 194–5; D. C. Woods, 'The operation of the Master and Servant Acts in the Black Country, 1858–1875', *Midland History*, 7 (1982), 93–115.

Furthermore, criminal prosecution of workers for breach of contract appears to have become more common over the course of the nineteenth century, even as the relations of production were becoming more modern. The evidence is patchy, because Master and Servant actions were generally heard only in magistrates courts, and no comprehensive data were collected and reported until the 1850s, but local studies by Douglas Hay indicate a rise in the number of Master and Servant offenders imprisoned between the last quarter of the eighteenth century and the first quarter of the nineteenth.[39] From 1857 to 1875 the picture is clearer: the number of criminal prosecution averaged about 10,000 per annum, fluctuating between an annual minimum of 7,385 and maximum of 17,082. The overall trend for these years is upward, with the final five years 1871–5 averaging 14,000 prosecutions annually.[40] Years of peak prosecution (1860, 1866, 1872) coincided with peaks in the trade cycle, and analysis of the data by Robert Steinfeld demonstrates that when unemployment rates were low employers resorted to the disciplining device of prosecutions more frequently.[41] Employers could be reasonably confident of a sympathetic hearing, because the legal process was massively biased in their favour. Cases could be heard by a local Justice of the Peace sitting alone, and such persons were usually well connected, economically and socially, with local employers; in fact in industrial districts they were often one and the same. For example, in 1859 almost 44 per cent of Black Country magistrates were iron and steel masters, and in a number of towns in the heart of the district they made up the entire local bench.[42] By mid-century in the Lancashire cotton town of Preston eleven of the nineteen magistrates were cotton masters.[43]

The geographical distribution of Master and Servant cases over the period 1857–75 shows a clear link between manufacturing and resort to law. In 1860, Cheshire, Derbyshire, Staffordshire and Shropshire all experienced more than 11.5 prosecutions per 10,000 population, with Lancashire, Durham and Yorkshire having between 8.5 and 11.5 prosecutions per 10,000 population. On the other hand, counties

---

[39] Douglas Hay, 'Master and Servant in England; using the law in the eighteenth and nineteenth centuries' in W. Steinmetz, *Private Law and Social Inequality in the Industrial Age* (Oxford, 2000), 227–264.

[40] Data from Judicial Statistics.

[41] Steinfeld, *Coercion*, 72–82.

[42] D. Phillips, 'Black Country Magistracy 1835–60', *Midland History*, 3 (1975–6), 161–90.

[43] H. I. Dutton and J. E. King, *'Ten Per Cent and No Surrender': The Preston Strike, 1853–1854* (Cambridge, 1981), 122.

such as Cumberland, Westmorland, Norfolk, Suffolk, Kent, Sussex, Oxfordshire, Dorset and Devon had fewer than 3.5 prosecutions per 10,000 population. In some towns in the Black Country, the rates were much higher: in Wolverhampton they reached a maximum of 45 per 10,000, and in Walsall 39 per 10,000.[44] Given that middle-class and elderly-headed households were largely untouched by this law, and with an average household size of around 5, these data suggest that in the industrial counties of England in the mid-Victorian period the annual chance of a working-class household suffering criminal prosecution for breach of labour contract lay between 1 in 150 and 1 in 200 – a sufficiently high rate for knowledge of the risk to be well known within working class communities. Once prosecuted, about 60 per cent of workers were convicted, and many of the 40 per cent that received a discharge did so because, under duress, they had agreed to return to work. Of those convicted, around one-quarter received a prison sentence (about 1,500 people a year), a quarter were fined, and the remainder suffered abatement of wages in order to compensate their former employer for losses incurred.[45]

Of course, breach of contract could as much be the result of action by the employer as by the worker, and the Master and Servant laws recognised this by providing explicit authority for workers to recover wages due.[46] In a sample of 670 Master and Servant cases from Walsall over an eighteen-year period from 1858, prosecutions by workers against employers accounted for 13.4 per cent of the total.[47] However, there was a structural asymmetry in the application of the law to these worker-originated cases. A master sued by a worker could be a witness in his own defence, but until 1867 a worker prosecuted by an employer could not give evidence on his own behalf (and thus frequently was unable to offer any defence at all). Furthermore, whereas it was a criminal offence for a worker to break a contract, punishable by up to three months' imprisonment with hard labour, breach of contract by an employer was a civil

[44] Steinfeld, *Coercion*, 80; Woods, 'Master and Servant'.
[45] Simon, 'Master and Servant', 186, n. 2; Steinfeld, *Coercion*, 75.
[46] Workers could also make claims for unpaid wages through the small debt courts, where their case was heard by a legally-trained judge or registrar. It seems likely that workers felt they received fairer treatment in the County Courts than from local Justices of the Peace in magistrates courts. One of the (unsuccessful) ambitions of organised labour's campaign in the 1860s for reform of Master and Servant law was for hearings to be transferred from magistrates to County Courts. On the very patchy evidence of the use of County Courts to settle disputes over employment contracts see W. Steinmetz, 'Was there a de-juridification of individual employment relations in Britain?', in Steinmetz, *Private Law*, 293–310.
[47] Woods, 'Master and Servant', 102.

offence only, with sanction against employers limited to payment of wages claimed, plus costs.[48] There was also an ambiguity about exactly what an employer's implied obligation was to a worker for the duration of a contract that specified a term of employment. Many employers sought to bind workers for a term without explicitly binding themselves to provide work, although there was a risk that, if challenged in court, such a contract might be declared void on grounds of lack of mutuality. But by the 1850s this issue had been resolved in favour of employers.[49] As long as the employer did not explicitly commit to provide a minimum amount of work, or a minimum level of wages, he could suspend a worker without pay, or put the worker on short time, without rendering the contract void, if he could justify such action by reference to the circumstances of the trade. Since most labour contracts were verbal rather than written, and since magistrates were more likely to take the word of an employer than a worker in any dispute over what was or was not promised, the chances of a worker being able to gain compensation from an employer for breach of contract were slight.

Despite the blatant unfairness of the Master and Servant laws, there is little sign that they engaged the interest of the early labour movement, apart from the brief flurry in 1844. Although the number of workers prosecuted under the Master and Servant laws far exceeded prosecutions under the combination and conspiracy laws, it was these latter laws that most exercised trade unions, because they directly impinged on the ability of workers to organise and act collectively. It was not until 1863 that a movement for reform of the laws of Master and Servant commenced, starting in the Glasgow Trades Council, gradually incorporating other Trades Councils and unions, receiving acknowledgement, if not outright support, from the National Association for the Promotion of Social Science,[50] and leading to an abortive private members' bill for reform of the law in 1864. A Select Committee was appointed to hear evidence from both sides of industry, and the ensuing Master and Servant Act, 1867, reflected a compromise.[51] 'Simple' breaches of

[48] Woods, 'Master and Servant', 93. Data relating to Master and Servant cases reported in the *Judicial Statistics* relate to criminal cases, and therefore probably omit any cases brought by workers against employers; see Steinfeld, *Coercion*, 75, n. 119.

[49] Steinfeld, *Coercion*, 164.

[50] A paper to the NAPSS in 1859 had argued that the Master and Servant laws violated the 'principle of equality which ought to pervade our laws.' A. Edgar, 'On the Jurisdiction of Justices of the Peace in Disputes between Employers and Employed arising from Breach of Contract', *Transactions of the National Association for the Promotion of Social Science, 1859* (London, 1860), 690.

[51] 30 and 31 Vict. c. 141. For a detailed account of the campaign for reform of the law see Simon, 'Master and Servant', 173–89, and F.M. Leventhal, *Respectable Radical: George Howell and Victorian Working Class Politics* (London, 1971), ch. 8.

contract would henceforth be punished solely with a fine, but 'aggra-vated' breaches which caused 'injury to persons or property' could still lead directly to imprisonment; employers and workers were now to be equally subject to these punishments. The loose phrasing of the 'aggra-vated misconduct' clause, together with the wide discretion allowed to local magistrates over interpretation of the law, meant that this reform fell well short of abolition of imprisonment for breach of contract. From a pre-reform level of around 1,500 custodial sentences per annum the number fell to around 500, although there was no reduction in the over-all number of prosecutions – in fact, as already noted, these rose to record levels during the economic boom of 1872–3.[52]

The continued application of Master and Servant laws against work-ers remained a bone of contention for organised labour; as the trade unionist T. J. Dunning complained, the law tended to categorise indus-trial labour almost under 'the old feudal notion of serfdom'.[53] In 1874 Frederick Harrison wrote a powerful critique of the amended Master and Servant law, arguing that it was 'a miserable remnant of class oppression'. He pointed out that although the 'aggravated misconduct' clause was technically neutral between employee and employer, 'the penalties of this clause, verbally so equal, fall exclusively on one class ... Workmen, as a fact, are imprisoned, and masters, as a fact, are not.'[54] As befitted a positivist who had trained as a barrister in the chambers of Sir Henry Maine, Harrison objected to the continued application of legal sanction on the basis of the status of the individual rather than the nature of the contract:

The contracts of commercial and ordinary affairs often involve very great inter-ests. Men are ruined, and families are desolated every day by deliberate breach of solemn engagements. When a contractor puts bad material in a bridge or a ship, he risks the lives of hundreds. The overtrading of a few speculators may bring on a national panic and the jobs of a knot of directors cause more suffer-ing than a bad winter. Now a breach of contract of this class amounts morally to a public crime, but where no penal statute is broken it is absolutely unpun-ished. Yet if a workman neglects a day's labour (price, say 5s.), he is liable

---

[52] It is likely that, in addition to those directly imprisoned for 'aggravated' breach of contract, some of those fined for 'simple' breaches would have ended up serving a prison sentence for non-payment of their fine.

[53] T. J. Dunning, 'Restraint of Trade', *Beehive*, 17 April 1869, quoted in E. Biagini, *Liberty, Retrenchment and Reform: Popular Liberalism in the Age of Gladstone* (Cambridge, 1993), 148. Dunning was secretary of the London Consolidated Society of Bookbinders from 1840 to 1871, and one of the most respected spokesmen for the union movement.

[54] Frederick Harrison, *Imprisonment for Breach of Contract, or, the Master and Servant Act* (Tracts for Trade unionists, no. 1, London, 1874), reprinted in Edmund Frow and Michael Katanka, *1868: Year of the Unions* (London, 1968), 141–9.

to three month's imprisonment. The sudden loss of a workman's labour may often be a serious matter, but it is preposterous to pretend that it can approach in consequence to the stoppage of a bank.[55]

It was less the eloquence of Harrison's critique, however, and more the newly elected Conservative government's desire to appeal to the expanded working-class electorate, that led to the repeal of the Master and Servant laws in 1875.[56] The Royal Commission on the labour laws appointed in 1874 recommended that penal sanction for 'aggravated' breach of contract be maintained, but the Employers and Workmen Act of 1875 carried though parliament by Home Secretary Richard Cross went much further than this by eliminating the concept of misconduct and misdemeanour from the legislation, and making breach of contract a purely civil offence for both parties.[57] From this date the legal treatment of employers and workers over issues of contract enforcement became symmetric. What the impact of this was on the working of the labour market is unclear. The fact that the Master and Servant laws were used right up to the point of their repeal, and with increased vigour in their final few years, indicates that employers believed they obtained real value from resort to law. Quite apart from the several thousand workers who were directly disciplined in the magistrates courts each year, there was a broader demonstration effect. As the vice-president of the Mining Association of Great Britain told the 1866 Select Committee, 'the moral effect of having the power is often sufficient'.[58] But sufficient for what? Woods has argued that the Master and Servant laws were used by employers for two distinct but related purposes – as an instrument of industrial discipline, especially with regard to strike activity, and as a means of restricting the free movement of labour.[59]

As the behaviour of the woollen manufacturer Mr Norton, cited above, makes clear, employers who were experiencing industrial action by their workforce could intimidate strikers by using the Master and Servant laws to threaten them with imprisonment. This was a much easier route than resort to combination or conspiracy laws, since it required no evidence to be furnished about the degree of organisation and collusion on the part of the workers. Furthermore, the Master and

---

[55] *Ibid.*, 142.

[56] Richard Shannon, *The Age of Disraeli, 1868–1881: The Rise of Tory Democracy* (London, 1992), 214–5.

[57] Steinfeld, *Coercion*, 210–33. It was still possible for a worker to be imprisoned as a result of breach of contract since failure to pay damages could lead to County Court action for recovery of debt, and thus to the same procedures as faced by other small debtors. See Chapter 2 above.

[58] *Select Committee on Master and Servant*, PP 1866 XIII, q. 1441.

[59] Woods, 'Master and Servant', 109.

Servant laws could be used against all striking workers, not just the ringleaders. When 500 stokers at the Beckton (east London) gas works went on strike in late 1872, each one of them was summonsed before the magistrates, and 24 of their number were imprisoned for six weeks with hard labour for 'aggravated' breach of contract.[60] The abolition of the Master and Servant laws in 1875, and the simultaneous legalisation of peaceful picketing by means of the Conspiracy and Protection of Property Act, clearly reduced the ability of employers to resist the collective demands of their workers through the use of State-sanctioned coercion. The significance of these legal changes was fully recognised by organised labour: the 8th Trades Union Congress in Glasgow in October 1875 carried a vote of thanks to the Conservative Home Secreatary, Cross, for his labour law reforms amid virtually unanimous applause. The following year George Howell, secretary to the parliamentary committee of the Trades Union Congress, described these Acts as 'a great boon to the industrial classes – as, in fact, the charter of their social and industrial freedom'.[61]

Abolition of the Master and Servant laws also reduced the capacity of employers to limit labour mobility. It should be noted that not all employment in mid-Victorian Britain was subject to Master and Servant restrictions, because some workers were explicitly engaged on the basis of 'minute contracts' which could be terminated at will by either party. Such contracts were the norm for Scottish (but not English) miners, and for unskilled dock workers.[62] However, Steinfeld, in his pioneering study of the content and context of the Master and Servant laws, concludes that 'employment at will was far from being the norm in England in the 1860s ... Most trades maintained contracts determinable on a fortnight's or a month's notice', and some still operated with annual contracts.[63] These arrangements enabled employers to restrict labour turnover and to restrain the use of wage premia in competitive bidding for scarce labour in local labour markets. Mary Dawson was just one of the many workers each year who found that pursuit of higher wages could lead to a prison sentence. There was, of course, a potential downside for employers who, during periods of trade depression, could

[60] Spain, 'Trade unionists', 112. For other examples of the use of Master and Servant laws against strikers in the cotton, iron and coal industries see Dutton and King, 'Ten Per Cent', 39; Steinmetz, 'De-juridification', 279.

[61] George Howell, A Handy-Book of Labour Laws (London, 1867), v.

[62] Gordon Phillips and Noel Whiteside, Casual Labour: The Unemployment Question in the Port Transport Industry 1880–1970 (Oxford, 1985), ch. 1; Eric Hobsbawm, 'Custom, wages and work-load in nineteenth-century industry', in his Labouring Men, 356, n. 43.

[63] Steinfeld, Coercion, 169.

find themselves committed to maintaining employment for their contracted workers. However, as noted above, by mid-century case law had
evolved so as to allow employers generally to shirk these obligations
without cost. Moreover, the fact that prosecutions under the Master
and Servant Acts continued at fairly high levels during periods of trade
depression indicates that employers felt they could benefit from apply-
ing these coercive laws even in slack labour markets. After 1875 it was
still possible for both employers and workers to pursue through the
civil courts claims for compensation for losses arising from breach of
contract. In addition to individual disputes, trade unions used the law
against employers who unilaterally broke formal collective agreements,
and some employers, particularly in the Durham coalfield, continued
to use mass summonses against strikers, although now their claims had
to be limited to financial compensation for proven losses. Overall, however, the number of breach of contract cases after 1875 was barely half
that of the early 1870s.[64]

The 1875 legislation clearly strengthened the bargaining position of
labour, but also important was the adoption by organised labour of new,
more aggressive, wage theories, following Mill's recantation of the concept of the 'wages fund'. The old political economy, which had been
widely accepted by organised labour, conceived of trade union wage
bargaining as an essentially zero-sum game, in which current wage vic-
tories above and beyond the 'natural' market rates would inevitably be
balanced by future losses. The new economic ideas of the 1870s and
1880s liberated unions from this conceptual straightjacket, and encouraged them to pursue action in defence of wages with increased vigour
and intellectual confidence.[65]

Both real wages and the labour share of national income rose over
the last quarter of the nineteenth century.[66] The proximate cause of the
rise in real wages was a secular decline in the cost of food, itself a function of greater imports of cheap grain, and later meat, from New World
producers. But the fact that workers were able to retain these gains by
resisting pressure for reductions in money wages is indicative of a real
change in the relative bargaining position of labour and capital. From
the mid-1870s the powerful combination of legal reform and ideological advance allowed labour to hold on to wage gains, an achievement
which coincides with the establishment of a labour market in Britain

---

[64] Steinmetz, 'De-juridification', 283.
[65] Eugenio F. Biagini, 'British trade unions'.
[66] Hunt, *Labour History*, 114; S. B. Saul, *The Myth of the Great Depression* (London, 1985), 33.

which, from a legal point of view, began to resemble the stylised model of classical political economy.

For the first three-quarters of the nineteenth century it is clear that the British labour market was not a 'free' market in the sense of work and wages being determined by the untrammelled interaction of supply and demand. The market for labour was constrained by legal rules, and these rules operated in a one-sided manner to coerce the sellers of labour. The objection by organised labour to these legal rules came not from the principled pursuit of 'free labour' in the sense of all contracts being terminable at will; there were clearly mutual advantages within some trades for workers, unions and employers to agree to fixed periods of notice. What workers and unions sought was legal symmetry and equality for capital and labour in terms of both the form of the legislation, and its application and enforcement in the courts. The 1875 Employers and Workmen Act unambiguously met the first of these demands, and to a large extent met the second.[67] However, even though the bargaining position of labour was strengthened from the mid-1870s, this does not necessarily mean that wages were henceforth simply determined by the balance of supply and demand in the labour market. Classical economists recognised that wages varied between different types of employment and in different places, and they constructed an elegant set of rational explanations as to how such variation fitted with a competitive process of wage equalisation. They faced the problem, however, that many wage differentials seemed in practice to be much larger or more rigid than could be accounted for by the theory.

Adam Smith set out five separate reasons why wages might vary between different types of employment.[68] Work varied in its pleasantness, difficulty, constancy and probability of success, and also in the degree of trust reposed in the worker. This formulation was retained and repeated by Mill, who thought that the relevant chapter of the *Wealth of Nations* 'contains the best exposition yet given of this portion of the subject'.[69] The implication of Smith's reasoning was that the net advantages offered by all occupations should tend to equality; differences in pay should reflect no more than the non-pecuniary rewards the occupations offer, together with the relative difficulty of qualifying

---

[67] Steinmetz notes that magistrates' practice under the 1875 Act appears to have been more even-handed than under the preceding Master and Servant Acts. Steinmetz, 'De-juridification', 283–93.

[68] Smith, *WoN,,* Book I, ch.10, part 1, 116–35.

[69] Mill, *Principles*, Book 2, ch.14, s.2.

for and following them.[70] In practice, as Smith and subsequent political economists noted, the world was not quite this straightforward, because institutions intervened to restrict the forces of competition from moving the labour market to equilibrium. Monopolies, guilds, compulsory apprenticeship and the settlement laws[71] were all identified by Smith as significant barriers to the free working of the labour market, but by the mid-nineteenth century these restrictions had all but disappeared. On the other hand, Mill introduced a new conundrum – the apparent existence of sex discrimination which led to the wages of women being 'generally lower, and very much lower, than those of men'. Mill suggested that such differences could frequently be accounted for by reference to supply and demand: the number of trades which through 'law and usage' were open to women was so limited that they were frequently 'overstocked' with willing female employees. However, he also accepted that 'when the efficiency is equal, but the pay unequal, the only explanation that can be given is custom; grounded either in prejudice, or in the present constitutions of society, which, making almost every woman, socially speaking, an appendage of some man, enables men to take systematically the lion's share of whatever belongs to both'.[72]

Mill's resort to the concepts of 'custom' and 'prejudice' to explain the apparently low wages of women seemed to weaken the automatic market process of equilibrium wage determination proposed by Smith. J. E. Cairnes tried to square this particular circle in 1874 by introducing the concept of non-competing groups, but in so far as this segmentation of the labour market into distinct groups was driven by culture or prejudice, this was little more than a semantic trick.[73] In 1890

[70] E. H. Phelps Brown, 'The labour market', in Thomas Wilson and Andrew S. Skinner, *The Market and the State* (Oxford, 1976), 245.

[71] The 1662 Law of Settlement gave overseers of each parish the power forcibly to remove from that parish any stranger who might become a burden on the funds available for relief of paupers. Individuals acquired a right of settlement by being born or married into a parish, by serving a full seven-year apprenticeship to a settled resident, or by renting or paying taxes on a property worth more than £10 per annum (a financial threshold that excluded the great majority of manual workers). The Settlement Laws acted as a significant barrier to the geographical mobility of labour. An amending statute in 1846 gave rights of settlement to individuals who could demonstrate five years' continuous residence; this time period was progressively reduced by 1865 to one year, by which date the practice of removing paupers to their place of settlement had largely fallen into abeyance.

[72] Mill, *Principles*, Book 2, ch.14, s.5.

[73] J. E. Cairnes, *Some Leading Principles of Political Economy* (London, 1874), 70–3. The related idea of segmented labour markets in which different groups of workers behave according to different decision rules was developed in the 1970s. The classic early contribution is P. Doeringer and M. Piore, *Internal Labor Markets and Manpower Analysis* (Lexington, MA, 1971).

Alfred Marshall came to the rescue of market ideology with his concept of the efficiency-wage. Marshall noted that just as the attributes of jobs vary, so to do the abilities and commitment of workers, and it is ability and commitment in any particular job that determines the efficiency of the worker:

> In order therefore to give its right meaning to the statement that economic freedom and enterprise tend to equalize wages in occupations of the same difficulty and in the same neighbourhood, we require use of a new term. We may find it in *efficiency-wages*, or more broadly *efficiency-earnings*; that is, earnings measured, not as time earnings are with reference to the time spent earning them; and not as piece-work earnings are with reference to the amount of output resulting from the work by which they are earned; but with reference to the exertion of ability and efficiency required of the worker.[74]

Marshall's insight – that apparent differences in wages paid for similar work may be due to differences in the characteristics of individual workers, as well as differences in the characteristics of the job – was a significant advance on the Smith/Mill view of pay differentials, but it has posed a major challenge for the empirical analysis of wage determination, because whereas money-wages are readily measurable, efficiency-wages are not. The efficiency-wage is a metaphysical concept; it exists because equalisation of it is necessary in theory to achieve long-run equilibrium in the labour market. It might be thought that for efficiency wages to be paid, employers must have some means of determining them, and workers must have some means of evaluating them, but the necessary mechanisms and metrics do not seem to exist at the point at which wages are actually set. In this respect the concept of the efficiency wage has some similarities to the concept of the wages fund – they are both reifications of abstract concepts that cannot be grounded in empirical processes. Labour economists have devoted a huge amount of time, energy and ingenuity to formalising and testing theories of compensating wage differentials, but in the absence of direct and independent measurement of worker ability and exertion and given the real difficulties in measuring individual productivity in any job which involves teamwork and joint production, it has proved possible neither to confirm nor refute Marshall's theory of the equalisation of efficiency wages.[75] In consequence many contemporary observers from

---

[74] Marshall, *Principles*, Book VI, ch. 3, 630–1.

[75] There is no shortage of theoretical explanations for why apparently different wages for similar or equally productive work do not represent a deviation from a rational process of long-run equalisation of efficiency wages, but in this area theory has run far ahead of empirical support. For reviews see: Sherwin Rosen, 'The theory of equalizing differences', and Glen G. Cain, 'The economic analysis of labor

Mill onwards, and many subsequent historians of nineteenth-century Britain, have continued to argue that custom has had a major role in determining the pattern of wages.

As we have seen, Mill thought 'custom' could account for the male–female wage gap, and subsequent scholars have identified a profound role for customary practices of wage setting. There is a large historiography relating to women's work which overwhelmingly argues that patriarchal institutions, both familial and commercial, structured the system of workplace authority and reward to diminish the return to female labour.[76] Customary expectations served to reduce the pay of women workers below that of their male workmates both directly and indirectly. Direct discrimination took the form of lower pay for equal work, as in the Lancashire cotton industry around 1830 when female mule spinners were employed at half the piecework rates of men.[77] Indirect discrimination could take the form of job segregation, as in the Prudential Insurance Company, where, from 1871, female clerks were formally excluded from the normal promotion ladder open to their male counterparts.[78] More common was an informal barrier to higher-status positions. For example, in the Courtauld silk mill at Halstead, Essex in the 1860s, all but a handful of female workers were confined to lower-grade winding and weaving tasks. Men, however, dominated overseeing, clerical and maintenance work, where earnings were at least twice the female level.[79]

Customary influences on wage setting seem to have extended well beyond the separate sphere of female employment. A classic article

---

market discrimination: a survey', both in Orley Ashenfelter and Richard Layard (eds.), *Handbook of Labor Economcs, volume 1* (Amsterdam, 1987), 641–92, 693–785; Lawrence F. Katz and David H. Autor, 'Changes in the wage structure and earnings inequality', in Orley Ashenfelter and David Card (eds.), *Handbook of Labor Economics, volume 3A* (Amsterdam, 1999), 1463–1555.

[76] Pam Sharpe, 'Continuity and change: women's history and economic history in Britain', *Economic History Review*, 48 (1995), 353–69; Maxine Berg, 'What difference did women's work make to the Industrial Revolution?', *History Workshop*, 35 (1993), 22–44; Jane Humphries, '"...The most free from objection...": the sexual division of labour and women's work in nineteenth-century England', *Journal of Economic History*, 47 (1987), 929–49; Sonya Rose, *Limited Livelihoods: Gender and Class in Nineteenth-Century England* (Berkeley, 1992); Deborah Valenze, *The First Industrial Woman* (Oxford, 1995).

[77] Mary Freifeld, 'Technological change and the "self-acting" mule: a study of skill and the sexual division of labour', *Journal of Social History*, 11 (1986), 334.

[78] Ellen Jordan, 'The lady clerks at the Prudential: the beginning of vertical segregation by sex in clerical work in nineteenth-century Britain', *Gender and History*, 8 (1996), 66.

[79] Judy Lown, *Women and Industrialization: Gender at Work in Nineteenth-Century England* (Cambridge, 1990).

from 1955 by Henry Phelps Brown and Sheila Hopkins argued, on the basis of a long-run survey of building workers' wages, that the pay differential between skilled and unskilled workers had barely changed over the seven centuries up to 1914. The explanation offered was that 'differentials were largely ruled by custom' and it required the exogenous shock of the First World War – conscription, rapid price inflation, and the 'dilution' of skilled trades with unskilled, often female, labour – to break the entrenched earnings norms within occupations.[80] Eric Hobsbawm also proposed that, up to about 1880, workers based their economic behaviour 'on custom, empiricism, or short-run calculation'. He suggested that 'the worker's wage calculation remained for long, and still to some extent remains, largely a customary and not a market calculation'.[81] Further research has provided indirect support for the idea of customary wage determination. E. H. Hunt has shown that regional wage differentials for workers in the building trades and in agriculture persisted over a hundred-year period during which the geographical and employment structure of the population changed significantly, as did the sectoral composition of the economy.[82] Nicola Verdon has argued that custom accounts for the constant (and low) level of female agricultural workers' wages through the nineteenth century.[83] Other historians have looked beyond wage data, and have used information on unemployment, indebtedness and nuptiality to argue that the British labour market in the nineteenth century exhibited pronounced and enduring regional diversity.[84] This is taken to imply that institutional rigidities, which may have included customary wage

[80] E. H. Phelps Brown and S. V. Hopkins, 'Seven centuries of building wages', *Economica*, 22 (1955), 195–206. For a more recent evaluation of the extent of customary wages in the early modern period see Donald Woodward, 'The determination of wage rates in the early modern north of England', *Economic History Review*, 47 (1994), 22–43.
[81] Eric Hobsbawm, 'Custom, wages and work-load in nineteenth-century industry', in his *Labouring Men*, 345, 347. William Reddy has gone further in claiming that the weight of culture and custom within working-class industrial communities in nineteenth-century Europe effectively prevented the emergence of a competitive market for wage labour. See William M. Reddy, *The Rise of Market Culture: The Textile Trade and French Society, 1750–1900* (Cambridge, 1984).
[82] E. H. Hunt, *Regional Wage Variation in Britain, 1850–1914* (Oxford, 1973); E.H. Hunt, 'Industrialization and regional inequality: wages in Britain, 1760–1914', *Journal of Economic History*, 46 (1986), 935–66.
[83] Nicola Verdon, *Rural Women Workers in Nineteenth-Century England: Gender, Work and Wages* (Woodbridge, 2002), 127.
[84] Humphrey Southall, 'The origins of the depressed areas: unemployment, growth, and regional economic structure in Britain before 1914', *Economic History Review*, 41 (1988), 236–58; Johnson, 'Small debts and economic distress', 65–87; Humphrey Southall and David Gilbert, 'A good time to wed?: marriage and economic distress in England and Wales, 1839–1914', *Economic History Review*, 49 (1996), 35–57.

setting, restricted the degree to which competitive pressures could generate flexibility in the labour market.

The belief that wage-setting practices in Britain were dominated by rigidity and custom throughout the nineteenth century and into the twentieth has not been universally accepted. A number of historical studies based on very different methodologies and theoretical perspectives have argued that customary labour practices were no match for the market pressures of nineteenth-century industrialisation. E. P. Thompson famously proposed that the employment pressures of industrial capitalism crowded out customary attitudes to time and work-discipline, and introduced a more regulated and monitored workplace environment.[85] He also suggested that by the early nineteenth century an older 'moral economy' was being subsumed by capitalist rationalisations, although he was cautious about the extent to which this interpretation could be transferred in its application from the specific locus of food riots to the more general analysis of 'just prices' and 'fair wages'.[86]

Coming from a very different intellectual position, the quantitative economic historian Jeffrey Williamson has argued vigorously that 'the wage structure exhibited enormous variability across the two centuries following 1710', and that it did so largely because of market pressures.[87] By extending his wage series beyond just the building trades examined by Phelps Brown and Hopkins, Williamson suggests that manual worker skill differentials changed (declined) markedly between the late eighteenth and early twentieth centuries. He also finds that, for the economy as a whole, the wage premium for skill rose up to 1871 and declined thereafter, which he interprets as a clear indication of a growing skills shortage through to the mid-Victorian period.[88]

A similarly neo-classical economic analysis has led Joyce Burnette to argue that the lower pay received by women workers in Britain during the late eighteenth and early nineteenth centuries had a rational, and market-based, explanation.[89] Although females typically earned

---

[85] E. P. Thompson, 'Time, work-discipline and industrial capitalism', *Past and Present*, 38 (1967), 56–97.

[86] E. P. Thompson, 'The moral economy reviewed' in his *Customs in Common* (London, 1993). See especially 336–42.

[87] J. G. Williamson, 'The structure of pay in Britain, 1710–1911', *Research in Economic History*, 7 (1982), 22.

[88] Jeffrey G. Williamson, *Did British Capitalism Breed Inequality?* (London, 1985), ch.3.

[89] Joyce Burnette, 'An investigation of the female-male wage gap during the industrial revolution in Britain', *Economic History Review*, 50 (1997), 257–81. For a recent analysis of female earnings in the cotton industry see H. M. Boot and J. H. Maindonald, 'New estimates of age- and sex-specific earnings and the male-female earnings gap in the British cotton industry, 1833–1906', *Economic History Review*, 61 (2008), 380–408.

between one-third and two-thirds of the male wage in the same employment, Burnette argues that this wage gap can be largely explained by
the lower value of work effort (in terms of time, physical strength and
skill) supplied by women. Burnette accepts that other forms of labour
market discrimination – such as actions by employers or unions to confine women to a small number of low-grade jobs – could and did occur
in the less competitive sectors of the nineteenth-century economy, but
she concludes that there is little empirical evidence to support the idea
that female industrial and agricultural wages were set according to customary rather than market pressures.[90]

There are two reasons for this long-running and deep-seated disagreement about the importance of custom in determining workers'
wages in nineteenth-century Britain. First, there is an ideological dispute between those who accept that the theoretical construct of competitive market equilibrium reflects underlying empirical processes,
and those who deny that such processes operate in practice. Second,
there is considerable disagreement about what actually happened to
wage differentials between different groups and over time.

The first of these disagreements is misconceived because it presents
competitive and customary wage determination as mutually incompatible processes. For many economists the competitive paradigm
within which they operate implies that, whatever the short-run impact
of the institutions of custom and tradition, in the long run the forces
of competition will drive out inefficient institutions by creating financial incentives to innovate. For many historians the socially embedded
nature of custom and tradition is so deeply-rooted that it is seen to create a dominant value-system which is independent of market pressures.
Neither position is tenable in its absolutist form. As we will see below,
competitive market forces were extremely important in establishing,
and changing, wage levels in nineteenth-century Britain, even in the
presence of customary wage-setting practices. On the other hand, it is
clear that employment and remuneration can be profoundly structured
by institutions, whether legal or customary. This chapter has already
demonstrated how coercive labour laws weakened the competitive position of labour; and below it will show that customary institutions also
had a long-term impact on pay and employment.

The second disagreement springs from the paucity, and the intrac-
tability, of information on nineteenth-century wages. Historical wages
data are seldom sufficiently detailed to sustain clear tests of alternative

---

[90] Burnette develops this position at some length in her *Gender, Work and Wages in
Industrial Revolution Britain* (Cambridge, 2008).

hypotheses. For example, it is often not known whether jobs with the same titles required identical levels of skill and effort; or whether different rates of pay for workers in the same job reflected real differences in the quantity or quality of the individual's output.[91] Rather than revisit the well-worked but disputed terrain of pay differentials according to skill or occupation, the approach taken here is to examine the relationship between earnings and age, in order to see the degree to which market competition and customary behaviour affected how much workers were paid for their labour.

It is well known that earnings tend to vary according to the age of the worker. Modern surveys of earnings find the effect of age to be substantial: for example, from the 1970s to the 1990s in Britain, the earnings of male manual workers aged 18–20 were barely 60 per cent of the earnings of similar workers aged 30–39, while workers aged 60–64 received 85 per cent of the wage for 30–39 year olds.[92] This age-specific pattern is of long standing: nineteenth-century wage data compiled by Bowley, Wood and Beveridge showed wages for 18–21 year olds to be consistently below 'adult' wages.[93] Pervasive differences in pay by age and gender may be an entirely rational response by employers to age- and gender-specific variations in the productivity of workers. For instance, hand-loom weavers accumulated skills through learning-by-doing, so we should expect younger, less-experienced workers like Mary Dawson to be less productive, and thus to receive lower wages, than their older and more highly skilled peers. And if weaving also required considerable strength and stamina to maintain high-quality output over a ten-hour shift (as was true until the widespread adoption of power looms in the early 1840s), then it is likely that, on average, adult male weavers would command higher wages than juveniles or adult women. Economists combine these various worker attributes of education, skill, strength, stamina and aptitude under the umbrella term 'human capital', and over the past thirty years have developed a sophisticated set of models to explain how human capital can account for variations in earnings by age and gender.[94] Skills are assumed to

---

[91] Williamson's conclusion about a rising wage premium for skill in nineteenth-century Britain has been strongly criticised for being derived from a narrow, unrepresentative and inconsistent evidential base. See R. V. Jackson, 'The structure of pay in nineteenth century Britain', *Economic History Review*, 40 (1987), 561–70; C. H. Feinstein, 'The rise and fall of the Williamson curve', *Journal of Economic History*, 48 (1988), 699–729.

[92] B. Black, 'Age and earnings', in M. B. Gregory and A. W. J. Thomson, *A Portrait of Pay, 1970–1982: An Analysis of the New Earnings Survey* (Oxford, 1990), 274–98.

[93] See the references in Feinstein, 'New estimates', 595–623.

[94] The pioneering work was by Jacob Mincer, *Schooling, Experience and Earnings* (New York, 1974).

be created by training, and to grow with age and/or work experience. Earnings are depressed at younger ages, since young workers receive part of their total employment compensation in the form of human capital. At older ages obsolescence and depreciation of human capital lead to a decline in productivity and a flattening and then decline in earnings. The overall profile of the relation between age and earnings is thus normally hump-shaped.

Many additional factors have been found to affect this underlying relationship between age and earnings: formal education should speed up the accumulation of skills and thus increase earning potential at younger ages; the application of mechanical power should reduce the wage premium paid for sheer physical strength, and thus reduce the advantage that adults have over juveniles; demography can have an impact, because a large 'baby-boom' birth cohort will lead to many juveniles entering the labour market at the same time, and this will tend to depress entry-level earnings; legislation can affect the structure of pay, for instance by prohibiting child employment (as the Factory Acts did, in stages, from 1833) or by setting a minimum wage (as was done by the Trades Boards Act of 1909). Over the course of the nineteenth century, therefore, as formal education in Britain expanded (and became compulsory from 1881), as industry, transport and agriculture became progressively mechanised, as the birth rate fell from its 1821 peak, and as new labour laws were implemented, we might expect to see a change in the relationship between age and earnings. What does the evidence show?

The analysis draws on three sets of age-specific earnings data: for 1833, the 1880s and the 1930s. The 1833 data relate to the earnings of over 21,000 males and 30,000 females employed in more than 200 textile factories around the country. For the 1890s the data refer to just over 1,000 males employed in the coal, iron and steel, textiles and glass industries. For the 1930s the data cover over 25,000 male and 10,000 female manual workers in London.[95] All the information relates to actual earnings, rather than to formal wage rates published by employers in local lists, or negotiated between employers and unions. Of course

---

[95] The data for 1833 was collected for the Royal Commission on the Employment of Children in Factories. The data for the 1890s is from a household budget study of British workers conducted by the American Bureau of Labor. The data for the 1930s is from the household survey conducted by the New Survey of London Life and Labour. For further information on the sources and analysis of these data, see Paul Johnson, 'Age, gender and the wage in Britain, 1830–1930', in P. Scholliers and L. Schwartz (eds.), *Experiencing Wages* (Oxford, 2003), 229–49; Paul Johnson and Asghar Zaidi, 'Work over the life course', in N. F. R. Crafts, I. Gazeley and A. Newell (eds.), *Work and Pay in Twentieth-Century Britain* (Oxford, 2007), 98–116.

the use of these data to make comparisons over time is constrained by geographical and sectoral variation. The 1830s data have wide geographical spread, whereas data for the 1930s are confined to London, and the 1880s data lack direct locational identifiers, but are probably biased towards the midlands and the north of Britain. All observations for the 1830s come from textile factories, those for the 1880s also include coal, iron and steel, whereas data for the 1930s reflect the character of the London labour force, with extensive manual employment in both services and manufacturing, but with almost no workers employed in textiles, or in coal, iron or steel. The 1830s data were derived from a survey of employers, whereas the information for the 1880s and 1930s has been extracted from household surveys. Nevertheless, there should be sufficient points of comparison to determine whether the relationship of earnings to age over time was responsive to changes in the age-specific human capital of the workforce, and to changes in the nature of work itself.

Figure 3.1 examines textile earnings data for 1833 to see whether there were significant differences in the relationship between age and earnings across different manufacturing areas. In order to allow for direct comparisons between regions and time periods which have different nominal levels of wages, the age-specific earnings data in the figures below are displayed relative to the average earnings of workers aged 30–34. It might be thought that the relationship between age and earnings in the most modern and mechanised manufacturing areas in 1833 would be different from that which existed in regions of traditional textile production where customary wage-setting practices may have been more likely to predominate. In fact, as Figure 3.1 shows, the age-earnings profiles for male workers up to age 42 were very similar in both the (modern) Lancashire cotton industry and in the (traditional) Wiltshire woollen industry where there was considerable worker resistance to mechanisation.[96] At higher ages the workers in Wiltshire fared relatively better than those in Lancashire, which may indicate that the fast pace of technological change in the more mechanised cotton industry particularly disadvantaged older workers who had not upgraded their skills.

This similarity in the shape of male age-earnings profiles is not confined to different branches of the textile industry, or to the 1830s. Figure 3.2 superimposes earnings data for the 1880s and 1930s on the Lancashire cotton data for 1833. Despite 100 years of massive

[96] J. de L. Mann, *The Cloth Industry in the West of England from 1640 to 1880* (Oxford, 1971), chs. 5 and 6.

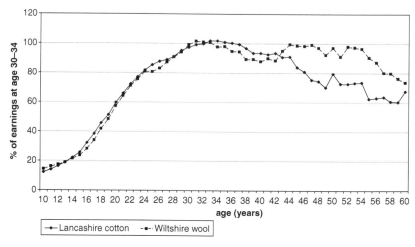

Figure 3.1 Earnings of male workers by age in 1833

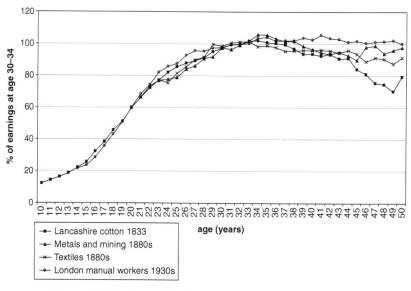

Figure 3.2 Earnings of male workers by age: 1830s, 1880s and 1930s

technological progress, productivity growth, expanded educational opportunity, demographic change, legal innovation and increased unionisation, there appears to have been practically no change at all in the relationship between age and earnings for male workers from their point of entry into the labour force until their early 40s. There was, of course, substantial sectoral change in the British economy over this period, but this can have had little impact on the overall relationship between age and earnings for manual workers, since there was almost no inter-sectoral variation in age-earnings profiles. Figure 3.2 reports two separate sets of data for the 1880s relating to males over 21 in metals and mining (526 workers) and textiles (470 workers). These two lines trace an almost identical path in Figure 3.2. The same is true for the data from inter-war London: the earnings profile for all male workers in 1930 (reported in Figure 3.2) is indistinguishable from the separate profiles (not reported here) for men employed in engineering (1,850 workers) and in clothing (556 workers), these being the two sectors of the metropolitan labour market closest to the employment included in the 1880s survey.

This long-run stability in the relationship between age and earnings is all the more remarkable because the entire basis of wage payment changed over the period considered. In the early nineteenth century, textile industry manual workers were typically paid piece-rates – that is, according to the volume and quality of the goods they produced: this was true in both the 'modern' and the 'traditional' textile regions.[97] But by the inter-war period, time-rates – that is, fixed payments by the hour, day or week – had become the norm. It seems implausible that the relative age-specific productivity of manual workers remained more-or-less invariant both between different economic sectors and over a century of unprecedented economic and technological change, yet that is the inference to be drawn from Figures 3.1 and 3.2 if we accept that age-specific earnings reflect age-specific productivity. An alternative interpretation is that the relationship between age and earnings reflects not the underlying age-specific productivity of the workers, but rather the inheritance of some customary expectations about the relative earnings of younger, prime-age and older workers.

A determining role for custom appears to be incompatible with standard economic assumptions about wage determination which posit that individual workers (and individual firms) maximise, that equilibrium is the norm, and that archaic or redundant wage forms will be readily abandoned in favour of remuneration systems that are technically more efficient. In fact we know that employers did use wages to compete with each other in order to attract the workers they needed – an example of this was the competition in Keighley in 1847 between the

---

[97] Adrian Randall, 'Work, culture and resistance to machinery in the West of England woollen industry', in Pat Hudson (ed.), *Regions and Industries* (Cambridge, 1989), 186; Huberman, *Escape*, 5.

woollen manufacturers Hattersley and Mitchell for Mary Dawson's services. It is also clear that wages reflected local patterns of supply and demand for labour. Wages in industrial Lancashire were, for both textile workers and agricultural labourers, some 30 per cent above equivalent wages in the largely agricultural counties of Somerset and Devon.[98] Furthermore, some wage relativities, such as that between men and women, did change considerably over time. In the 1830s the average 30-year-old female textile worker earned roughly 40 per cent of the equivalent male wage, whereas by the 1930s a 30-year-old woman earned about 60 per cent of the male wage. The nineteenth-century labour market was undoubtedly responsive to competitive pressures in many respects, yet not, apparently, when it came to the relation between earnings and age. Why not? The answer lies in the powerful role of custom in determining this aspect of the wage structure.

It is helpful here to introduce the concept of 'path dependence'. This term has been extensively used in economics since the 1980s to convey a sense that history matters, that current economic systems are, to some degree, the products of their own past. This is, however, a very loose usage of what is intended to be a much more precise concept. A process can be thought to be path dependent if choices made at an early stage serve to *lock in* that process to a particular pathway of development.[99] Examples that are commonly used by economists to illustrate path dependency typically relate to technological choice. For example, the QWERTY typewriter keyboard was designed to slow down typists, and thereby reduce the risk of keys jamming on early mechanical typewriters. With modern word processors the keyboard layout can be reprogrammed at trivial cost, but we continue to use the (inefficient) QWERTY layout because this is what the great majority of users are familiar with. There may be long-run savings to be gained from adopting a more efficient layout, but the short-run costs to users of re-learning how to type are so great that we find ourselves *locked in* to QWERTY.[100] Another example might be the 'standard' railway gauge

---

[98] Hunt, *Regional Wage Variation*; Johnson, 'Age, gender and the wage'.
[99] The literature on path dependence in economics is huge. For a short introduction and guide to further literature see Paul A. David, 'Path dependence, its critics and the quest for "historical economics"', in Pierre Garrouste and Stavros Ioannides (eds.), *Evolution and Path Dependence in Economic Ideas* (Cheltenham, 2001), 15–40.
[100] Paul David initiated the debate with his 'Clio and the economics of QWERTY', *American Economic Review*, 75 (1985), 332–7. Further contributions are referenced in David, 'Path dependence', 36–8. For a critique and counter-argument which denies that economic actors will persist in the use of sub-optimal technologies or institutions, see S. Liebowitz and S. Margolis, 'The fable of the keys', *Journal of Law and Economics*, 33 (1990), 1–25; idem, 'Path dependence, lock-in, and history', *Journal of*

of 4 feet 8½ inches. The technological (and other) parameters that led to the choice of this gauge in the nineteenth century are no longer paramount, and if a new railway system were being built from scratch in the early twenty-first century it would probably be optimal to adopt a different gauge. However, the cost of converting existing railways to a different gauge would be huge, and the construction of a new line to a dimension different to that of the rest of the network would significantly reduce its usefulness. Hence twenty-first-century railways are *locked in* to a nineteenth-century technological standard.[101] In the case of railways the lock-in is due to the cost of altering the physical capital, whereas with the typewriter it is due to the cost of altering the human capital of millions of typists, but the effects are similar.

How might the idea of path dependence be applied to the relationship between age and earnings in the nineteenth-century labour market? The parallel is not immediately obvious, because wage payment systems do not embody an expensive physical technology, and change to them does not appear to involve significant cost in terms of either physical or human capital. A cotton or woollen master could instigate a change to the relative earnings of workers of different ages at short notice and at trivial administrative cost. It would seem to make sense to do so if age-specific labour productivity altered over time because of, for example, mechanisation or improved education. Yet in fact age-specific wage relativities appear to have been locked in throughout the nineteenth, and well into the twentieth, century. To ascribe this rigidity to 'custom' is to offer description rather than explanation. As Arthur Stinchcombe has trenchantly observed, it is 'difficult to explain why many types of organisations retain structural peculiarities after their foundation without falling into tautologous statements about "tradition", "vested interests" or "folkways" not being changeable by formal regulation'.[102] Explanation of customary behaviour requires that the mechanisms that maintain and perpetuate this behaviour among the various groups affected be identified.

Law, Economics, and Organization, 11 (1995), 205–26. This counter-argument seems to me to rely on the belief that there exists a poorly-specified Darwinian process within the economy which will ultimately eradicate inefficient institutions.

[101] D. Puffert, 'The standardization of track gauge on North American railways, 1830–1890', *Journal of Economic History,* 60 (2000), 933–60.

[102] Arthur Stinchcombe, 'Social structure and the founding of organizations', in James G. March, *Handbook of Organizations* (Chicago, 1965). Reprinted in Arthur Stinchcombe, *Stratification and Organisation* (Cambridge, 1986), 196–220 at 217. Stinchcombe's early work on historical causation explored from a sociological perspective many of the same issues relating to the persistence of institutional forms that have subsequently attracted the attention of economists who use the concept of path dependence.

The path-dependent mechanism that operated to maintain stable age-specific wage premiums within a wide range of manual occupations was clearly not driven by the cost of changing either physical or human capital. In fact, the standard economic models of path dependence are less relevant here than models drawn from political science which emphasise the collective nature of many actions.[103] Consider the position of a single textile manufacturer – say Mr Mitchell of Keighley – who recognises that the introduction of mechanisation (the power loom) has fundamentally changed the relative productivity of juvenile and adult weavers by reducing the physical demands of the job. If it is assumed that Mitchell's overall revenue was constrained by the competitive environment of the Yorkshire woollen market, then he could reward the increased productivity of juveniles only by reducing the wages for adult workers.[104] If workers responded immediately (or as rapidly as was allowed by the Master and Servant laws) to these price incentives, Mitchell would soon find himself swamped with juvenile workers attracted by the higher wages and devoid of adults who would seek to maintain their customary wages by taking employment elsewhere. If, as seems likely, workers of different ages are not completely interchangeable in terms of skills and responsibilities, Mitchell's attempt to bring age-specific pay more in line with age-specific productivity would probably leave him with a workforce so unbalanced in age structure that its overall productivity would be diminished.

Quite apart from the questionable short-run economic gains for a go-it-alone employer, there was also the potential cost of peer-group pressure. Even in Yorkshire and Lancashire, the most modern part of the British textile industry in the early-Victorian period, production was highly fragmented with large numbers of small firms operating at each stage of the manufacturing process and tied to each other through close trading and credit networks.[105] An antagonistic action by one employer, such as abandoning locally-agreed wage payment systems, could lead to both commercial and social ostracism by the rest of the employer

---

[103] See Paul Pierson, 'Increasing returns, path dependence, and the study of politics', *American Political Science Review*, 94 (2000), 251–67; Paul Pierson, 'Not just what, but *when*: timing and sequence in political processes', *Studies in American Political Development*, 14 (2000), 72–92, and the several commentaries appearing in the same issue. Also useful is James Mahoney, 'Path dependence in historical sociology', *Theory and Society*, 29 (2000), 507–48.

[104] This assumption is consistent with a model of a perfectly competitive market in which all producers are price-takers. It is also a realistic representation of the Yorkshire woollens market in the mid-nineteenth century.

[105] P. Hudson, *The Genesis of Industrial Capital: A Study of the West Riding Wool Textile Industry, c. 1750–1850* (Cambridge, 1986); Huberman, *Escape*.

community. In towns in which employers constituted a critical mass of magistrates and councillors, exclusion from this group could result in a costly loss of influence over employment-related court cases or council decisions. It could also lead to a loss of status within the often tightly knit middle-class social world of nineteenth-century industrial towns.[106]

Despite the large number of textile employers in the major cotton and woollen towns of Lancashire and Yorkshire in the mid-nineteenth century, and despite their evident commercial competition with each other over the purchase of inputs and the sale of outputs, they did not operate as atomistic employers (as assumed in economic models of a perfectly competitive market), because they were linked by multiple and overlapping social networks. Mark Granovetter has argued that all attempts at purposive action are 'embedded in concrete, ongoing systems of social relations', and that the social content with which continuing economic relations are overlaid 'carries strong expectations of trust and abstention from opportunism'.[107]

There were, therefore, two separate forces militating against any change in customary age-related wages. The embeddedness of market relationships meant that an employer who broke with local wage conventions in order to align wages more closely with productivity might well see any financial advantage from this move diminished because of his exclusion from socially and economically valuable local networks. We should note, however, that social relations between employers did not prevent opportunistic attempts to poach workers (as Mitchell did in the case of Mary Dawson), and in some respects the Master and Servant laws can be seen as a formal legal mechanism to restrict short-term wage competition between employers which could not be fully contained by purely social sanctions. The second force, which seems to be more compelling in terms of long-run stability of wage relativities, was the problem of collective action. A change to age-specific wage relativities in order to reflect the changing nature of work and changing characteristics of workers across the nineteenth century had the characteristics of a classic 'prisoners' dilemma'. If all employers adopted a

---

[106] R. J. Morris, *Class, Sect and Party: The Making of the British Middle Class, Leeds 1820–1850* (London, 1990); R. H. Trainor, *Black Country Elites: The Exercise of Authority in an Industrial Area, 1830–1900* (Oxford, 1993).

[107] Mark Granovetter, 'Economic action and social structure: the problem of embeddedness', *American Journal of Sociology*, 91 (1985), 481–510, at 487, 490. For an interesting critique of the use of the concept of embeddedness within economic sociology see Greta R. Krippner, 'The elusive market: embeddedness and the paradigm of economic sociology', *Theory and Society*, 30 (2001), 775–810.

more accurate and efficient payment structure, they could all be better off, but if only one (or a small number) of employers adopted this
new structure, they would likely experience higher costs of production
because they would be incapable of retaining a balanced labour force.
Thus the rational decision for each individual employer was to persist
with the prevailing structure of age-specific wage relativities, regardless
of whether it was technically efficient.

Does this mean that employers were powerless in the face of customary wage payment practices? Not at all. The most likely response
of any employer who found that technology was making certain age
groups more productive, was not to try to change the customary age-
earnings profile, but rather to work around this customary structure by
changing the proportion of workers of different ages. This is, of course,
exactly what happened with the mechanisation of the textile industry in
the nineteenth century – men were replaced in large numbers by child
and female workers, but the age-earnings profiles for manual workers
in Lancashire cottons and Yorkshire woollens remained virtually the
same as in traditional (non-mechanised) textile areas, and the same as
in virtually all other sectors of the economy. This was also, according
to Mill, what occurred throughout the professions:

All professional remuneration is regulated by custom. The fees of physicians,
surgeons, and barristers, the charges of attorneys, are nearly invariable. Not
certainly for want of abundant competition in those professions, but because
the competition operates by diminishing each competitor's chance of fees, not
by lowering the fees themselves.[108]

The previous chapter showed that legal and economic theorists in
Victorian Britain ascribed to a model of contractual relationships which
was premised upon the idea that the law and the market were neutral
facilitators of free bargains and effective competition. In practice, the
law relating to the recovery of debts was anything but neutral; small
debtors were treated with enduring, even increasing, harshness, while
commercial debtors, and from 1861 large personal debtors, were given
the opportunity to shed a significant proportion of their debt through
the legal process of bankruptcy. Henry Maine's influential belief
about the shift in social organisation from status to contract simply
ignored the fact that, with respect to recovery of debt, the Victorian law
was riven with status distinctions. The same was true of employment
law. Until 1875 workers could be subject to criminal sanction simply
for behaving in a self-interested manner, even though such behaviour

---

[108] Mill, *Principles*, Book II, ch. iv, s. 3.

was supposed to be the natural mainspring of the economy which kept it in harmonious balance. Again we see that the law was structured by status distinctions which were designed to privilege the interests of employers. Rather than supply and demand being guided by the free market to produce optimally efficient outcomes, they were constrained and channelled by market institutions to produce outcomes that invariably favoured the interests of capital over labour. Economic activity was also constrained and channelled by custom, particularly with respect to wages, where entrenched social expectations about the appropriate returns to age, sex, skill and status set the broad structure of pay differentials. It was, of course, true that wages were higher where labour was scarce, but it was not the case that wages were determined in an absolute manner by supply and demand. The price of different sorts of labour was set according to broad social expectations, and it was at the margin that this price could be shifted by the balance of supply and demand. The effect of competition was thus apparent within the limits set by custom. We see, therefore, that Victorian conceptions of competition based on freedom of contract and free labour were idealistic, rather than realistic, representations of market structures.

Part II

Institutions

> Unlike the laws of Production, those of Distribution are partly of human institution: since the manner in which wealth is distributed in any given society, depends on the statutes or usages therein obtaining. But though governments or nations have the power of deciding what institutions shall exist, they cannot arbitrarily determine how those institutions shall work. The conditions on which the power they possess over the distribution of wealth is dependent, and the manner in which the distribution is effected by the various modes of conduct which society may think fit to adopt, are as much a subject for scientific enquiry as any of the physical laws of nature.[1]
>
> John Stuart Mill, *Principles of Political Economy* (1848)

John Stuart Mill was well aware of the contingent nature of economic institutions. Although governments could legislate to promote, regulate or restrict trade and exchange, their capacity to direct economic activity was constrained 'by the various modes of conduct which society may think fit to adopt'. Legislators could enact statutes, but they had control of only a small number of indirect levers with which to influence economic behaviour. Military might – which Britain possessed in abundance throughout Victoria's reign – supported imperial ambition, both economic and political, but had little impact on domestic economic governance. The tax system did not come into contact with the vast majority of domestic economic activity, focusing instead on a limited range of customs, excise and property imposts. And in England the common law foundations of the legal system interposed very extensive room for judicial interpretation of any statute, such that the original legislative intent could be drastically revised without any formal recourse to Parliament.

The weakness of direct and coercive economic power within the British State, particularly compared with the major continental European economies, together with a broad commitment among British politicians and public intellectuals to a political economy of free trade and minimal regulation, created among contemporaries – and subsequent historians – the impression that economic development occurred largely

[1] Mill, *Principles*, Preliminary Remarks, para. 31.

independently of either government promotion or government restriction. An apparent case of benign neglect fostering healthy development. Yet Victoria's reign in fact witnessed the passage of foundational laws which created the joint stock company, the dominant economic institution of modern capitalism.

The chapters in this section examine the process whereby the British government decided to sanction the passage of these foundational laws, and the process whereby the formal statutes were adopted, adapted and interpreted by economists, judges, financiers, businessmen and journalists to create, by 1900, the institutional core of corporate capitalism. What may seem, at first sight, to be a simple evolutionary story of economic necessity driving institutional and legislative modernisation, turns out to be a complex tale of diverse interest and unpredictable outcomes. The outcomes were determined not by competitive pressure but by social choices about the desirability or acceptability of various modes of economic conduct.

4   The incorporation of business

On the evening of Saturday 7 October 1893 a distinguished and expect-
ant audience gathered in the Savoy Theatre for the premiere of a new
light opera penned by the redoubtable team of W. S. Gilbert and Sir
Arthur Sullivan. This creative duo were at the height of their fame: their
immediately previous collaboration, *The Gondoliers*, had run to universal acclaim for 554 consecutive performances, and Queen Victoria had
requested a special performance for herself and her court at Windsor
Castle. Yet despite this appreciation from the heart of the British establishment, there was always a satirical edge to Gilbert and Sullivan pro-
ductions. Gilbert, the librettist, had already directed his rapacious wit
at a range of British institutions including the legal system (*Trial by
Jury*, 1875), the aristocracy (*Iolanthe*, 1882) and the snobbery of the
class system (*The Gondoliers*, 1889). In this new production, *Utopia
(Limited), or the Flowers of Progress*, his target was the limited liability
joint stock company. The plot, absurd as always, centred on the imagi-
nary Pacific island of Utopia where the King, in pursuit of all things
modish and English, decides to follow contemporary business fashion
and convert every one of his citizens into a limited liability company.
The audience loved it. *The Times* judged this new production a great
success; George Bernard Shaw, then music critic of *The World*, thought
it the most enjoyable of all the Gilbert and Sullivan operas.[1]

The stock in trade of opera libretti are adultery and unrequited love.
To construct a comic opera about the technical apparatus of company
law would at first sight seem as bizarre as writing a pop song about
the intricacies of capital gains tax. That Gilbert and Sullivan managed this implausible feat with considerable success is testament not
just to their artistic skills, but also to their keen appreciation of the
late-Victorian middle-class mind set. Joint stock companies were big
news in the 1890s. The Transvaal gold rushes of the late 1880s led
to a rash of speculative mining companies being floated and traded

---

[1] *The Times*, 9 October 1893, p. 6.

on the London Stock Exchange (the 'Kaffir circus'), and to considerable public and press discussion of the benefits and risks of investing in such concerns.[2] At the same time, thousands of established businesses which had long operated quite contentedly as sole proprietorships or partnerships, chose to take advantage of a legal opportunity that had existed since mid-century for conversion to joint stock limited liability companies. It was this normalisation of the company which provided Gilbert and Sullivan with their opportunity to poke fun at the indiscriminate nature of company formation. As Mr Goldbury, the company promoter, explained to the King of Utopia:

> Stupendous loans to foreign thrones
> I've largely advocated
> In ginger-pops and peppermint-drops
> I've freely speculated
> Then mines of gold, of wealth untold
> Successfully I've floated
> And sudden falls in apple-stalls
> Occasionally quoted
> And soon or late I always call
> for Stock Exchange quotation
> No scheme too great and none too small
> for Companification.[3]

'Companification' – the substitution of an impersonal corporate legal entity for the sole proprietorship or partnership – has long been seen by economic analysts and commentators as *the* defining element of modern capitalism. In 1933 Adolf Berle and Gardiner Means produced their path-breaking analysis of *The Modern Corporation and Private Property* in which they wrote that 'the modern corporation may be regarded not simply as one form of social organisation but potentially (if not yet actually) as the dominant institution of the modern world'.[4] Alfred Chandler has memorably identified the 'visible hand' of corporate management

---

[2] The nominal capitalisation of South African mining companies newly registered in Britain averaged just over £1m per year for the period 1880–4, but soared to over £10m in 1888 and £14m in 1889. A second speculative South African mining boom occurred in 1895–6. See Jean-Jacques van Helton, 'Mining, share manias and speculation: British investment in overseas mining, 1880–1913', in J. J. van Helton and Y. Cassis (eds.), *Capitalism in a Mature Economy* (Aldershot, 1990), 159–85. The dubious, and in some cases fraudulent, nature of the speculative mining companies floated during the 'Kaffir circus' was used by Arnold Bennett as the central device of his short story 'The fire of London', published in his *The Loot of the Cities* (London, 1905).

[3] See the libretto at Gilbert and Sullivan Archive: http://math.boisestate.edu/gas/utopia/html/index.html

[4] Adolf A. Berle Jr. and Gardiner C. Means, *The Modern Corporation and Private Property* (New York, 1933), 356.

in the modern multi-unit business enterprise as the driving force of US economic growth since the 1880s.[5] The economic and ideological dominance of the modern corporation is one of the few points of agreement between detractors and supporters of modern capitalism. As far as critics are concerned, the corporation 'is a pathological institution, a dangerous possessor of the great power it wields over people and societies'.[6] Anti-globalisation campaigners believe that multi-national corporations are 'now reaching out to establish the hegemony of a culture of greed and excess in virtually every country in the world'.[7] But for advocates of western capitalism, the company is 'the most important organisation in the world ... the basis of the prosperity of the West and the best hope for the future of the rest of the world'.[8]

It is certainly true that the investor-owned joint stock company is the most prominent economic organisation in the 'capitalist' economic systems of Western Europe, North America and Japan, and that it is an important economic form in almost all countries. It is a commonplace among economists that investor-owned companies, and the financial markets which facilitate the trade in company shares, represent, in most circumstances, the most efficient way to organise and finance the large-scale production of goods and services. In fact there is a powerful view which insists that a specifically American form of investor-owned company, based on the superior flexibility of Anglo-American common law over continental European civil law systems, can to a large degree explain America's long-run advantage in economic performance over her major competitors.[9] It is not appropriate here to unpick the provenance of these claims about the relative efficiency of different forms of capitalist organisation in the early twenty-first century, though it is perhaps worth drawing attention to Henry Hansmann's insistence that 'investor ownership is not a logically necessary concomitant of free markets and free enterprise'.[10] Hansmann notes that much market activity, even in modern America, is conducted by institutions with quite different organisational forms – mutual companies in insurance,

[5] A. Chandler, *The Visible Hand: The Managerial Revolution in American Business* (Cambridge, MA, 1977).
[6] Joel Bakan, *The Corporation: The Pathological Pursuit of Profit and Power* (London, 2004), 2.
[7] David C. Koten, *The Post-Corporate World* (West Hartford, CT, 1998), 33.
[8] J. Micklethwait and A. Wooldridge, *The Company* (London, 2003), 2.
[9] Rafael La Porta, Florencio Lopez-de-Silanes, Andrei Schleifer and Robert Vishny, 'Legal determinants of external finance', *Journal of Finance*, 52 (1997), 1131–50; Rafael La Porta, Florencio Lopez-de-Silanes, Andrei Schleifer and Robert Vishny, 'Law and finance', *Journal of Political Economy*, 106 (1998), 1133–55.
[10] Henry Hansmann, *The Ownership of Enterprise* (Cambridge, MA, 1996), 1.

not-for-profit firms in education and healthcare, owner cooperatives in housing, employee cooperatives in law and accounting, producer cooperatives in farming. The joint stock company is clearly a contingent, not a natural, form of economic organisation.

However, the almost automatic association made by most economists today between the joint stock company and economic efficiency carries within it an implicit historical assertion: that the evolution and use of the joint stock company in the nineteenth century was itself a contributory factor in the expansion of economic activity and sustained rise in the rate of economic growth that occurred in North America and Western Europe between 1800 and 1900.[11] There is no direct way of determining whether this assertion is supported by empirical evidence: economic growth on both sides of the Atlantic was temporally associated with the rise of the joint stock company, but it was likewise temporally associated with the expansion of international trade, technological progress, rising levels of literacy and increasingly democratic systems of national governance. It is possible to construct loose accounts as to why any or all of these factors may have had a positive impact on the rate of growth of the economy in the nineteenth century, but it is not possible to construct consistent and convincing tests of their relative importance. This and the following chapter therefore take a different approach. Rather than attempt to measure the impact of joint stock organisation on the economy at large, they instead examine a related proposition – that the evolution in design and use of the joint stock company form was a response to the growing needs of a developing economy for a more flexible and efficient way of organising business activity. This proposition conceives of the legal structure as a servant of the economy, and of legal innovation as an essentially functionalist response to the changing technological parameters of the economic system. Such a view is consistent with the dominant paradigm within the literature on law and economics, which sees the law (especially the Anglo-American common law) as an inherently efficient creator and transmitter of rules and norms which adjust to the changing needs of a dynamic market in order to facilitate optimal decision-making and resource allocation.[12] The underlying

---

[11] For a rare and recent challenge to this orthodoxy see T. Guinnane, R. Harris, N. Lamoreaux and J-L Rosenthal, 'Putting the corporation in its place', *Enterprise and Society*, 8 (2007), 687–729.

[12] One of the formative texts is Richard A Posner, *Economic Analysis of Law* (Boston, 1972). The major contributions to this position have emerged from US scholars who collectively dominate the law and economics field. For an early and powerful British statement of the functionalist position see C.A. Cooke, *Corporation, Trust and Company* (Manchester, 1950), ch. 1.

process here is one of natural selection. Legal forms which no longer serve the interests of economic actors fall out of use and eventually disappear; meanwhile, new economic opportunities provide an incentive to adapt existing laws to suit a new environment, and to create entirely new legal structures where necessary.

This functionalist interpretation of the legal system, though favoured by most of those economists who pay attention to such issues, is by no means universally accepted. There exists a quite different viewpoint among many legal scholars who emphasise the relative autonomy of a legal system which has its own self-referential system of jurisprudence and reasoning, its own professional structure, and its own, somewhat isolationist, social networks.[13] From this perspective, change in a civil law system occurs only when the core rationale for any particular legal process is repeatedly challenged by cases which cannot be accommodated within the existing framework of precedent and jurisprudential reasoning. Legal changes made to accommodate social or economic innovation may lag these innovations by many years or decades.

It has recently been suggested by Ron Harris that a middle way between functionalism and autonomy may have characterised the English approach to commercial law in the eighteenth and nineteenth centuries. Autonomy at the top of the legal system – the formal doctrines and processes of legislation and the higher courts – was balanced by clear economic instrumentality in the way in which businessmen and their lawyers operated on and around the margins of the law, especially in the lower courts. However, Harris suggests that even this compromise position is too stark, since in practice the balance between autonomy and functionalism waxed and waned over time, and varied according to the specific institutional and economic setting.[14]

This chapter sets out to address the functionalist proposition that the rise of the joint stock company in nineteenth-century Britain was driven by the needs of a dynamic and expanding market economy. The specific focus is on the impact that incorporation and the issue of shares had on business proprietors. Implicit in the functionalist case lie two interrelated ideas: that incorporation offered distinct efficiency gains over alternative forms of business organisation; and that evidence of these gains was sufficiently conclusive to persuade the mid-Victorian legislature to extend the benefits of incorporation to many previously excluded businesses. The following chapter then examines the related

---

[13] See, for example, Mark Kelman, *A Guide to Critical Legal Studies* (Cambridge, MA, 1990).

[14] Harris, *Industrializing English Law*, 3–12.

but distinct issue of limited liability, and the particular salience this had (and continues to have) for investors in joint stock companies. General access to incorporation and limited liability are often spoken of in the same breath, but in fact they are distinct legal privileges which were introduced into English law by different acts at different points in the nineteenth century, and it is therefore appropriate to give them separate attention. Chapter 6 then presents a detailed case study evaluation of the economic benefits of the introduction in Victorian Britain of the joint stock limited liability form. As noted above, it is not possible to conduct a convincing direct test of the economy-wide impact of incorporation, but Chapter 6 makes use of institutional diversity within the insurance sector in the nineteenth century to take a targeted look at this issue.

The joint stock company was not a creation of the nineteenth century; examples from the mid-sixteenth century include the Muscovy and the Levant Companies, which were organised to develop England's trading routes with Russia and Turkey respectively.[15] Yet it was a series of acts during Victoria's reign – the 1844 Companies Registration Act, the 1855 Limited Liability Act, the 1856 Joint Stock Companies Act, and the 1862 Companies Act – that created the legal framework for incorporation and share ownership which remains, in essence, the basis of corporate capitalism today.[16] This legislation transformed incorporation from being a rare privilege bestowed by government on large businesses with narrow, often strategic, purposes, to being a generally accessible legal form available to almost any undertaking, regardless of scale, purpose or importance.

The defining characteristic of a commercial corporation is that it is conceived of in law as an artificial person which can sue and be sued in its own right, independently of those persons who have combined collectively to form the corporation.[17] It allows individuals to pool their

[15] W. R. Scott, *The Constitution and Finance of English, Scottish and Irish Joint-Stock Companies to 1720* (2 vols., Cambridge University Press, 1910–12).

[16] 1844 Companies Registration Act, 7 & 8 Vict. c. 110; 1855 Limited Liability Act, 18 & 19 Vict. c. 133; 1856 Joint Stock Companies Act, 19 & 20 Vict. c. 47; 1862 Companies Act, 25 & 26 Vict. c. 89. L.S. Sealy, *Company Law and Commercial Reality* (London 1984) has noted (at 1–2) that a company lawyer from the late-nineteenth-century period would have no difficulty in comprehending modern company law, which retains the key elements of this Victorian legislation.

[17] There was an extensive discussion among legal scholars at the beginning of the twentieth century about the relationship between the State and groups, such as corporations, that exist inside it. Those who were influenced by German legal theory argued for the 'real personality' of the corporation (i.e. that corporate personality has a bearing on the reality of corporate life), while mainstream English jurisprudence

resources – and if they so desire, their energy and business acumen – in order to conduct business in a manner distinct from that of a sole trader or partnership. An individual trading under his or her own name is personally responsible for commercial actions taken and decisions made; partners in a business typically share joint and direct responsibility for the success or otherwise of the venture. In a corporation, on the other hand, the owners of the business – the shareholders – are not held responsible for the actions of the company, for although their shareholding imparts ownership, they do not directly control the company, which in law has an autonomous legal personality. If a corporation errs, the shareholders may lose their wealth, but not their liberty.

As with other aspects of economic development during industrialisation, the evolution of the corporate form in Britain did not pass unnoticed by the classical economists. Despite the individualistic premise of much of the economic analysis in the *Wealth of Nations*, Adam Smith devoted considerable effort to explaining how collective bodies – states, companies and interest groups – might interact, and sometimes interfere, with the smooth working of the competitive market economy. Smith has often been interpreted as being hostile to both the principles and practice of joint-stock companies; he did not deal explicitly with them until the third (1784) edition of the *Wealth of Nations*, where he condemned, at some length, the status and actions of companies granted 'exclusive privileges'.[18] He acknowledged that there could be a valid case for allowing monopoly trading rights for a limited period in order to compensate merchants for the high risk associated with the initiation of 'a new trade with some remote and barbarous nation', but in the cases of the Royal African Company and the East India Company he had no doubt that long-term monopoly had led to inefficiency and high costs.[19] On the other hand, he recognised that the Hudson Bay Company appeared to function efficiently without legal entry restrictions, and he noted that 'a joint stock company, consisting of a small number of proprietors, with moderate capital, approaches very nearly to the nature of a private copartnery, and may be capable of nearly the same degree of vigilance and attention'.[20]

accepted the artificial personality of the corporation. See the 'Editors' Introduction' in F. W. Maitland, *State, Trust and Corporation*, edited by D. Runciman and M. Ryan (Cambridge, 2003).

[18] Smith, *WoN*, Book V, ch.1. The material on joint stock companies included in 1784 appears to have been drafted as early as 1774. See G. M. Anderson and R. D. Tollison, 'Adam Smith's analysis of joint-stock companies', *Journal of Political Economy*, 90 (1982), 1237–56.

[19] Smith, *WoN*, Book V, ch. 1, 754.   [20] *Ibid.*, 744.

Far from being intrinsically hostile to the joint stock company, Smith viewed it as an economic organisation that should be subjected to his general test of efficiency and fitness for purpose – could it survive and prosper in a competitive market.[21] He recognised both strengths and weaknesses. For owners there were three key advantages to incorporation – liquidity, limited liability and scale economies. In a partnership no individual partner can transfer their share to another person without the consent of all other partners, and any partner can at any time withdraw from the partnership and demand payment for their share of the common stock. In a joint stock company, on the other hand, shares can be freely transferred at whatever price the market deems appropriate.[22] Furthermore, in a partnership each partner is 'bound for the debts contracted by the company to the whole extent of his fortune. In a joint stock company, on the contrary, each partner is bound only to the extent of his share.'[23] Liquidity and limited liability together allowed joint stock companies to raise capital on a scale beyond the capacity of any sole trader or partnership:

This total exemption from trouble and risk, beyond a limited sum, encourages many people to become adventurers in joint stock companies who would, upon no account, hazard their fortunes in any private copartnery. Such companies, therefore, draw to themselves much greater stocks than any copartnery can boast of.[24]

Yet Smith saw the potential scale of joint stock companies as an inherent weakness as well as a strength. A multitude of owners cannot directly manage the affairs of a large concern, and have to devolve responsibility to a small body of managers:

The directors of such companies, however, being the managers of other people's money than their own, it cannot well be expected, that they should watch over it with the same anxious vigilance with which the partners in a private copartnery frequently watch over their own. Like the stewards of a rich man, they are apt to consider attention to small matters as not for their master's honour, and very easily give themselves a dispensation from having it. Negligence and profusion, therefore, must always prevail, more or less, in the management of the affairs of such a company. It is upon this account that joint stock companies for foreign trade have seldom been able to maintain the competition

[21] Anderson and Tollison, 'Adam Smith's analysis'.
[22] Smith, *WoN*, Book V, ch. 1, 740.
[23] *Ibid.*, 740–41. It should be noted that there was some legal ambiguity about whether all early joint stock companies incorporated by Royal Charter or Act of Parliament had limited liability. See Cooke, *Corporation*.
[24] Smith, *WoN*, 741.

against private adventurers. They have, accordingly, very seldom succeeded without an exclusive privilege; and frequently have not succeeded with one.[25]

In this striking passage Smith recognises that there exists a potential conflict of interest within a joint stock company between managers and shareholders. This insight – a century and a half before Berle and Means identified the separation of ownership and control as a central feature of the modern corporation, and almost two centuries before the 'agency problem' made its way into the core syllabus of institutional economics – led Smith to conclude that there existed only four sectors in which the advantages of large-scale capital could outweigh the costs of managerial negligence – banking, insurance, canals and waterworks. In these trades, Smith believed, it was possible to reduce internal operations to a routine which would constrain managers to behave without undue negligence or profligacy. This list of trades appears to reflect those few domestic business activities in which joint stock firms operated and prospered in the late eighteenth century.[26]

In the first half of the nineteenth century classical economists added little to Smith's brief analysis of the costs and benefits of incorporation (although, as will be seen in Chapter 5, they did have further things to say about the related but distinct issue of limited liability).[27] Mill repeated Smith's concern about the agency costs associated with joint stock companies, particularly the lack of 'zeal' of paid managers, although he cautioned that 'Adam Smith fixed his observation too exclusively on the superior energy and more unremitting attention brought to a business in which the whole stake and the whole gain belong to the persons conducting it'.[28] Mill proposed that the fidelity of managers could be enhanced through incentive payments (profit-sharing), while careful selection could ensure the appointment of persons with more appropriate skills than could be anticipated within a small-scale partnership.[29] On balance he thought the benefits of scale economies would typically outweigh the losses from managerial shirking, and thus that corporations were more likely to dominate where the market is large, and partnerships where the market is more restricted.

[25] *Ibid.*, 741.
[26] H. A. Shannon, 'The first five thousand limited companies and their duration', *Economic History* (a supplement to the *Economic Journal*), 2 (1932), 396–424; Anderson and Tollison, 'Adam Smith's analysis', 1244.
[27] C. E. Amsler, R. L. Bartlett and C. J. Bolton, 'Thoughts of some British economists on early limited liability and corporate legislation', *History of Political Economy*, 13 (1981), 774–93.
[28] Mill, *Principles*, Book 1, ch. 9, s. 2.   [29] *Ibid.*, 141.

By the end of Victoria's reign, Alfred Marshall was both extending and qualifying Mill's analysis of the characteristics and function of joint stock companies. He concurred that a great strength of the corporation was its ability to expand without limit, and noted that company amalgamations were frequently promoted on the grounds that shareholders would reap the benefits of economies of scale.[30] On the other hand, he elaborated on Mill's analysis of agency costs, recognising that 'joint stock companies are hampered by internal frictions, and conflicts of interest between shareholders and debenture holders, between ordinary and preferred shareholders, and between all of these and the directors; and by the need for an elaborate system of checks and counterchecks'.[31] He also recognised that the joint stock form was 'plastic', and that if 'a group of wealthy capitalists retain the complete effective control of all the affairs of a company in their own hands, they can act with as much freedom and vigour as if they remained in simple partnership'.[32] Thus, although the increase in the number of joint stock companies has resulted in 'the general democratisation' of the ownership of business, the control of these companies lay in the hands of a small number of directors and managers, leaving the shareholders 'almost powerless'.[33] As to how this tension between the interests of owners and controllers might be resolved, Marshall put his faith not in the competitive ordering of the market, but in moral values: 'it is a strong proof of the marvellous growth in recent times of a spirit of honesty and uprightness in commercial matters, that the leading officers of great public companies yield as little as they do to the vast temptations to fraud which lie in their way'.[34]

Smith, Mill, Marshall and their fellow economists did not devote much space in their published works to the organisation of business. They all recognised that corporations had a capacity to raise capital and operate on a larger scale than did sole proprietors or partnerships. They also recognised the 'agency problem' that arises with the divorce of ownership and control, although they differed over the importance of this problem, and the extent to which it could be mitigated through incentive structures designed to align the interest of managers with those of shareholders. Overall, however, their writings do not suggest that they considered the organisational form of business to be a significant factor

---

[30] A. Marshall, *Industry and Trade: a Study of Industrial Technique and Business Organization* (London, 1919), 303, 331.
[31] Marshall, *Principles*, Book VI, ch. 7, s. 6.   [32] Marshall, *Industry and Trade*, 317.
[33] *Ibid.*, 303, 314.   [34] Marshall, *Principles*, Book IV, ch. 12, s. 4.

in the extent or efficiency of economic activity. As long as businesses – whether partnerships or companies – were not allowed to exercise any anti-competitive privileges, the market would determine which type of organisational structure was most appropriate for each type and scale of economic activity.

Yet this philosophical obeisance to the concept of a neutral market failed to acknowledge a reality of which lawyers were well aware – that the market was a nexus of institutions and rules with specific legal definitions, that these definitions embodied a multiplicity of obligations and constraints, and that the obligations and constraints were themselves subject to change over time through both judicial decision and legislative enactment. Nowhere was this clearer than in the case of incorporation, since the British state had chosen, from 1720 to 1825, to enact a general prohibition on the formation of joint stock limited liability companies.

The Bubble Act of 1720 made illegal the formation of any unincorporated joint stock company, and the issue of transferable shares therein.[35] Incorporation could still be sought and obtained by means of a Royal Charter or a private Act of Parliament, but this could be a long, costly and uncertain process.[36] From a functionalist perspective it would seem that this blanket prohibition on unincorporated companies must have increased the overall cost of economic activity, and restricted its scale and rate of growth during the early stages of industrialisation. This was certainly the viewpoint offered in the pioneering work carried out in the 1930s into the early history of incorporation in England. Hunt is typical in claiming that:

the history of the business corporation or joint stock company in England during one hundred and fifty years following the statute of 1720 is the story of an economic necessity forcing its way slowly and painfully to legal recognition against strong commercial prejudice in favour of 'individual' enterprise, and in the face of determined attempts of both legislature and courts to deny it.[37]

---

[35] 6 Geo I c.18. The Act acquired its popular name because it was passed at around the same time as the speculative investment mania known as the South Sea Bubble, and it has commonly (though erroneously) been considered to represent a legislative attempt to prevent future bubbles. In fact the Act was sponsored by the South Sea Company as part of a concerted effort to restrict competition from other joint stock companies. See Harris, *Industrializing*, 60–81.

[36] Leone Levi, 'On Joint Stock Companies', *Journal of the Statistical Society*, 33 (1870) 1–41. But see Harris for qualification.

[37] Hunt, *Business Corporation*, 13. See also H. A. Shannon, 'The coming of general limited liability', *Economic History*, 2 (1931), reprinted in E. M. Carus-Wilson (ed.), *Essays in Economic History* (1954), 358–79; G. Todd, 'Some aspects of joint stock companies, 1844–1900', *Economic History Review*, 4 (1932), 46–71.

This is now the mainstream interpretation; in their recent history of corporate finance, Baskin and Miranti state that 'Industrialization was further advanced by the more efficient concentration of capital in business units made possible by the liberalization of laws controlling the formation of joint-stock companies.'[38]

Harris has recently revisited this issue, and has produced a more nuanced account. He concludes that the total capital of joint stock undertakings in England rose five-fold between 1740 and 1810 to reach £90 million, with the majority of growth coming in the form of companies – both incorporated and unincorporated – involved in transport, shipping, mining and public utilities.[39] Furthermore, he notes that through the ingenious work of various lawyers and businessmen, the unincorporated company found ways of using trusts and other legal devices to systematise governance and the transferability of shares, and to sue and be sued using a common name. An unincorporated group of individuals could not collectively own property, but property could be held for the group in trust. A deed of settlement set out the terms by which trustees appointed by the shareholders could use the company's funds for the purposes specified. The company could then act through its trustees rather than as a collection of individuals.[40] Nonetheless Harris sees the unincorporated company as seriously deficient compared to its incorporated alternative in terms of its ability to achieve a separate legal identity, or to offer limited liability to its shareholders.[41]

The deficiency stemmed in large part from the vagaries of English common law. Although clever lawyers often succeeded in their creative use of legal instruments to compensate for the inherent inadequacies attributable to the dubious legal standing of the unincorporated company, sometimes they encountered equally clever lawyers arguing against them in court. In these circumstances the decisions of judges were unpredictable, and not always consistent with legal precedent, where such could be found. Worse still, an increasing amount of complex partnership litigation, and all of that relating to trusts, was considered to fall under equity rather than common law jurisdiction, and thus ultimately to join the queue of the many thousands of cases pending at the Court of Chancery, where final judgment could take as long as thirty years.[42]

Harris moderates the earlier view of Hunt, Shannon and others that the Bubble Act seriously retarded the growth in scale and range of activities of joint stock companies. Yet he endorses their largely functionalist

---

[38] J. B. Baskin and P. J. Miranti, Jr., *A History of Corporate Finance* (Cambridge, 1997), 130.
[39] Harris, *Industrializing*, 193–8.   [40] Cooke, *Corporation*, 86–7.
[41] Harris, *Industrializing*, 165–7.   [42] *Ibid.*, 159–65.

interpretation of company law reform as a response to economic pressure when he writes 'the courts, Parliament and the government were forced, one by one, to deal with the totally new scale of the employment of joint stock by the business sector and with all the problems related to this new phenomenon'.[43] A speculative investment boom in 1825, led by South American mining companies, but involving also a spate of unincorporated company formations in gas, insurance, canal, railways and other activities, extended public awareness of the principles and practice of joint stock organisation.[44] Almost simultaneously the government repealed the Bubble Act and abolished the long-standing corporate monopolies that existed in banking and marine insurance.[45]

From 1825 onwards there were consistently over 200 companies listed in the *Course of the Exchange*, which was the semi-official journal of the London stock exchange. Around one-third of these were canal companies, with insurance and gas light companies together representing another third of the total.[46] A further mania for company formation, concentrated in railways and banking, occurred in 1834–6, and on the eve of the 1844 Act there were at least 720 companies known to the London stock market, with a total capitalisation of over £210 million.[47] Harris concludes that this growth was the result of 'the repeal of restriction, the introduction of new technology, and cyclical booms. One by one new sectors were conquered by the joint stock business company, which became a more familiar and integral component of England's economic success.'[48]

---

[43] *Ibid.*, 198.

[44] H. English, *A Complete View of the Joint Stock Companies Formed during 1824 and 1825* (London, 1827). Disraeli was one of a large number of active pamphleteers engaged in 'puffing' the South American mining stocks.

[45] Marine insurance was the legal monopoly of the Royal Exchange and London Assurance companies until the promoters of the Alliance Insurance Co. successfully moved for abolition of the monopoly in 1824. The Bank of England's monopoly of joint stock banking was abolished in 1826, from which date joint stock banks of issues were permitted to operate if more than 65 miles from London. The Bank Charter Act of 1833 confirmed that non-issuing joint stock banks were permitted even in London. The first of these, the London and Westminster, was established in 1834, and it became the largest common-law partnership ever to exist in England. B. Supple, *The Royal Exchange Assurance: A History of British Insurance 1720–1970* (Cambridge, 1970), 198–9; J. Clapham, *The Bank of England: A History* (Cambridge, 1944), vol 2, 134; Harris, *Industrializing*, 207–17; Jefferys, 'Trends', 65.

[46] Harris, *Industrializing*, 219.

[47] A parliamentary return of 1846 identified 947 companies registered after the 1844 Act which had been in existence prior to its passage, but it is not possible to reconcile these data with the number of companies known to the Stock Exchange prior to 1844. *Ibid.*, 222.

[48] *Ibid.*, 223.

This interpretation has recently been challenged by Taylor, who sees rather less responsiveness in the legal structures surrounding the operation of joint stock companies. He suggests that a primary motive for the repeal of the Bubble Act was to relieve Parliament of the avalanche of petitions for private bills of incorporation that coincided with investment booms (almost 300 such petitions were laid before parliament in 1825).[49] And although the repeal of the Bubble Act meant that unincorporated companies were no longer illegal, they were still subject to the obstacles and constraints placed by the common law on actions carried out by a collectivity of individuals. Taylor argues that

there had been very little change in popular and official attitudes to joint stock companies, and speculation therein, by the end of the 1830s ... Despite legislation in 1825, 1834 and 1837, companies were in a similar legal position in 1840 as they were in 1800, due largely to the common law interpretation of unincorporated companies, and to the government's desire to maintain its discretion over granting privileges of incorporation.'[50]

Gladstone's Joint Stock Companies Registration Act of 1844 can be seen either as a further step on the long road to full legitimation and democratisation of the joint stock company, or as another haphazard move to respond to immediate problems generated by the inconsistencies within corporate law. Harris identifies a long list of structural and contingent, legal and economic, ideological and personal factors relevant to the form and timing of the 1844 Act, and concludes that this legislation was 'not determined in a systematic manner solely by either economic developments or internal legal dynamics'.[51] Yet in almost the same breath he suggests that the pre-1844 legal framework had restrained entrepreneurial spirit in England throughout the preceding century, and thus he seems to go a good way down the functionalist line, even if he questions whether the legal framework which was ultimately arrived at was rationally selected to achieve economic optimality.[52]

Taylor is sceptical, and sees this key piece of legislation as being more haphazard in origin, and less positive in purpose. The 1825 Act delegated to the Board of Trade the power to advise the Crown on applications for charters of incorporation (with unlimited liability), and this power was restated by the 1834 Trading Companies Act.[53] But this

---

[49] James Conrad Taylor, '"Wealth makes worship": attitudes to joint stock enterprise in British law, politics and culture, c. 1800–c. 1870', University of Kent PhD thesis, 2002, 121. A revised version has been published as James Taylor, *Creating Capitalism: Joint-Stock Enterprise in British Politics and Culture, 1800–1870* (Woodbridge, 2006).

[50] *Ibid.*, 146–7.   [51] Harris, *Industrializing*, 288.

[52] *Ibid.*, 288–92.   [53] Cooke, *Corporation*, 124–5.

route to quasi-incorporation was less popular and no more certain than the tortuous path of seeking a private Act of Parliament,[54] and it was similarly constrained by the stance of political economy towards joint stock companies. Smith had suggested that the joint stock company was necessary, in a competitive economy, only where the scale or riskiness of activity was such that it was beyond the capacity of prudent men to organise and finance it as a partnership. The Board of Trade repeatedly reflected this Smithian principle by rejecting applications for incorporation via Letters Patent on the grounds that the proposed capitalisation of a company was too small to warrant the granting of special privileges.[55] It is clear, therefore, that throughout the 1820s and 1830s there was a consistent assumption across both Tory and Whig administrations that incorporation should be viewed as a privilege to be dispensed – by either Parliament or the Crown – to large-scale undertakings that were deemed to be in the 'public interest', broadly defined.[56] Ordinary commercial ventures were considered to be unworthy of any such privilege, and were therefore supposed to compete with each other on a level playing field established by the common law of partnership.

In reality this playing field was far from level, at least as far as creditors were concerned. Common law required that in any suit between partners and third parties, or between members of the same partnership, all partners had to be joined to the action as parties by being named. In the case of a small business operated by a handful of readily identifiable partners, this legal requirement presented few difficulties. Not so, however, in the case of an unincorporated company established under a trust deed. It was the shareholder-partners, not the trustees, who owned the company and were ultimately liable for its actions and debts, but there was no ready way of establishing the identity of these shareholders. There was no requirement for there to be any public list or register of shareholders, and this made the task of identifying and naming each and every partner in a large undertaking laborious to the point

---

[54] Over the period 1840–4 there were 19 applications to the Board of Trade for Letters Patent, of which 11 (58%) were successful, whereas over the same period 527 private bills for incorporation were presented to Parliament, of which 353 (67%) led to Acts being passed. Taylor, 'Wealth', 149.

[55] See, for example, the case of Scottish Porter and Ale Brewery Company in Minutes of Lords Committee of Privy Council for Trade on Granting Letters Patent, 4 November 1834, Appendix 3 of *Report on the Law of Partnership* by Mr Bellenden Kerr, reprinted as Appendix I of the *First Report of the Select Committee on Joint Stock Companies*, PP 1844 vii.

[56] Cooke, *Corporation*, 119–20.

of impossibility.[57] Witnesses to the 1837 Board of Trade investigation into the law of partnership concurred that the obligation of naming all partners in any legal action, and the right of each partner to be individually represented in the action, amounted to a virtual 'denial of justice' in the case of creditors of large unincorporated companies.[58]

This would not have been the first – or last – occasion on which justice had been denied to some parties because of the attachment of the legislature and courts to an apparently dysfunctional principle of procedure, but this circumstance was seen to bear more heavily from the later 1830s when some of the companies formed during the 1834–6 investment boom ceased trading and reneged on their contracts. It seems, however, that it was the fraudulent design of some of these companies, rather than the more prosaic issue of appropriate legal process, that precipitated further public investigation and legislation. A Select Committee on Joint Stock Companies was established in 1841 with a narrow remit to investigate the machinations behind a number of intentionally fraudulent joint stock insurance companies that had been established during the 1830s. This was a matter of considerable public interest; the extraction of at least £250,000 from gullible annuitants and policyholders by the West Middlesex and General Annuity Association was brilliantly parodied by Thackeray in his description of the workings of the Independent West Diddlesex Fire and Life Assurance Company, published in the autumn of 1841 in his story of the *Great Hoggarty Diamond*.[59] The select committee had not completed its enquiry when it was suspended on the fall of the Melbourne ministry, but was reconvened in 1843 by the newly appointed President of the Board of Trade, Gladstone, and its terms of reference were widened to examine not just 'modes of deception', but also the general status of joint stock companies.

Despite this expanded remit, the report issued by the committee was focused almost exclusively on the issues of fraud and malpractice, rather than on the legal status of the unincorporated company. As far as Gladstone and his fellow committeemen were concerned, in the case of intentionally fraudulent companies 'the remedy is easy: publication

---

[57] A proposal to compel joint-stock companies to register the names of their partners in the Court of Chancery was defeated in parliament in 1824; Hunt, *Business Corporation*, 52.

[58] *Report on the Law of Partnership* by Mr Bellenden Ker, PP 1844 vii. This denial of justice worked symmetrically, since it was equally laborious for a large unincorporated company to take action against any third party.

[59] Thackeray's story of 'the History of Samuel Titmarsh and the Great Hoggarty Diamond' was published in four instalments in *Fraser's Magazine*, September–December 1841.

of the Directors, of the Shareholders, of the Deed of Settlement, of the amount of the Capital, and whether subscribed or not subscribed, nominal or real, would baffle every case of fraud'. For those companies where the problem lay not with the initial design and intent, but with subsequent operational failure, the committee felt the problem could be met 'by the periodical holding of meetings, by the periodical balancing, audit, and publication of accounts, and by making Directors and officers more immediately responsible to the shareholders'.[60] These recommendations formed the basis of the Joint Stock Companies Registration and Regulation Act of 1844, and thus established the framework of modern company law.

The genesis of the 1844 Act thus appears to be much more closely linked to popular concern about company fraud than to the interest that some businessmen and lawyers had in regularising the legal standing and improving the efficiency of large unincorporated companies. Taylor has acutely remarked that 'companies were not to be brought within the law because they had achieved respectability, but because they needed to be made respectable'.[61] Respectability was to be assured through a system of compulsory registration of all partnerships (other than banks) with twenty-five or more members and freely transferable shares.[62] Existing companies as well as future formations were required to register with the newly created Registrar of Joint Stock Companies. Not only would putative companies have to submit a listing of the names, occupations and addresses of their promoters, but once fully established each company had to register the details of all officers, directors and shareholders. The books of the company had to be balanced and audited annually, and the balance sheet and auditor's report had to be deposited with the Registrar and distributed to shareholders in advance of the ordinary meeting. The underlying philosophy here was consistent with the prevailing ethos of political economy. The state was to interfere only to ensure that relevant information was placed in the public domain; the principle of *caveat emptor* was presumed to apply to anyone contemplating investing in or dealing with a registered company. John Stuart Mill, who was to commence writing his *Principles of Political Economy* a year after the passage of the 1844 Act, concurred with the approach taken by Gladstone in this legislation.[63] Mill thought

[60] *First Report of the Select Committee on Joint Stock Companies*, PP 1844 vii, iv.
[61] Taylor, 'Wealth', 152.
[62] The Joint Stock Banks Act, 1844, continued to require banks to petition the Board of Trade for Letters Patent if they wished to incorporate.
[63] Mill began *Principles* in the autumn of 1845. N. Capaldi, *John Stuart Mill: A Biography* (Cambridge, 2004), 201.

that hitherto the laws on joint stock companies had been 'most unreasonably jealous of allowing such associations to exist' but that they had also 'generally neglected the enforcement of publicity' which was 'the best security to the public' that could be achieved.[64]

The 1844 Act transformed incorporation from being a privilege controlled by the state and granted on highly specific terms, to being a legal status obtained through conformity with a bureaucratic process. There was a fair amount of public discussion of this legislation – *The Times*, reflecting the tenor of the Select Committee's investigation, called it the 'Anti-Bubble Bill'[65] – though it barely raised a murmur in parliament, where Gladstone felt it met with 'universal approval'.[66] The immediate impact appeared to be the exact opposite of that intended; within twelve months of the Act receiving Royal Assent the country was experiencing a bigger investment bubble than ever before – the so-called 'railway mania'. There was a huge surge of provisional company registrations in 1845; over 1,500 in total, of which 1,149 were railway undertakings.[67] There is little evidence, however, that the 1844 Act stimulated this speculative bubble, though it is clear that the registration requirements of the Act could not prevent the flotation of fraudulent companies in an environment of quite excessive investor credulity. In fact, because railway companies always required special acts of parliament to gain the rights of compulsory purchase necessary for the construction of their routes, the provisional registration requirement of the 1844 Act did not diminish the substantial economic, political and engineering challenges faced by these companies in realising their initial ambitions. Provisional registration simply provided a better means than hitherto of monitoring and measuring the scale and extent of railway promotion.

The relevance of the introduction of general incorporation for the rest of the economy seems to have been muted. Table 4.1 reports the distribution of (unlimited) English companies by broad economic sector, distinguishing between companies already in existence in September 1844 and required to register under the new Act, and those newly formed companies that completed registration in the period up to July 1856. It is clear that the reconceptualisation of incorporation from being a privilege to being a right had little impact on the extent to which businessmen in different sectors of the economy availed themselves of this facility. In particular, it is evident that by mid-century very few manufacturing enterprises had made use of the joint stock form of organisation.

---

[64] Mill, *Principles*, Book V, ch. 9, ss. 5–7.   [65] Taylor, 'Wealth', 157.
[66] *HCDeb*, 10 June 1844, col. 475.   [67] Levi, 'Joint Stock', 24.

Table 4.1. *Sectoral distribution of joint stock companies*
(a) in existence prior to 1844, and (b) formed and
registered 1844–56[68]

	(a) 1844	(b) 1844–56
Gas, water, utilities	309	229
Insurance and finance	220	260
Mining	112	108
Railways	109	20
Shipping	51	46
Manufacturing	45	57
Miscellaneous	33	46
Markets and public halls	31	85
Brewing and food	23	30
Land and buildings	14	29
TOTAL	947	910

Source: Shannon, 'First five thousand', 420.

There was a further wave of company law reform in the mid 1850s when general access to limited liability was added to the general right of incorporation. This was a politically – and in the views of some contemporaries, morally – contentious development, and issues raised by this further stage in the development of company law will be discussed in Chapter 5. Access to limited liability probably made incorporation more immediately attractive to some businessmen, but Figure 4.1 shows that there was no step-change in the rate of incorporation from 1856. The scale of incorporation rose to significant levels only in the 1880s; according to Jefferys, it was the period 1885–1914 that witnessed 'the triumph of the company in almost all spheres of economic life'.[69]

How far was this gradual adoption by business of incorporation a result of the economic imperatives identified by the classical economists? Smith had identified the scale of a business as the primary reason for resort to incorporation, since large concerns could not readily be financed by a small number of partners. He also noted that the division of a company into freely transferable shares gave owners of capital increased liquidity, while limited liability reduced the risk of large-scale loss for owners. Set against these potential benefits was the potential cost of the divorce of ownership and control between shareholders

[68] An alternative listing of these early companies by Levi produces both a slightly higher total and, using different sectoral headings, a slightly different but broadly consistent distribution. See Levi, 'Joint stock', 24–5.
[69] Jefferys, 'Trends', 142.

Figure 4.1 UK company registrations: 1844–1913

and managers. An economic account of this 'triumph of the company' should, therefore, reveal a clear shift in these benefits and costs of incorporation.

The growth of the British economy in the second half of the nineteenth century was associated with and contributed to the rise of the large-scale company. There exists a long-standing critique of British business performance which blames the small scale and family control of enterprise for the sluggish growth of the British economy compared to both the USA and Germany in the late nineteenth and early twentieth centuries. It is certainly true that Britain did not experience the same degree of merger and acquisition activity that led in America to the creation of huge industrial combines. The largest American company, US Steel, had a capitalisation in 1902 that was fifteen times greater than Imperial Tobacco, the UK's most highly valued manufacturing company, and a workforce five times larger than the UK's largest manufacturing employer, the Fine Cotton Spinners and Doublers

Association.[70] Even so, by 1905 the largest fifty manufacturing firms in the UK all had an issued share capital of over £1 million. Yet although large-scale corporations were very important in some industrial sectors, the majority of joint stock companies were characterised more by the small scale than by the large scale of their capital. Table 4.2 reports, for 1856–68 and for 1896–1905, the distribution by size of the nominal capital of newly registered companies. In both periods it can be seen that close to half of companies were established with nominal capital of less than £10,000, and no more than 2 per cent with capital greater than £1 million. Moreover, the paid-up capital was frequently only a small proportion of nominal capital. For the years 1863–6 estimates published by *The Times* indicated that the sums actually deposited for partly paid-up shares in 876 new companies offering shares to the public represented less than one-tenth of the nominal capital.[71] In 1870 Leone Levi felt that 'the practice of advertising a large nominal capital, often out of all proportion to the amount of *bonâ fide* subscribed or required, which obtains in small as well as in large companies, is wrong in the extreme'; it certainly rendered information on company capitalisation highly problematic.[72] Nevertheless it seems evident from these data that a need to raise a capital sum beyond the capacity of the average partnership could account for only a small proportion of company incorporation throughout the second half of the nineteenth century.

If the scale of companies' commercial activity can account for only a fraction of incorporation, then perhaps it was the desire for increased liquidity that motivated the majority. In principle owners could extract capital from their business more easily if it were an incorporated company rather than a partnership, because company shares could be freely traded whereas sale of a share in a partnership required the agreement of all partners. The practice, however, was rather different. In 1913 there existed over 60,000 registered companies in the UK, but the total number of securities quoted on the London Stock Exchange was little over 5,000, and only about one in ten of these could command a ready market.[73] Thus a high level of liquidity was attained by the shareholders of fewer than 1 per cent of registered companies. This state of affairs

---

[70] Christine Shaw, 'The large manufacturing employers of 1907', *Business History*, 25 (1983), 42–59; Leslie Hannah, *The Rise of the Corporate Economy* (2nd edn, London, 1983), 22.

[71] £35.6 million was subscribed, against an authorised capital of £373 million; *The Times*, 29 December 1866. Hunt notes that in these four years a further 2,627 companies which did not proceed to offer shares to the public were registered, with a nominal capital of a further £326 million. Hunt, *Business Corporation*, 146.

[72] Levi, 'Joint Stock', 11.

[73] Michie, *London Stock Exchange*, 94–5.

Table 4.2. *Distribution of nominal capital of newly registered companies: 1856–68 and 1896–1905*

Nominal capital (£)	Percentage of companies	
	Registered 1856–68	Registered 1896–1905
1–4,999	29.4	30.6
5,000–9,999	13.0	15.2
10,000–49,999	30.6	32.8
50,000–99,999	11.3	8.3
100,000–499,999	10.5	11.6
500,000–999,999	3.1	0.9
1 million +	2.0	0.5
Number of companies	*7,009*	*39,852*

Sources for 1856–86: Levi, 'Joint stock', 12. For 1896–1905: Company Law Amendment Act, Appendix volume [Cd 3053] PP 1906 XCVII, 104.

did not arise because the stock market failed to provide shareholders in most companies with the attribute of liquidity which they desired, since the great majority of companies were formed under rules which explicitly prevented free trade in shares.

A parliamentary enquiry in 1906 into the operation of company law noted that 'a large and increasing proportion of the companies under the Acts are classed in common parlance as private companies', the characteristics of which were generally that they had fewer than twenty shareholders, and that they restricted the right of free transfer of shares.[74] Company law stipulated a minimum of seven shareholders, and many companies were founded at this minimum level. Shannon's pioneering research into the archival records of early registered companies concluded that around 15 per cent of companies founded 1875–83 were 'private', and that a further 30–45 per cent were either 'abortive' or 'small'. It is unclear how he drew distinction between these separate categories, since among the criteria he used to determine whether a company was private included the number and nature of shareholdings and the nominal value of shares.[75] A sharper picture emerges from later in the century; of the 1,328 companies registered in the first half of 1890, 87 per cent had ten shareholders or less.[76]

---

[74] *Report on Company Law Amendment Act* [Cd 3052], PP 1906 xcvii, 17.
[75] H. A. Shannon, 'The limited companies of 1866–83', *Economic History Review*, 4 (1933), 290–316.
[76] P. Ireland, 'The rise of the limited liability company', *International Journal of the Sociology of Law*, 12 (1984), 247.

The 1907 Companies Act provided the first explicit recognition of the private company as a distinct legal entity, defined by three criteria: (i) it did not raise capital from the public; (ii) it had no more than fifty shareholders; (iii) its articles of association restricted the right to transfer of the company's shares.[77] By December 1914 private companies accounted for more than three-quarters of all registered companies.[78] As Cottrell has noted, the triumph of the registered company in the last decades of the nineteenth century was 'essentially due to private partnerships turning themselves quietly into private limited companies'.[79] These private companies were predominantly partnerships – very often family firms – which had converted their legal status but which had not altered at all what they did or how they did it. Conversion did little or nothing to increase liquidity for the owner-shareholders, since there was no public market for these shares. In fact the articles of association of the private company typically confined the sale of shares to existing shareholders, thereby deliberately recreating the practice, if not the form, of a partnership. A good example of the sort of constraint that could be written into the articles of association can be seen in the case of the biscuit manufacturer Huntley and Palmers. When this partnership incorporated in 1898, the articles explicitly referred to 'George Palmer' and 'Samuel Palmer' shares (these being the original partners), and required that they be offered to that same branch of the family before being offered to the other.[80]

This case demonstrates also that the characteristics of a private company were not confined to small enterprises. In 1907 Huntley and Palmers employed 6,500 workers, and had an issued capital (all held within the family) of £2.4 million, which placed it 33rd and 36th respectively on rankings of the largest UK manufacturing companies by employment and by capitalisation.[81] In fact Shaw has estimated that about one-third of the largest hundred manufacturing companies in 1907 were private rather than public companies.[82] It is therefore apparent that incorporation was not a necessary condition for the development of large-scale manufacturing enterprise in late-Victorian Britain, and it is also clear that in the great majority of cases incorporation was not sought in order to give owner-shareholders significantly enhanced liquidity.

[77] Storrar and Pratt, 'Accountability v. privacy', 259–91. For an analysis of the pattern of development of limited liability private companies in France, Germany and the US, as well as in Britain, see Guinnane et al., 'Putting the corporation in its place'.
[78] F. Lavington, The English Capital Market, (London, 1929), 201.
[79] Cottrell, Industrial finance, 163.
[80] T. A. B. Corley, Quaker Enterprise in Biscuits: Huntley and Palmers of Reading, 1822–1972 (London, 1972), 156.
[81] Shaw, 'Large', 52; Hannah, Rise, 187.   [82] Shaw, 'Large', 46.

The third economic rationale for incorporation identified by Smith was limited liability. The association he drew between incorporation and limited liability, which he derived from knowledge of the organisational form of the chartered trading companies, did not hold for the early registered companies, which were formed with unlimited liability up to 1856 (banks and insurance companies continued to operate with unlimited liability until 1858 and 1862 respectively). The motivation for these early company formations must have lain elsewhere, but from 1856 the opportunity to restrict liability to the sums invested in the business provided an incentive for owners to incorporate, even though, as will be shown in the next chapter, the value of this facility may well have been overestimated by both contemporaries and subsequent historians. Yet corporations did not maintain their monopoly of limited liability; this privilege was extended in stages to partnerships. In 1865 'sleeping' partners who were not actively engaged in the day-to-day management of the business were granted access to limited liability, and from 1907 this was available to all partners – yet little use was made of these facilities. Levi noted that twenty years after it was introduced the provision relating to sleeping partners was almost entirely ignored,[83] and full limited partnership status was adopted by only 557 partnerships between 1908 and 1913, during which period almost 40,000 new limited liability companies were formed (the majority of which, of course, were small private companies).[84]

The economic advantages of incorporation identified by the classical economists do not seem sufficient to account for the scale, timing and character of company formation in Victorian Britain. This suggests that there may have been other attributes associated with incorporation which motivated owners of business to undertake a conversion from partnership to corporation. Two case studies from the banking sector in the 1850s provide useful insight; the issues are particularly clear-cut because all banks at this time, whether partnerships or corporations, operated under conditions of unlimited liability.

A tale of two banks

In 1843 Catherine Gore, one of the most prolific and popular novelists in England, dedicated her new work, *The Banker's Wife*, to her trustee

[83] Leone Levi, 'The progress of joint stock companies with limited and unlimited liability in the United Kingdom, during the fifteen years 1869–84', *Journal of the Statistical Society of London*, 49 (1886), 241–72.
[84] Ireland, 'Rise', 258; *61st Abstract of Statistics* [Cd 7636], PP 1914–16 lxxvi, 363.

and friend Sir John Dean Paul, senior. Sir John was the leading partner
in the private banking firm of Strahan, Paul and Bates located at 216
The Strand, and custodian of the hard-earned capital that Mrs Gore
had accumulated from two decades of relentless publication of 'silver-
fork' novels.[85] *The Banker's Wife* told a moral tale of greed and hubris as
the banker Richard Hamlyn of Dean Park used and abused his clients'
funds to promote his own social advance. 'This man of universal credit',
wrote Mrs Gore of Richard Hamlyn, 'was but a more polished, more
cautious, more solid swindler, in the amount of thousands, where swin-
dlers in the amount of tens or hundreds are sentenced to the hulks.'[86]
But in dedicating the work to Sir John Dean Paul, senior, Mrs Gore was
at pains to explain that her book was 'intended to exhibit the failings
of an individual, not as an attack upon a class'. As for Sir John, he had,
in her view, added to the distinction of the ancient banking house that
bore his name.[87] More than that, he was an active philanthropist, serving at various times as Steward of King's College Hospital, Treasurer of
the Asylum for Female Orphans, Chair of the Benevolent and Provident
Institutions for Governesses, and Vice-President of both the Royal
Maternity Charity and the Society for Improving the Conditions of the
Labouring Classes.[88] But even as Sir John was receiving this encomium
from Mrs Gore he was stealing her money. In 1847, acting as trustee for
Mrs Gore who was then residing in France, he sold £23,000 of Consols
on her behalf, on the grounds that a better rate of interest could be
obtained by investing in Exchequer Bills, but in reality this money was
simply appropriated by the firm.[89]

This cavalier attitude towards client funds had existed within the
bank at least since 1816, and by 1849 the business was effectively insolvent, but it continued to trade. In January 1852 John Dean Paul, junior,
succeeded to his father's baronetcy, assumed the role of senior partner
within the bank, and continued to misappropriate depositors' funds in
a desperate attempt to avoid moral and financial bankruptcy. As one of
the most prominent Anglican evangelicals of his day, Sir John, junior,

---

[85] For brief details of Mrs Gore's life see the *Oxford DNB*; for a discussion of her economic novels see N. Russell, *The Novelist and Mammon* (Oxford, 1986).
[86] C. Gore, *The Banker's Wife* (London, 1843), quoted in Russell, *Novelist*, 73, n. 24.
For the use of bank failures as a central moral device in Victorian novels see Timothy
L Alborn, 'The moral of the failed bank: professional plots in the victorian money
market', *Victorian Studies*, 38 (1995), 199–226.
[87] Gore, *Banker's Wife*, 'Dedication'.
[88] His name is associated with all these roles in various charity advertisements placed in
The Times between 1832 and 1848.
[89] *The Times*, 19 October 1855, 6.

had a reputation to preserve.[90] Moral probity was supposed to extend to all financial affairs, great or small, and Sir John was diligent in his prosecution of mendicants who attempted to obtain charitable donations of a few shillings under false pretences.[91] He was also generous with his time to his many chosen causes; as a contemporary wrote: 'There was scarcely a society belonging to the Evangelical section of the Church of England in which the baronet of the Temple Bar Bank did not hold the honorary office of treasurer, trustee, or committee-man, and from which his firm did not, in consequence, enjoy more substantial advantage as the custodians of their funds.'[92] But as for these funds put in his charge by the bank's depositors, he seemed to care very little.

The financial position of Strahan, Paul and Bates – precarious, tending towards the hopeless – was well known in the City by the early 1850s, and this led to the withdrawal of inter-bank lines of credit, even when Sir John tried to bolster his professional connections with the offer of a somewhat desperate 7 per cent interest rate.[93] The underlying causes of this financial malaise were common to many other nineteenth-century private banks: poor stewardship of funds, unlucky or imprudent long-term investments, and withdrawal by partners of an income far in excess of operating profits.[94] In addition, the partners had pursued, from the late 1840s, a reckless lending policy in an attempt to recoup past losses. More than £130,000 had been lent to the Mostyn colliery in a series of transfers initially intended to produce a high rate of return, and subsequently to shore up the colliery company to prevent a default on the original mortgage. Furthermore, over £300,000 was lent, without any tangible security, to two speculators engaged in railway and civil engineering projects in Italy and France. Confidence finally collapsed on Friday 8 June 1855. Although clearly insolvent, the bank continued to trade until the close of business on Saturday 9th, thereby allowing depositors with privileged information to withdraw their funds, and concentrating misery on the trusting and the ignorant. Bankruptcy proceedings revealed that liabilities exceeded £750,000, and at least £113,000 of client funds and securities had been

---

[90] E. J. Garnett, Aspects of the relationship between protestant ethics and economic activity in mid-Victorian England. Oxford University D.Phil thesis, 1986, 52. See generally Chapter 1 on evangelical attitudes to commerce and to fraud.

[91] *The Times*, 1 May 1852, 7.

[92] D. M. Evans, *Facts, Failures and Frauds: Revelations Financial, Mercantile, Criminal* (London, 1859), 109.

[93] *The Times*, 15 June 1855, 9.

[94] Both Paul and Strahan, a distant cousin, maintained large and hospitable London and country residences. Paul's family estate at Rodborough, near Stroud, was subsequently sold, in distress, to Lord John Russell.

misappropriated by the partners. As far as *The Times* was concerned, 'We have never had a grosser instance of villany than that of this "most seeming virtuous" banker who, with his pockets stuffed full of the securities which he had abstracted from his customers, could go down to Exeter-hall, and take the chair at some religious meeting of which he was the leader and the idol.'[95]

Barely fifteen months later *The Times* was again fulminating that 'In the annals of commercial fraud we have never heard or read of more outrageous acts of rascality.'[96] But it was no longer Strahan, Paul and Bates who were the target of this invective, but instead the directors of the Royal British Bank, which had just become insolvent with liabilities of over £500,000. This bank had been established as a joint stock venture in 1849, and was intended to provide deposit and loan facilities to the rapidly expanding retail, wholesale and small manufacturing sector in the metropolis.[97] The initial capital of £100,000 was divided into £100 shares of which half was called up; by the time the bank closed for business, additional share offers had increased the total sum subscribed to £158,000. The reasons for this banking collapse must have seemed wearily familiar to contemporaries: operating expenses that were well in excess of profits; directors who had granted loans to themselves against which little or no collateral was offered in security; and a disastrous investment of over £100,000 in an unprofitable Welsh mine. Loans to managers and directors were recorded in a private ledger, and did not appear in the annual balance sheet, but the auditor's report did not reveal this irregularity, perhaps because one of the auditors himself was the recipient of a secret loan of £2,000.[98]

The collapse of both the Royal British Bank and of Strahan, Paul and Bates was the result of a combination of managerial incompetence and managerial fraud. The scale of the losses were similar, the distribution of misery among depositors (and in the case of the Royal British Bank, among shareholders too) was widespread. But the different legal status of these banks – the one a joint stock company, the other a partnership – made a fundamental difference to the course of legal process against the perpetrators of the frauds, and to the punishments imposed.

There was no ambiguity about who was responsible for the bankruptcy in the case of Strahan, Paul and Bates: the three partners were

[95] *The Times*, 13 September 1855, 6. Exeter Hall, a non-sectarian meeting hall on the Strand with a capacity of 3,000, provided a venue for the meetings of a large number of evangelical organisations and charities.

[96] *The Times*, 24 September 1856, 6.

[97] Prospectus of the Royal British Bank (1849). Goldsmiths' Library.

[98] *The Times*, 13 March 1857, 9.

joint owners of their eponymous bank (even though Bates, the former chief clerk, joined as a salaried partner in 1842 and took no share in the profits). Bankruptcy proceedings were swift, as was the arrest of the partners on a charge of misdemeanour with respect to the unauthorised sale of securities. Equally swift was the granting by the Governor of the Middlesex House of Correction in Clerkenwell of irregular privileges to the three well-connected prisoners: they were allowed free movement between cells, unlimited visits from family and friends, and special supplies of fruit and wine. The governor had been assured by Strahan that he would be rewarded for his trouble; in fact he was reprimanded and removed from office by the Middlesex magistrates.[99] Perhaps the prisoners should have seen this as an omen of their diminishing ability to forge their own futures.

The first ploy they adopted in their trial at the Old Bailey was to argue that the voluntary declaration of their guilt which they had made on oath before a Commissioner in Bankruptcy should absolve them from any criminal charges, on the grounds that bankruptcy legislation explicitly prevented evidence disclosed under oath in any compulsory investigation from being used in a criminal prosecution. This received short shrift from the Attorney General who led the prosecution: he described it as an attempted fraud on the act of Parliament. Strahan and Bates then argued that although they were partners, they were not aware of the full extent of the misappropriations. Judge Alderson noted in his summing up that:

a partner was responsible civilly for the acts of his co-partner, but not criminally. In a criminal act, to make a man liable he must be personally, in some way or other, a party to the act, that was, if he did not personally perform or take part in the act itself, he must authorise it in some way or other, or be cognisant of it. At the same time, it must not be forgotten that Strahan and Bates were partners, and as such, must naturally be supposed to know of what was going on in the concern.[100]

The jury had no doubts that Strahan and Bates had full knowledge: it took them just twenty minutes to find all three men guilty of fraudulently disposing of securities entrusted to them as bankers. Judge Alderson, after noting the good education and high social standing of Sir John Paul, concluded that 'as I cannot conceive any worse case under the Act, I can do nothing else but impose the sentence therein provided for

---

[99] *The Times*, 19 October 1855, 9.
[100] This reportage of the summing up is taken from Evans, *Facts*, 143. *The Times* (29 October 1855, 9) reports the summing-up with slightly different phrasing, but identical meaning.

the worst case – namely, the most severe punishment, which is, that you be severally transported for 14 years'.[101] Times had changed: the banker Henry Fauntleroy, found guilty of a similar charge thirty-one years earlier, had been hanged at Newgate.

Directors of the Royal British Bank fared rather better. In the immediate aftermath of the bank's collapse they were spared close attention because of a legal farrago caused by overlapping jurisdictions. The bank's shareholders, who had unlimited liability, obtained a winding-up order from the Court of Chancery, and a manager was duly appointed to draw up an account of assets and liabilities, together with an estimate of the amount to be raised by calls upon shareholders, which would be proportionate to the number of shares held. Two weeks later, however, a depositor (and thus a creditor) of the bank filed a petition in the Court of Bankruptcy, and an official assignee was appointed. Under bankruptcy proceedings each shareholder was potentially liable for the debt due to every creditor. When officers of the Court of Bankruptcy went to seize the bank's premises they found them to be occupied by officers of the Court of Chancery who refused to relinquish possession. Meanwhile each of the 280 shareholders, who through Chancery were attempting to manage an orderly attribution of liability, found that they could be personally pursued by each of the bank's creditors for the entire debts of the bank. Among these shareholders were sixty-seven 'gents', twenty-eight spinsters, and ten widows, together with butlers, household servants, clerks, shopkeepers, artists and publicans – a group described by *The Times* as 'a class of small people ... who live entirely outside of the great commercial world, are wholly unacquainted with trade on a large scale, and to whom, therefore, all the machinery of this great world of business and all its proceedings are as simple mysteries as if they were matters of another world'.[102]

When the affairs of the bank came before the Bankruptcy Court in April 1857 the details of directorial appropriations became clear.[103] Humphrey Brown, MP for Tewskesbury and director since 1853, had borrowed £70,000 on the strength of a deposit of £18 14s. and some worthless paper guarantees. John McGregor, MP for Glasgow and founding Governor of the bank, had borrowed over £7,000 on a similar basis; likewise the bank's general manager (£30,000) and the bank's solicitor (£7,000). Yet these actions constituted no crime; instead they

---

[101] *The Times*, 29 October 1855.   [102] *The Times*, 18 September 1856, 8.
[103] For a detailed account of the legal proceedings following the bank's collapse, see James Taylor, 'Company fraud in Victorian Britain: the Royal British Bank scandal of 1856', *English Historical Review*, 122 (2007), 700–724.

reflected merely commercial imprudence on the part of the bank in accepting low-grade collateral from depositors who happened also to be directors or officers of the bank. With evident exasperation *The Times* noted that 'It is difficult for the non-legal mind to understand how a definition of fraud can be so limited as to exclude the case of the Director or Manager of a joint-stock bank who diverts to his own use £30,000 of the funds belonging to the concern, who does this secretly, and who deposits in place of the money a packet or two of worthless paper.'[104]

Legal minds were equally discomfited. Within a month of the bankruptcy court hearing, the Attorney General, Sir Richard Bessell, had introduced the Fraudulent Trustees Act which made it a misdemeanour, punishable by up to seven years in prison, for any director or officer of a corporation to take fraudulently for his own use any property of the company, to falsify or destroy the books of the company, or to circulate false statements as to the circumstances of the company. However, the Act did not have retrospective sanction, and the only resort open to the Attorney General was to bring an action against the directors and officers of the Royal British Bank for conspiracy to defraud the public. Arrests ensued – that of Humphrey Brown being delayed somewhat by the disguise he adopted of a wig and green spectacles – and a criminal trial finally commenced in February 1858, almost eighteen months after the demise of the bank.[105]

The trial hinged on the issue of whether the company report and balance sheet issued in December 1855 was knowingly falsified by the directors and officers of the bank. Directors who had appropriated funds on the basis of worthless collateral but who had resigned from the board prior to this date could not be touched by this action, whilst other directors who had not extracted loans from the bank, but who were members of the board at this date, were charged with joint liability in this conspiracy. A special jury consisting solely of metropolitan merchants found all seven defendants guilty; three – including Brown – were sentenced to a year's imprisonment, three received lesser custodial sentences, and one received a token fine of one shilling.[106] Even these modest punishments were not quite what they seemed. An appeal against the convictions was rejected in May 1858, but just two months later all but one of the directors had gained his freedom in response to petitions relating variously to good character and ill health.

[104] *The Times*, 24 September 1856, 6.   [105] *The Times*, 12 June 1857, 5.
[106] A transcript of the trial is provided by Evans, *Facts*, 280–386.

Humphrey Brown even had the temerity to stand again for election as MP for Tewkesbury in 1859 – without success.[107]

The collapse of the Royal British Bank and of Strachan, Paul and Bates had similar causes, and similar consequences in terms of the scale of financial loss for depositors, but for the perpetrators the sentences were very different – one year's imprisonment versus fourteen years' transportation. The sentences were commuted in various ways, but the huge difference in treatment remained: Brown served just five months, while Sir John Paul managed, though the exertions of his friends in high places, to avoid heavy labour in the convict quarries of Portland, to be disembarked from the convict ship *Nile* just before it set sail for Western Australia, and to be released after four years of incarceration.[108] The difference in treatment stemmed from fundamental legal presuppositions about the responsibilities of partners and directors. Partners were presumed to be jointly liable for the actions of their partnership, unless it could be shown in an unambiguous way that they did not have, and could not have been expected to have, knowledge of actions deemed to be illegal. Company directors, on the other hand, could not be held responsible for illegal actions of the company unless it could be shown that they had consciously and deliberately attempted to deceive and defraud the public. Even this legal constraint did not exist prior to the 1857 Fraudulent Trustees Act, and, as shown in Chapter 7 below, company law remained extremely weak with respect to disclosure of accurate financial information through to the end of the century. Rather than the State vigorously pursuing commercial fraudsters through the courts, it was generally left to shareholders to exercise vigilance over directors and managers, though frequently they possessed neither the information nor the capacity to do this.[109]

It is clear, therefore, that in addition to the economic advantages of incorporation – the ability to raise large capital, the transferability and liquidity of the company share, and the limited liability offered to investors – there was an important legal advantage for owners. Incorporation, even in the form of a private company with 99 per cent of the shares owned by one person, allowed the owner to hide behind

---

[107] *The Times*, 5 July 1858; 8 March 1859.
[108] *The Times* (7 September 1857, 10) reported that Strachan, Paul and Bates had all set sail on the convict ship *Nile*, but the ship indents reveal that none of them were on board when the ship docked in Freemantle on 1 Jan 1858. For the privileges received by Paul in Portland prison see *The Times*, 26 December 1862, 8; for details of his early release see *The Times*, 18 October 1858, 4; 8 March 1859, 10.
[109] Taylor, 'Company Fraud', 722–4.

the veil of corporate personality and to distance himself from the legal obligations of partnership or sole proprietorship. Of course, most businessmen were not consciously or deliberately fraudulent, and it would be wrong to suggest that the incorporation wave of the 1880s and 1890s was driven by a desire to avoid criminal action for fraud. However, what the corporate veil also did was provide owners with an effective means of securing their personal assets against claims from commercial creditors. To see how this was achieved we need to look in more detail at the second key element in the rise of the company in nineteenth-century Britain – limited liability.

5 The limitation of liability

It seldom happens that technical aspects of company law are seen as holding sway over national destiny, but in the mid-nineteenth century limited liability was believed by some of its more militant supporters and opponents to have just this power. It was variously claimed that limited liability would induce widespread economic and moral degeneration, and that it would liberate and stimulate industry and commerce throughout the entire nation. The issue was debated with vigour and passion, for it brought into high relief Victorian uncertainties about the natural order of the economic world; for some, limited liability was at the centre of a battleground between God and Mammon.

In the view of the political economist J. R. McCulloch, limited liability was unnatural and unnecessary:

> In the scheme laid down by Providence for the government of the world, there is no shifting or narrowing of responsibilities, every man being personally answerable to the utmost extent for all his actions. But the advocates of limited liability proclaim in their superior wisdom that the scheme of Providence may be advantageously modified, and that debts and obligations may be contracted which the debtors, though they have the means, shall not be bound to discharge. Borrow, say they, as much as you please, and pay as little as you like, – the less, it would seem, the better![1]

McCulloch's conception of a natural economic order was profoundly different from that of many mid-century free-traders, for whom it meant an economy untrammelled by legal constraint or privilege. Robert Lowe, who as Vice-President of the Board of Trade introduced the limited liability legislation to parliament in 1856, set out the *laissez-faire* case thus:

> [Limited liability] is not a question of privilege; if anything it is a right ... The principle is the freedom of contract and the right of unlimited association – the right of people to make what contracts they please on behalf of themselves,

---

[1] J. R. McCulloch, *Considerations on Partnership with Limited Liability* (London, 1856), 10–11.

whether those contracts may appear to the Legislature beneficial or not, as long as they do not commit fraud or otherwise act contrary to the general policy of the law.[2]

Boyd Hilton has strikingly identified the introduction of general limited liability as the moment when God lost out to Mammon, when a Liberal Tory 'evangelical or retributive' version of free trade was superseded by a more optimistic, expansionist and commercial Whig/Radical vision of the free market. By mid century, beliefs in the idea of evangelical providentialism, original sin, moral trial, and redemption or damnation at the Day of Judgement were on the wane. For Hilton, limited liability was a 'case of the well-off investing class softening the rigours of capitalism *at the very point* where it threatened themselves. In the same way the repeal of hell-fire can be regarded as unbuttoning a system of spiritual capitalism *at just the point* where the upper classes felt vulnerable.'[3]

Despite the vehemence of some of the contemporary debate, it is far from clear that the limited liability legislation had any major impact on the economy or, once the flurry of dispute about the legislation had died down, that it was viewed as an economic or moral watershed by the majority of parliamentarians, capital owners and businessmen (or even, according to Jane Garnett, by the majority of evangelicals).[4] John Bright, speaking at the 1856 annual general meeting of the Manchester Chamber of Commerce, the majority of whose members had consistently opposed limited liability, told the audience that expectations about the likely effects of the legislation 'have been grossly exaggerated on both sides'.[5] *The Economist* agreed: 'Never, perhaps, was a change so vehemently and generally demanded, of which the importance was so much overrated.'[6] The following year *The Economist* reiterated that 'We shall be surprised if encouragement be really given by this act to the formation of companies,' and the data on company registration confirms this – there was no surge in activity in the mid-1850s (see Figure 4.1 above).[7] Even Hilton recognises that limited liability did not cause any major political confrontation, and that the moral realignment

[2] *HCDeb*, 1 Feb 1856, col. 129. Lowe's speech was subsequently reprinted as Robert Lowe, *Speech on the Amendment of the Law of Partnership and Joint Stock Companies* (London, 1856).
[3] Boyd Hilton, *The Age of Atonement: The Influence of Evangelicalism on Social and Economic Thought, 1785–1865* (Oxford, 1988), 255, 277.
[4] Garnett, 'Relationship between protestant ethics and economic activity', 272–86.
[5] Quoted in A. Redford, *Manchester Merchants and Foreign Trade, 1794–1858* (Manchester, 1934), 216.
[6] *The Economist*, 1855, 84–5.   [7] *The Economist*, 28 June 1856, 700.

signalled by the legislation would have had little if any impact on the majority of the well-to-do who were 'carefree by disposition'.[8] So was limited liability anything more than a technical tidying-up of company law, a logical but minor addition to the 1844 Act that had gone half way to giving all corporations the array of legal privileges long since available to chartered companies? This chapter will sketch the genesis of the 1856 limited liability legislation to see how far it was the result of a functional response of the legal system to a pressing economic need. It will then move on to examine how limited liability worked in practice in the second half of the nineteenth century, before reviewing the combined effect of both incorporation and limited liability on the rights, duties and status of capitalists in Victorian Britain.

The principle of limited liability – meaning that investors in a corporation are liable for no more than the amount they agree to invest – was long established in English company law. The chartered trading companies had offered shareholders this protection since the sixteenth century, as had almost all the canal and railway companies established by private act of parliament since the 1780s.[9] As has been shown in Chapter 4, Adam Smith and most of his eighteenth-century contemporaries advanced a dual justification for the extension of this royal or parliamentary privilege to such business ventures: their purpose was beneficial to the public good, and their activities necessitated the subscription of capital on a scale far larger than that of any partnership. The focus of debate in the middle years of the nineteenth century was whether this privilege should be extended to all enterprises regardless of their type or scale of activity.

The pros and cons of general limited liability did little to engage the intellectual energy of political economists. McCulloch's condemnation was not so much a battle-cry to rally forces for the defence as an idiosyncratic voice in the wilderness. Discussion of limited liability, or even use of the term, is entirely absent from the major writings of David Ricardo, James Mill, Nassau Senior, and Senior's successor as Drummond Professor of Political Economy at Oxford, Richard Whately.[10] In fact, the only serious consideration came at the behest of parliament, in evidence collected by H. Bellenden Ker, the commissioner appointed in

---

[8] Hilton, *Atonement*, 297, 277.   [9] Scott, *Constitution and Finance*.
[10] The relevant works are: David Ricardo, *On the Principles of Political Economy and Taxation* (London, 1817); James Mill, *Elements of Political Economy* (London, 1821); Nassau Senior, *An Outline of the Science of Political Economy* (London, 1836); Richard Whately, *Introductory Lectures on Political Economy* (London, 1832).

1836 to investigate the workings of the law of partnership. This context is significant: Bellenden Ker's enquiry was explicitly focussed on partnerships rather than companies, and thus considered the issue of limited liability almost solely with respect to sleeping partners – that is, investing partners who supplied capital but who did not take an active role in the management of the enterprise. It had been repeatedly argued in parliament since 1818 that sleeping partnerships modelled on the French *société en commandite* would provide a stimulus to economic activity by encouraging a greater flow of capital into commercial uses.[11]

In 1836 Bellenden Ker received evidence from two political economists, Thomas Tooke and Nassau Senior, though in neither case did their views run to more than a couple of printed pages. Senior, although he had not considered limited liability to be worthy of mention in his *Outline of the Science of Political Economy* published in the same year, submitted evidence in which he argued for the benefits of partnership *en commandite*. Investment in an unlimited partnership demanded of the investor considerable attention to internal management in order to monitor and regulate exposure to risk. Few people unaccustomed to business could do this, and, suggested Senior, even experienced men of commerce were unwilling to expend the time and effort involved when their stake in the partnership was small. As a result, he believed, small sums that otherwise would be productively invested in commercial undertakings were instead diverted into the chartered trading companies or foreign loans.[12]

However, on this subject as on so many, political economy did not speak with one voice. Tooke, a founder member with Ricardo, Malthus and James Mill of the Political Economy Club, opposed the idea of sleeping partnerships on four separate grounds. First, he suggested, the legislation was not necessary because British enterprise was already characterised by 'an abundance, I should almost say an exuberance, of capital'.[13] Second, and in good Benthamite fashion, he argued that it would be inconsistent with rational legislation to grant limited liability to partnerships comprising just a handful of sleeping partners but to deny it to companies where the number of non-managing investors might be ten or more times greater. His third objection was jurisprudential, and was based on a natural law argument:

---

[11] John Saville, 'Sleeping partnerships and limited liability', *Economic History Review*, 8 (1956), 418.

[12] *Report on the Law of Partnership* by Mr Bellenden Ker, reprinted as Appendix I of the *First Report of the Select Committee on Joint Stock Companies*, PP 1844 vii. Evidence of Nassau Senior, 300.

[13] *Ibid.*, Evidence of Thomas Tooke, 270.

On the slightest reflection, however, it must be obvious that the *commandite* is a privilege, and has not the shadow of foundation as a natural right. The general, if not the universal, rule of commercial transaction is, that the individual is liable, to the full extent of his means, for the engagements entered into by himself, or on his behalf, or jointly with others; and it is only by the interposition of a special law that he can be shielded from the more general one of being answerable, in all cases, by the whole value of his property, and, in some cases, by his person, for such engagements.

Finally, Tooke suggested, with an institutional variant of Gresham's Law, that 'inferior' limited liability businesses would drive out the 'better instrument' of the unlimited partnership:

A person possessed of certain property, being desirous of increasing his income beyond mere interest of money, by embarking a given sum in trade, without risking the remainder of his fortune, which would be at stake if he employed it himself, or by a clerk or agent, would only have to invest the manager of it with the character of a partner in *commandite*, in order to have the benefit of all the chances in his favour which might attend a hazardous undertaking (involving transactions on credit), while, if all the adverse chances should occur, so as to entail losses to the amount of twice or three times the capital (no uncommon occurrence in trade), he would be accountable only for the sum he has subscribed. This mode of business holds out such advantages over a common partnership, that unless the formalities prescribed should prove to be too troublesome to be generally complied with, it would be extensively acted upon, and might gradually supersede the latter mode for all establishments trading on a capital within the prescribed limits.

Tooke's arguments about natural law and about institutional selection were both extremely prescient, and, as will be shown below, remained central to the debate over limited liability until almost the end of the century. It is not clear what attention Bellenden Ker paid to the views of either Senior or Tooke; he may well have given more weight to the evidence received from various bankers, lawyers and merchants, the great majority of whom opposed the concept of *en commandite* partnership. Ker's 1837 report rejected the idea of limited liability for sleeping partners, and the issue then lay dormant for more than a decade, with little discussion inside or outside parliament. When it was revived in 1850 the impetus came not from investors, businessmen, or *laissez-faire* advocates of freedom of contract, but rather from a group of middle-class philanthropists and Christian Socialists.[14] Robert Slaney, the radical MP, led a dogged, if narrowly based, campaign in the House of Commons over several years to reform the law of partnership in favour of working men. He argued that the legal framework placed restrictions on the

---

[14] Saville, 'Sleeping partnerships', 419.

development of industry and enterprise and retarded social improvement, thereby disadvantaging the working classes. Slaney's persistence led to Select Committee investigations in both 1850 and 1851 into the legal framework regulating both investment and partnership.[15]

There were two strands of objection to the current state of the law. The first, articulated particularly by Slaney, was that unlimited liability placed restrictions on socially useful investments such as the construction of housing for the working classes, markets, baths and washhouses.[16] The restrictions took two separate forms. First, promotion of such socially useful enterprise by an unlimited corporation was constrained by a shortage of capital, since investors, who were reluctant to expose their entire assets by taking a small shareholding, tended instead to invest in government stock or chartered companies. Second, the capacity of such enterprises to secure limited liability status through acquisition of a charter was constrained by the conservative approach of the Board of Trade in acceding to applications, and by the high cost involved – over £1,000 in the case of the Metropolitan Association for Improving the Dwellings of the Industrial Classes.[17] For Slaney, these were not just financial impediments, but significant obstacles to the achievement of a broader economic democracy that would embrace working men. Limited liability partnerships would, he argued, promote 'the enfranchisement of capital'.[18]

The second objection, coming especially from Christian Socialists,[19] was that the partnership laws inhibited the capacity of working men to combine to form producer cooperatives by exposing them to unreasonable levels of risk.[20] Because producer cooperatives involved the mutual sharing of profit, members were deemed to be conjoined in partnership, and were thus liable for the losses and debts incurred by any other partner. John Stuart Mill, one of the witnesses to the 1850 Select Committee and a supporter of cooperative associations as a bulwark against antagonism between capitalist and worker, added a further dimension which linked the issues of socially useful investment and producer cooperatives:

[15] *Select Committee on Investments for the Savings of the Middle and Working Classes*, PP 1850 xix; *Select Committee on the Law of Partnership*, PP 1851 xviii.
[16] *HCDeb*, 20 Feb 1851, cols. 842–50.
[17] *SC Savings of the Middle and Working Classes*, evidence of E.V. Neale, qq. 389–91.
[18] *HCDeb*, 20 Feb 1851, col. 848.
[19] Slaney was not a Christian Socialist, though he was sympathetic to their support for the working classes in general, and producer cooperatives in particular.
[20] *SC Savings of the Middle and Working Classes*, evidence of E. V. Neale, qq. 212–4; Thomas Hughes, qq. 431–2; L. Jones, qq. 985–6.

The great value of limitation of responsibility, as related to the working classes, would not be so much to facilitate the investment of their savings, not so much to enable the poor to lend to the rich, as to enable the rich to lend to the poor.[21]

The report of the 1850 Committee made a general observation that the law of partnership inhibited worker cooperatives, but it fell short of specific recommendations, and it fell on deaf ears in the House of Commons where it was not discussed. The 1851 Committee covered similar ground, and produced similar recommendations although, as Loftus has noted, the second report was subtly different in tone. The language of social reform and democratisation apparent in the 1850 report, which reflected the dominance of Christian Socialists among the witnesses (six out of seventeen), was replaced by a more formal and legalistic analysis.[22] However, the moral arguments advanced by Slaney and the Christian Socialists about the role of limited liability in promoting social harmony through partnership between labour and capital were to a large extent accommodated in June 1852 by the passage of the Industrial and Provident Societies Act (also promoted by Slaney). This legislation extended the provision of the 1850 Friendly Societies Act to cooperatives, and although it did not grant formal limited liability to such societies, it explicitly excluded the creditors of any insolvent member from any claim on the assets of other members. Therefore, although Slaney had introduced into parliament in February 1852 a motion for the appointment of a Royal Commission to further investigate the laws of partnership, by the time the Commission set to work the entire focus of the investigation had shifted from working men to manufacturers, traders and financiers.

The 1854 report of the Royal Commission on Mercantile Laws is significant not for its conclusions and recommendations ('although the details of our mercantile laws may require correction ... it would be unwise to interfere with principles which ... have proved beneficial to the general industry of the country')[23] but for the complete lack of consensus in the evidence collected. The commissioners were 'much embarrassed by the great contrariety of opinion ... Gentlemen of great

---

[21] *Ibid.*, q. 847. For Mill's supportive analysis of worker cooperatives see his *Principles*, book IV, ch. 6, s. 6.

[22] D. Loftus, 'Capital and community: limited liability and attempts to democratize the market in mid nineteenth-century England', *Victorian Studies*, 45 (2002), 104; Saville, 'Sleeping partnerships', 422.

[23] *Royal Commission on the Assimilation of Mercantile Laws in the UK and amendments in the law of partnership, as regards the question of limited or unlimited responsibility*, PP 1854 xxvii, Report, 7.

experience and talent had arrived at conclusions diametrically oppo-site ... it is difficult to say on which side the weight of authority in this country preponderates.'[24] Shannon, and more recently Bryer and Taylor, have classified the seventy-four replies from UK respondents to a questionnaire distributed by the commission to seek views on limited liability from interested parties.[25] Overall, forty-three were in favour of the extension of limited liability, and thirty-one against, but within each broad category of respondent, opinion was divided. Among the inner circle of the Bank of England, the governor and two directors opposed any extension, but the former governor, the deputy governor and two other directors were in favour.[26] Business communities were equally divided: chambers of commerce were generally opposed to any liberalisation, though not all their members were; of the thirty-seven representations received from the merchant and manufacturing com-munity, seventeen were in favour of extension and twenty against.[27]

Very little of the discussion within or without the commission related to universal limited liability – even the most defensive of the commis-sioners, the Scottish judge Lord Curriehill, recognised that there was scant support for the idea of exempting all partners from liability, and the central issue of debate was the merit or otherwise of *en comman-dite* partnership. Curriehill argued that even the extension of limited liability to sleeping partners would be hugely damaging – fraud and speculation would multiply while the supply of commercial credit to honest (unlimited) business would be curtailed.[28] The distinguished barrister G. W. Bramwell countered with the *laissez-faire* case, argu-ing that 'the interest of a community is best consulted by leaving to its members, as far as possible, the unrestrained and unfettered exer-cise of their own talents and industry. The restraint of limited liability partnerships offends against this rule.'[29] Individuals should be free to choose to transact with either limited or unlimited partnerships, and market competition would determine which organisational form pro-duced better (lower cost) outcomes.

In the nineteenth century, as now, royal commissions were often seen as instruments to close down discussion of a complex issue rather than to resolve it, and the anodyne majority view of the commissioners

---

[24] *Ibid.*, 5.
[25] Shannon, 'Limited liability', 358–79; R. A. Bryer, 'The Mercantile Laws Commission of 1854 and the political economy of limited liability', *Economic History Review*, 50 (1997), 37–56; Taylor, *Creating Capitalism*, 151.
[26] Bryer, 'Mercantile Laws', 44; Hunt, *Business Corporation*, 129.
[27] Cottrell, *Industrial Finance*, 50–1; Bryer, 'Mercantile Laws', 43.
[28] *RC Mercantile Laws*, 14–15.   [29] *Ibid.*, Report, 23.

seemed well suited to achieve this end. However, the first report of the commission had been sitting on the shelf for just two months when, on 27 June 1854, Robert Collier, liberal MP for Plymouth and frequent speaker on matters of legal reform, introduced to the House of Commons a general motion to modify the law of partnership in favour of limitation of liability for investors.[30] This clearly struck a chord with the majority of members present. Although both the Attorney General and the Home Secretary, Palmerston, appealed to Collier not to press for a vote, and promised government attention to the issue, the mood of the House – expressed 'by loud cries' – was that the motion be put, and it was duly carried.[31] Far from shelving the issue, this debate forced the government's hand.

By the autumn of 1854 the Board of Trade had determined not to grant any further charters for limited liability incorporation on the grounds that a change in the law was pending. Perhaps also the government had been stung by Robert Lowe's withering critique of this process for granting charters:

But of all the systems, the very worst is surely to forbid limited liability, and then vest in a Minister holding his seat by a Parliamentary majority the power of suspending the law in favour of such associations as he thinks fit. If the law be right, it ought to be enforced; if wrong, to be repealed. I should as soon think of allowing the Secretary of the Treasury to grant dispensation for smuggling, or the Attorney General licences to commit murder.[32]

In June 1855 the Vice-President of the Board of Trade, E. P. Bouverie, introduced two separate bills, one to amend the law of partnership, the other to apply limited liability to companies. The first of these proposed that loans to partnerships should be able to bear interest varying with profit, thereby effectively enabling *en commandite* partnerships. The second proposed an amendment to the 1844 Act that would allow joint stock companies, other than in banking and insurance, to be formed with limited liability. This recognised the lack of competence of the Board of Trade to determine whether any application for a limited liability charter was in the public interest; the only real test of this was success or failure in the market.[33] The partnership bill ran out of parliamentary time and lapsed at the end of the session, and the limited liability bill reached the statute book only after being rushed through

[30] The original report was filed in Chancery on 27 April 1854.
[31] *HCDeb*, 27 June 1854, cols. 752–800.
[32] Lowe's evidence to RC Mercantile Laws, quoted by Collier in parliament. *Ibid.*, col. 756.
[33] Shannon, 'Limited liability', 377.

both Commons and Lords; there was some protest about the process, but little dissent over substance in either House.

Just forty-six companies had been registered under this legislation, which required that their name end with the term 'Limited', when, in February 1856, Robert Lowe, now Vice-President of the Board of Trade, introduced both a new Joint Stock Companies Bill to supersede the Acts of 1844 and 1855, and a new Partnerships Bill. The latter fell on a technical point of drafting,[34] but the former passed through both Houses with little debate. By the Joint Stock Companies Act of 1856, seven or more persons could become a body corporate with limited liability by registering a memorandum of association. These companies had to declare their name and objects, and provide a set of rules for internal regulation, which could simply be the model set provided in an appendix to the Act. A balance sheet had to be presented at the annual meeting, but otherwise the previous safeguards of a minimum paid-up capital, registration of prospectuses, and the scrutiny of the Registrar, were removed.[35]

The adoption of general limited liability in 1856 creates a puzzle: why did parliament fail to enact the proposal for *en commandite* partnerships, which had been extensively discussed over the previous five years, yet readily agree to extend limited liability to corporations even though there had been few direct calls for this in the public debate? Shannon suggests that the legislature was moved by the realisation that capital would be more productively employed under conditions of limited liability, but he produces no direct evidence in support.[36] Moreover, the arguments presented in the early 1850s to the select committees and royal commission about unproductive investment were almost all framed with reference to sleeping partnerships rather than corporations. Jefferys takes a more specific line on agency, asserting that the reform reflected the investment needs and growing influence of a 'body of capitalists not directly engaged in trade'. Again the influence, let alone the preferences, of these Home Counties *rentier* capitalists, remains hidden from view; Cottrell has convincingly trounced this interpretation, although Bryer has recently attempted to revive it within an explicitly Marxist interpretation of the mid-nineteenth-century legislation.[37] Hunt, appealing to a general 'spirit of the age', suggests that economic necessity and a rationalistic acceptance in parliament of the

---

[34] *HCDeb*, 11 Mar 1856, cols. 2200–01.
[35] Saville, 'Sleeping partnership', 429–301; Shannon, 'Limited liability', 377–9;
[36] Shannon, 'Limited Liability', 379.
[37] Jefferys, 'Trends', 9; Cottrell, *Industrial Finance*, 45–8; Bryer, 'Mercantile Laws'.

laissez-faire case carried the day.[38] More recently Taylor has refashioned this idea, arguing that the discourse of the 1850s had repositioned companies from being seen as quasi-public bodies sanctioned by the state for specific purposes, to being conceived of as entirely private entities over which the state had no right or duty of control.

Taylor's interpretation warrants elaboration, because it speaks to the 'natural law' argument that surrounded limited liability. In 1836 Thomas Tooke had articulated the natural law case against limited liability by stating that a general rule of commercial transaction is that the individual must be liable to the full extent of his means. That this position derived from law was clear; that it was natural was far from self-evident. The unlimited liability of a sleeping partner seemed to derive from the 1793 case of *Waugh* v. *Carver*, which itself drew on the alleged authority of a case in 1775 (*Grace* v. *Smith*) which in fact did not affirm the liability of a dormant partner. In commenting on *Grace* v. *Smith*, Sir William Blackstone had defined the nature of partnership thus: 'The true criterion when money is advanced to a trade is to consider whether the profit or premium is certain and defined; or casual, indefinite and depending on the accident of trade. In the former it is a loan; in the latter, a partnership.'[39] The huge influence of Blackstone's *Commentaries* on the teaching and practice of English law – they went through twenty-three successive editions in the ninety years after initial publication in the 1760s and spawned a plethora of extracts and digests produced for students – ensured that this opinion became an authority in its own right.[40] The justification for partners carrying unlimited liability for partnership debts was then elaborated in *Waugh* v. *Carver* on the grounds that 'he who takes a share of the profits of a business, takes part of the fund on which creditors rely for payment'.[41]

The requirement that partners accept liability 'to the last acre and the last shilling' was evidently a principle derived not from Providence but from Blackstone – which made it even more robust in the eyes of the English bench. Yet by mid century it was being challenged from within the legal profession as well as from without. In the 1851 Select Committee the Commissioner in Bankruptcy, R. G. Fane, presented a detailed juridical analysis of the genesis of this principle, and concluded that it was based on mistaken political economy: 'creditors neither can nor do rely on profits for payment. Profits do not exist till creditors are

---

[38] Hunt, *Business Corporation*, 116–17.
[39] *Grace* v. *Smith*, 2 Wm Blackstone 1000, quoted in Hunt, *Business Corporation*, 130.
[40] Oxford DNB.
[41] 2 Wm Blackstone 235, cited in Hunt, *Business Corporation*, 130.

paid.'[42] In fact, virtually all the discussion in the select committees, royal commission and in parliament, from both advocates for and opponents of limited liability, was motivated by practical concerns about the likely impact on credit, speculation, fraud and the level of economic activity. Little attention was paid to the more abstract and general issue of the relationship of individuals to any group of which they were a member and the role of the state in sanctioning the associational form of the group, despite the fact that the concept of *en commandite* partnership blurred the conceptual distinction that existed in English law between the fictive personality of a corporation and the real personality of an individual. It was not until the very end of the nineteenth century that the eminent legal historian F. W. Maitland, heavily influenced by the German jurist Gierke, opened up a debate about whether corporate personality inherently involved state concession, or whether it was a matter of legal recognition of 'real' arrangements made by private actors.[43]

Mid-Victorian pragmatists were not troubled by such fine legal and philosophical niceties, and there is little in the debates and discussions of the 1850s that dwells on the fictive personality of the corporation. Taylor is right to argue that companies were repositioned in the public discourse from being seen as quasi-public to being seen as private bodies, but this had happened in the 1840s – a combination of the 1844 Act which allowed them to be formed by a purely administrative process, and the experience of private speculative gain and loss in the 'railway mania' of 1844–5. The timing of the introduction of general limited liability in 1856 remains something of a puzzle; happenchance – the parliamentary embarrassment caused by Collier's motion, and the installation at the Board of Trade of the militant *laissez-faire*-ist Lowe – had its part to play. Can it be seen as a functionalist response by the legal system and legislature to pent-up economic pressure for reform? The 'contrariety of opinion' revealed to the 1854 royal commission suggests that the pressure was far from strong or uniform. One important reason for this was that unlimited liability in practice was not what it seemed, because it had already been significantly attenuated by a variety of legal devices.

The idea that every partner in every enterprise – including, of course, shareholders in the unlimited corporations formed under the 1844 Act – was liable to his or her last acre and shilling was yet another fiction of

---

[42] *SC Law of Partnership*, evidence of G. C. Fane, 74–5.
[43] Maitland, *State, Trusts and Corporation*. For comments on Maitland's view on unincorporated bodies, see Harris, *Industrializing*, ch. 6.

the Victorian legal system. A variety of devices had been invented by lawyers specifically to constrain personal liability. Over time, as these were tested in the courts, an informal regime of quasi-limited liability emerged, although it was in the nature of judge-made law for there to be always some risk attached to reliance on such devices. One simple means of limiting the liability of partners was to specify the extent of liability in contracts with third parties. This became common practice in the large unincorporated insurance companies that were formed once the monopoly of the London Assurance and Royal Exchange over marine insurance was removed in 1824. However, few businesses other than insurance made use of a detailed written contract for each and every transaction, and even when this was done, the liability of partners could be limited only with respect to contractual claims; noncontractual claims based on torts were not affected by contractual limitations.[44] Individual liability in large unincorporated companies was also constrained by the practical difficulty that any creditor faced in bringing action against the partners. Each shareholder – and in the larger companies there could be hundreds – could file a separate defence, and any alteration in the share-holding (an almost daily event in any actively traded stock) could require the plaintiff to revive his suit.[45]

Even in small, stable partnerships the liability of partners was circumscribed by rules of priority developed in Chancery since at least the early eighteenth century, and clearly established from 1794. Creditors did not have open access to the individual assets of partners and the collective assets of the partnership. According to what became known as the 'jingle rule' of asset partitioning, business creditors who contracted with the partnership had first to resort to the jointly held partnership property, and private creditors who contracted with partners as individuals first had to resort to the separate property of these partners, and neither group could pursue a claim against assets in the other category until all claimants on that estate had been paid in full.[46]

A further limit on individual shareholder liability in unlimited companies and partnerships was introduced by the Winding-Up Acts of 1848 and 1849, which permitted shareholders to petition the Court of Chancery for dissolution and winding-up of their company in the event of bankruptcy or insolvency. A winding-up order was a means of apportioning the debts of the company proportionately among shareholders,

---

[44] Harris, *Industrializing*, 143–4; Cooke, *Corporation*, 166–8.

[45] *Report on the Law of Partnership* by Mr Bellenden Ker, 248–50.

[46] J. Getzler and M. Macnair, 'The firm as an entity before the Companies Acts', in P. Brand, K. Costello and W.N. Osborough (eds.), *Adventures of the Law* (Dublin, 2005), 267–88.

thereby relieving each individual shareholder of the risk that they might be called on, under bankruptcy proceedings, to make good the entire debts of the company from their personal estate.[47] However, as became clear in the case of the Royal British Bank, the overlapping jurisdictions of the Courts of Chancery and Bankruptcy still left a good deal of uncertainty in practice over the likelihood that shareholders would be pursued by creditors for the entirety of their estate.

The uncertainty that common law principles imposed on all parties involved with unlimited companies – directors, shareholders and creditors – was brought into high relief by the extraordinary circumstances and aftermath of the 'railway mania' of 1844–5. When the bottom dropped out of the stock market in October 1845 a huge number of investors were left holding almost worthless paper in the thousand or so railway companies that had been provisionally registered over the preceding nine months. Kostal, who has examined the causes and consequences of this 'mania' in some detail, shows that the crash created 'a vast and tangled web of indebtedness', and the English courts became the locus of a long, drawn-out power-play between various actors seeking to recoup their losses and shed their liabilities.[48] The first shot was fired by trade creditors of the failed companies. Since provisionally registered companies had issued to subscribers only letters of allotment, and had yet to convert these into formal shares, the initial targets were the provisional directors named in the prospectuses, many of whom were included for the eminence of their title or local reputation rather than their knowledge of railway affairs. Initially, the courts held the provisional directors to be liable as partners, or quasi-partners, for the debts of the company, but subsequent judgments conceived of the issue as one of contract rather than partnership, and absolved the directors from personal liability unless the plaintiff could demonstrate that the debt resulted from an express contract entered into in person by the defendant.

The next round of engagement was between the original subscribers for shares and the provisional directors. Subscribers had paid deposits to the provisional companies, in return for which they received letters of allotment, which were promises to issue shares once the registration process had been completed. A lively secondary market in these letters of allotment meant that, if prices rose, fortunate subscribers could make significant capital gains well before registration was completed and shares were issued. But once the market collapsed many

[47] Cooke, *Corporation*, 146–51.
[48] Kostal, *Railway Capitalism,* ch. 2, from which this account is taken.

subscribers turned to the provisional directors for reimbursement of their deposit, arguing breach of contract. Again some initial early decisions in favour of subscribers were reversed by a ruling in 1847 that purchasers were bound by their purchase, and that the rule of *caveat emptor* should apply. Subscribers received the paper that they had paid for, and whether that paper tuned out to be valuable or worthless was a matter to be determined by the laws of supply and demand in the market, and was not the responsibility of the provisional directors.

The third round of litigation was brought by provisional directors against subscribers. The letters of allotment typically specified when and where deposits on shares should be made, but once the market value of these letters and shares had dwindled, allottees were understandably reluctant to throw good money after bad by paying the cash deposits. Directors brought suits for breach of contract against subscribers, and the substantive grounds for these were strong. After some initial success, these actions foundered in the courts on procedural grounds. Provisionally registered companies were unincorporated bodies until the point of full registration and therefore their directors did not have the authority to sue collectively. Technically every provisional director was a party to the contract with each allottee, and thus had to be named as a co-plaintiff in any action – a time-consuming and expensive process made yet more difficult by the frequent changes to the composition of provisional company committees. Thus in the one area of post-mania litigation where breach of contract was unambiguous, the procedures of the English courts ensured that it was almost impossible to bring a successful prosecution.

The extent of flexibility and ambiguity that English law brought to the issue of limited liability for partners and for corporations goes some way to explaining the lack of consensus within the financial and mercantile communities in the 1850s. Investors in limited liability companies certainly benefited from the protection of their personal assets. However, the great majority of companies formed in the latter part of the nineteenth century were small private concerns in which the investor-shareholders were also the director-owners, and they were therefore also directly exposed to the downside of limited liability in that, as trade creditors, their claim over the assets of proprietors of other small businesses was also limited. Even for *rentier* capitalists the introduction of general limited liability in 1856 (extended to include joint stock banks in 1858 and insurance companies in the consolidating Companies Act of 1862) did not provide absolute protection of personal assets in the event of corporate insolvency, because most shares were only partly paid-up at point of issue (to about 25 per cent of nominal value), and if the company became insolvent, shareholders were liable to the full nominal value of the shares they held. Although subsequent calls increased the general level of company capitalisation, in 1885 the unpaid liability of shares of public companies quoted on the Stock Exchange still averaged almost 40 per cent of the nominal value.[49]

The circumscribed nature of limited liability in the case of partly paid-up shares was brought home forcefully in the financial panic following the collapse of the bill-broking house of Overend and Gurney in 1866. Shares in other companies on which only a small amount of the nominal value had been paid up became unsaleable because potential buyers were not prepared to take on the liability; this was particularly true for banking shares because banks were perceived to be particularly at risk during the panic, and because banking shares were typically issued with small paid-up proportions on large denomination shares (£20–£50 or more).[50] There was no provision in the 1862 Act for companies to reduce their nominal capitalisation or subdivide their shares, and this prompted commercial interests, led by the company promoter David Chadwick, to mobilise for further legal amendment. The 1867 Select Committee on Limited Liability Acts led to an amending act which permitted companies to reduce their capitalisation and the value of their shares and also, as a result of a late amendment in the House of Lords, allowed companies to be formed with limited shareholders and unlimited directors. Unsurprisingly this additional company form attracted few takers: in 1886 Levi noted that 'scarcely any companies' of this type had been established.[51] Given the choice, almost everyone opted to limit their liability: between 1862 and 1906 almost 98,000 new joint stock companies were registered in the United Kingdom with limited liability, and just 151 with unlimited liability.[52]

From 1856 to the 1890s there remained a lingering legal tension between individual and corporate liability that was inherent in the fictive personality of the corporation and the real personality of sole proprietors and partners. As had so often been the case hitherto, it was not legislation but the courts that determined where the limits of liability actually lay, and as in the past, it took the courts several goes to reach a

---

[49] A. Essex-Crosby, 'Joint-Stock Companies in Great Britain, 1890–1930', M.Comm. thesis, University of London (1938), 26.

[50] Todd, 'Some aspects of joint stock companies', 46–71; J. B. Jefferys, 'The denomination and character of shares, 1855–1885', *Economic History Review*, 16 (1946), 45–55; Cottrell, *Industrial Finance*, 58–9, 84.

[51] Levi, 'Progress', 244.

[52] *Annual Return relating to Joint Stock Companies for 1906*, PP 1907 lxxvi, 78–9. This return does not specify how many, if any, companies were formed with the hybrid limited/unlimited form sanctioned by the 1867 Act.

firm conclusion. What brought matters to a head was not further delib-
eration in parliament, or speculation on the stock exchange, or changes
in the fortunes of any of the country's major banking or trading or
manufacturing companies, but rather the activities of a bootmaker in
Whitechapel High Street.

The wisdom of Salomon

Like most migrants, the boot maker Aron Salomon arrived in Britain
with few assets other than the clothes he wore. He had been born in
Rhenish Prussia – the most westerly part, bordering Belgium and the
Netherlands – in about 1837, and he subsequently found his wife,
Schoontje, across the border in Holland.[53] In 1862, when their first son
was born, they were living in Bermondsey, although they do not appear
in the census records of the previous year. In 1865, when their third
son was born, they were living in Spitalfields, possibly in the Peabody
Buildings erected in 1864 on Commercial Street to house the artisan
and labouring poor of London, which is where they were residing with
their five children aged between 9 years and 9 months at the time of the
1871 census. Also living with them were Schoontje's nephew Adolph
Anholt, who worked as a boot manufacturer's apprentice, probably
under Aron, and a 17-year-old 'nurse girl' who helped to care for the
young family.

Ten years later and the family had grown with the birth of a further
three children, and had also moved out of the Peabody Buildings and
just around the corner to 28 Whitechapel High Street where Aron ran
a boot manufacturing business. He had become a naturalised British
subject by 1881, although his wife Schoontje remained a Dutch citizen
to the end of her days, despite anglicising her name to Jeanet.[54] The
three eldest sons, Emanuel (19), Salomon (17) and David (15) were also
recorded as boot manufacturers. In addition to the ten family members, the premises at 28 Whitechapel High Street housed two domestic servants. The 1880s were a good decade for the Salomon family;
by 1891 they had moved far up the social scale and were now to be

---

[53] Details relating to household composition and residence are derived from the manuscript censuses from 1871–1901. Alternate spellings appear in different years – Aaron
Solomon in 1871, Aaron Salomon in 1881, and Aron Salomon – the name under
which the legal actions were brought – in 1891 (although *The Economist* misreported
the name as Aron Salomons).

[54] She is recorded as Schoontje in the censuses from 1871 to 1891, as Jennette in the
1901 census, and as Jeanet in the probate register for 1912. Her personal effects, valued at £278, were left to her eldest son, Emanuel.

found in Bloomsbury, at 36 Bedford Place. They had not quite reached the fashionable heights of Russell Square, which lay at the end of their street, and which housed, among others, the Pankhurst family, but this was a social and economic, as well as physical, world away from the Peabody Buildings in Whitechapel.[55] Aron's business was clearly a success, helped no doubt by the efforts of three of his sons and a German nephew who worked for him. Having moved to a fashionable address, in 1892 Aron decided further to follow the fashion soon to be satirised by Gilbert and Sullivan by converting his business into a limited liability company.[56]

By this date Salomon was no longer a mere maker of boots, but instead was a leather merchant, hide factor and wholesale and export boot manufacturer. He had been successful in winning government contracts and the business was generating a profit of between £1,000 and £2,000 per annum. In July 1892 Aron Salomon commenced the process of converting his solely-owned business into a joint-stock limited liability company. The first act was to appoint a trustee for the future company with whom a preliminary agreement over the value of assets could be negotiated. The person nominated to take this role was none other than Adolph Anholt, Schoontje's nephew and former lodger. The trustee agreed, on behalf of the putative company, to buy the goodwill of the business for £7,500, leases for £2,500, and fixtures and fittings for £6,000, all to be paid for in fully paid-up shares. Bills in hand and book debts, valued at almost £6,800, were to be paid for in cash, and the stock in trade, valued at £16,000 was to be paid partly in shares and partly in cash or debentures (debentures were bonds secured by a floating charge on the assets of the company).[57] These valuations were all determined by Aron Salomon and were, it was subsequently claimed in court, considerably higher than the amounts appearing in the balance sheet of the business. Nevertheless, on 28 July 1892 the company was formed to carry out this agreement. The nominal capital of Aron Salomon and Company (Limited) was £40,000, divided into 40,000

---

[55] In the maps produced by Charles Booth's social survey of London in 1898, Bedford Place was coded red – 'middle class, well-to-do' – while Russell Square was coded yellow – 'upper-middle and upper classes, wealthy'. Commercial Street was coded purple – 'Mixed – some comfortable, others poor'. See http://booth.lse.ac.uk/

[56] Details of Salomon's business, insolvency and the subsequent court cases, are derived from court records (National Archives J14/35, J14/307) and court reports in *The Times*, particularly 21 December 1893, 29 May 1895, 17 November 1896.

[57] For the significance of floating charges in commercial finance see J. Getzler, 'The role of security over future and circulating capital: evidence from the British economy *circa* 1850–1920' in J. Getzler and J. Payne (eds.), *Company Charges: Spectrum and Beyond* (Oxford, 2006), 227–51.

shares of £1 each. By chance this was exactly the average capitalisation of the 2,505 new limited companies registered in 1892; Salomon had apparently created a very ordinary company. The memorandum of association was signed by the required seven persons – Aron, his wife Schoontje, his daughter Sophie, and the four sons Emanuel, David, Salomon, and Moritz – each of whom was allotted one share apiece. On 2 August the seven subscribers to the company met and appointed Aron Salomon as Managing Director at a salary of £500 a year, and then appointed both Emanuel and Salomon Salomon to directorships at a salary of £148 a year. Aron Salomon was also appointed as Chairman of the new company, while another son, Asher – aged just 17 – became Treasurer. Then, on 12 August, the newly formed company executed the agreement drawn up between Aron Salomon and the trustee, Adolph Anholt, and thereby purchased the business. Three weeks later, 20,000 paid-up shares were allotted to Aron Salomon as payment for goodwill, leases and fittings, and debentures for £10,000 were sealed and ordered to be given to Aron.

At this point, the preliminary agreement had been fully executed, and Aron Salomon's business had been converted from a sole proprietorship to a limited liability company. Aron still had absolute control of the business – he was managing director, chairman of the board, and majority shareholder, owning all but six of the 20,007 issued shares. In August 1892 the business was in a sound condition and was generating a significant surplus. However, according to subsequent court evidence of Emanuel Salomon, a succession of strikes in the boot trade led to a loss of government contracts and a slide from profit to loss.[58] To raise additional funds Aron Salomon borrowed £5,000 from Edmund Broderip, using the 100 debentures of £100 each as security. In February 1893 these original debentures were returned to the company and cancelled, and fresh debentures to the same amount were issued to Broderip to secure repayment of his loan, with Aron Salomon named as the beneficial owner.

By September 1893 the company had defaulted on the payment of interest on the debentures, and Broderip initiated an action to enforce his security. A winding-up order was made, and a liquidator was appointed at the instance of the unsecured creditors, who were owed close to £8,000. At this point Aron Salomon issued a counter-claim

---

[58] The early 1890s was a period of considerable tension between employers and workers in the boot and shoe trade, culminating in a major lock-out in 1895. See Alan Fox, *A History of the National Union of Boot and Shoe Operatives, 1874–1957* (Oxford, 1958), ch. 21.

against Aron Salomon and Company (Limited) on the basis that, as beneficial owner of the debentures, he had a preferential claim on the assets of the company. Thus began a series of cases that commenced in the High Court in 1894, moved on to the Court of Appeal in 1895, and reached the House of Lords in 1896 in the definitive case of *Salomon v. A. Salomon and Co. (Limited)*.

The company, now represented by the liquidator, claimed that the formation of the company was a sham, because Aron Salomon effectively remained as sole proprietor, and that the debentures had been intentionally used to allow Salomon to rank 'as a creditor of his own business in priority to persons who are in substance his own creditors and to take the whole business and assets away from them'. Mr Justice Vaughan Williams was clearly in sympathy with this argument. He concluded that the company was a mere fraud because the business was owned and wholly controlled by Aron Salomon and nobody else. He then ingeniously shifted the substance of the case from company law to the law of principal and agent, by concluding that the company was employed by Aron Salomon as his agent, and that under the law a principal is bound to indemnify the agent for actions undertaken at the principal's bidding. Vaughan Williams asserted that the creditors of the company were, in effect, the personal creditors of Aron Salomon, and the use of the debentures was a deliberate attempt to defeat the rightful claims of unsecured creditors.[59]

This judgment seemed completely to undermine the principle of separate corporate personality as established by the Companies Acts, and Aron Salomon was given leave to appeal. Three months later, the Court of Appeal substantially affirmed the decision of Vaughan Williams, but by reference to a different set of legal principles. Lords Justice Lindley, Lopes and Kay concluded that although A. Salomon and Co. (Limited) had been formed entirely in accordance with the requirements of the 1862 Companies Act, the *intention* lying behind the formation of this 'one man company' was not consistent with the law which explicitly removed the privileges of incorporation from companies with fewer than seven members. Lindley demurred from the logic of Vaughan Williams's decision because 'as the company must be recognised as a corporation, I feel a difficulty in saying that the company did not carry on business as a principal'. Nevertheless, he was of the view that judgment should be given against Aron Salomon because he had defied the spirit of the law, if not the letter:

---

[59] *The Times*, 15 Feb 1895, 14.

Mr Aron Salomon's liability to indemnify the company in this case is, in my view, the legal consequence of the formation of the company in order to attain a result not permitted by law. The liability does not arise simply from the fact that he holds nearly all the shares in the company. A man may do that and yet be under no such liability as Mr Aron Salomon has come under. His liability rests on the purpose for which he formed the company and on the way he formed it, and on the use which he made of it. There are many small companies which will be quite unaffected by this decision. But there may possibly be some which, like this, are mere devices to enable a man to carry on trade with limited liability, to incur debts in the name of a registered company, and to sweep off the company's assets by means of debentures which he has caused to be issued to himself in order to defeat the claims of those who have been incautious enough to trade with the company without perceiving the trap which he has laid for them.[60]

Lord Lopes came to the same conclusion using rather more colourful language: 'It would be lamentable if a scheme like this could not be defeated. If we were to permit it to succeed, we should be authorising a perversion of the Joint Stock Companies Acts ... To legalise such a transaction would be a scandal.'[61]

It is surprising that it took so long for the legitimacy of the 'one man company' to attract judicial attention. When Robert Lowe had first introduced the Joint Stock Companies Act to Parliament in 1856 he had explicitly recognised the problem of indistinct responsibility that would arise if limited liability were to be extended to small partnerships and sole proprietorships:

There appears to me to be something incompatible and inconsistent between the character of a man acting as a principal in trade, and that of a person being a corporator, and whose liability as such shall be limited. There would be a constant ambiguity whether such a person was trading as a principal or as a private individual ... Everything would always be said to have been done by the corporation and nothing by the individual, and a door to vexation, quibbling and perjury would be opened which it is most desirable to keep closed.[62]

Nevertheless, the opportunities created for sole traders by the 1856 Act were quickly recognised by lawyers. Edward Cox, barrister and recorder of Falmouth, Devon, was one of a number of lawyers to produce manuals of advice on how to 'get up' a limited liability company. There was considerable demand for such manuals, with Cox's work going through seven successive editions by 1870. Cox noted that the law did not specify any minimum number or proportion of shares to be held by each of the seven or more members of a limited liability

[60] *The Times*, 29 May 1895, 3.   [61] *Ibid.*
[62] *HCDeb*, 1 Feb 1856, col 113.

company, and therefore a trader need do no more than 'give one £1
share to each of his children (if of age), brothers or sisters, parents or
servants, and keep the remaining shares himself, and he will obtain the
advantages of incorporation'. He foresaw that 'traders in difficulties
will easily save themselves from the personal inconvenience of bankruptcy or insolvency, by immediately converting their business into a
Limited Liability Corporation'.[63] Aron Salomon was far from being the
first sole proprietor to put this plan into practice; where he was an inno-
vator was in the use of debentures to obtain preferred creditor status
over the assets of the company. It was this that seemed so to offend the
sensibilities of the Appeal Court judges.

Salomon took his case onwards from the Court of Appeal to the
House of Lords, where judgment was delivered by the Lord Chancellor
and Lords Watson and Herschell in November 1896. They were unanimous in reversing the decision of the Court of Appeal, and withering in
their criticism of the earlier judgments. They could not understand how
Mr Justice Vaughan Williams could deem the company to be an agent
of Aron Salomon: 'either the limited company was a legal entity or it
was not. If it was, the business belonged to it and not to Mr Salomon. If
it was not, there was no person and no thing to be an agent at all; and it
is impossible to say at the same time that there is a company and there
is not.' Nor could they comprehend how the Appeal Court judges could
deem the company to have been contrary to the spirit of the law. The
statute did not require persons subscribing for shares to be unrelated to
each other, nor did it specify any limit on the number of shares for which
a single member could subscribe. The Lord Chancellor summarised:

The truth is that the learned Judges have never allowed in their own minds the
proposition that the company has a real existence. They have been struck by
what they have considered the inexpediency of permitting one man to be, in
influence and authority, the whole company, and assuming that such a thing
could not have been intended by the Legislature, they have sought various
grounds upon which they might insert into the Act some prohibition of such
a result.

But, he concluded, it was not appropriate for any Judge to insert into an
Act of Parliament limitations which are not to be found in the letter of
the law. He further surmised that Aron Salomon's predicament was the
result of misfortune rather than dishonesty or unworthy intent.[64]

[63] Edward W. Cox, *The New Law and Practice of Joint Stock Companies with and without
Limited Liability* (4th edn, London, 1857), xviii–xix.
[64] *The Times*, 17 Nov 1896, 13.

The Law Lords' decision must have been very welcome news for Aron Salomon, but scant compensation. His business had become insolvent, and the long drawn-out legal action had exhausted his financial resources. The house in Bedford Place, and the rest of his personal assets, were sacrificed to this case. By the time it had reached the House of Lords in 1896, Aron Salomon was listed in the court titles as a pauper. He moved back to the East End, where he died, in Hackney, less than six months after the Lords' decision. It had been a Pyrrhic victory; his personal effects at death were valued at £503.[65]

It had taken the English judiciary forty years to give full and unequivocal effect to the Joint Stock Companies Act of 1856. Whether the legislature had ever intended to sanction one-man companies of the sort created by Aron Salomon remains a moot point. In hearing Salomon's appeal the Lord Chancellor was adamant that the only way of determining the will of parliament was to look at the letter of the law, though if he had looked back to the House of Commons debate of 1 February 1856 he would have seen that the Act's sponsor, Robert Lowe, was explicitly opposed to the creation of such companies. What is clear is that it took the judiciary several decades to accept that, in all cases, a properly constituted joint stock company had a real legal personality independent of any or all of its members. This shift in legal position occurred not in response to significant pressure from economic interests, but instead because of jurisprudential arguments in which moral presumptions derived from the working of the law of partnership were at first attached to, and then de-linked from, the law of incorporation. Judges were initially hesitant to abandon all oversight of company activity to the principle of *caveat emptor*, and this is understandable given some of the wilder excesses of company promotion in the second half of the century (discussed further in Chapter 7 below). Implicitly the judges feared that in the absence of legal constraints, individuals taking shelter behind the corporate veil would consistently break their contracts and fail to pay their debts. This was a deeply entrenched belief; it was the advantage to be gained from being able to renege on debts that had led Thomas Tooke in 1836 to assert that 'inferior' limited liability companies would drive out the better instrument of the unlimited partnership.

---

[65] He died on 13 May 1896 at 167 Amhurst Rod, Hackney. Details from the Probate Register for 1897.

In fact, as noted above, there was no rush to incorporate in the immediate aftermath of the 1856 legislation, partly because investor and proprietor liability could be limited to some degree through a variety of
other legal devices, partly because of lack of understanding of how the
new law would work in practice. Nor was there any obvious decline in
commercial probity; the courts did not become awash with commercial
claims and counter-claims. Yet both commercial morality and commercial practice were changed by the companies legislation of Victoria's
reign. To get a clear sense of what had changed it is necessary to consider the combined impact of joint stock incorporation and limited liability on the rights and duties of ownership, and to do this requires a
brief digression into jurisprudence.

In Chapter 4 it was noted that the distinction between ownership
and control of companies can be traced back to the writings of Adam
Smith, and that it has been commonplace in industrial economics since
the managerialist analysis of Berle and Means. However, economists'
conceptions of ownership are often simplistic: ownership is commonly
defined in terms of the right of a residual claim on the assets of an
organisation after all other legitimate claimants have been paid; thus
shareholders own the classical capitalist firm, policyholders own mutual
insurance companies, and so on.[66] Yet the conflicting judgments in the
case of *Salomon* v. *Salomon and Co. (Ltd)* reveal 'ownership' to be a
much more complex and ambiguous term in the context of a joint-stock
corporation.

Take a simple example of the contingent nature of shareholder ownership. If S, as sole proprietor, owns outright a bootmaking enterprise,
he takes all the profit (as residual claimant) and can freely enter the
premises without fear of breaching the law of trespass. But if S owns
outright some shares in a company that runs a bootmaking business
he is still a residual claimant, but he cannot freely enter the workshop,
and if he enters except by invitation of the company he is committing
trespass. Even if S buys up *all* the shares, he still cannot freely enter the
workshop, because that property is owned by the company, not by him
as the sole shareholder. So shareholder ownership is more circumscribed
than personal property ownership. How much is it circumscribed?

This is where jurisprudence comes in. Conceptions of ownership
are culturally and historically specific, and they cannot be reduced
to a single simple definition. But in a classic exposition of the nature
of ownership, A. M. Honoré identified eleven separate characteristics
of ownership, and argued that if a sufficient number are identified, then

[66] Berle and Means, *Modern Corporation.*

it is sensible to describe the resulting relationship as ownership.[67] The eleven characteristics present in full ownership are:

   i. the right to possess; that is, to have exclusive physical control of an asset;
  ii. the right to use the asset;
 iii. the right to manage the asset, such as by contracting with others over its use;
  iv. the right to income derived from use of the asset;
   v. the right to capital, including the right to consume or destroy the asset;
  vi. the right to security, and hence immunity from arbitrary appropriation;
 vii. the right to transmit the asset to others;
viii. absence of term, thus giving full ownership in perpetuity;
  ix. duty not to cause harm to others through use of the asset;
   x. judgment liability; that is, the liability of the owner's interest in the asset to be used to settle debts;
  xi. residual control; that is, reversion of full ownership rights when any pre-existing ownership rights accorded to other parties lapse.

None of these characteristics is a necessary constituent of ownership, and much of that which is commonly thought of as ownership is circumscribed in relation to one or more of these characteristics. For example, although the majority of homes in the UK today are 'owner-occupied', the ownership rights are typically constrained because the homes are mortgaged (thus compromising characteristic *vii* – the right to transmit) or are leasehold (compromising characteristic *viii* – absence of term).

Table 5.1 shows these same criteria applied to different aspects of corporate ownership. A sole trader whose business is not encumbered with any restrictive contracts or covenants has full ownership of the business in relation to all eleven characteristics. The same holds true for the ownership by partners of their partnership, except for the requirement that the partners have to reach joint agreement over the transmission of their assets to others. A company shareholder likewise has full ownership rights over his or her shares. However, the shareholder's ownership rights over the shares do not directly extend to ownership rights over the company. The legal constitution of the share as an entirely autonomous form of property – a primarily nineteenth-century legal and conceptual development – externalised the shareholder from the

---

[67] A. Honoré, 'Ownership', in A. G. Guest (ed.), *Oxford Essays in Jurisprudence* (Oxford, 1961), 107–47.

Table 5.1. *Characteristics of corporate ownership*

	Sole trader over own business	Partners over partnership	Company shareholder over share	Company shareholder over company	Directors over company
Possession	Yes	Yes	Yes	No	Yes
Use	Yes	Yes	Yes	No	No
Management	Yes	Yes	Yes	Some	Yes
Income	Yes	Yes	Yes	Some	No
Capital	Yes	Yes	Yes	Some	No
Security	Yes	Yes	Yes	No	Some
Transmission	Yes	(Jointly)	Yes	No	Yes
Unlimited term	Yes	Yes	Yes	Yes	No
Duty not to harm	Yes	Yes	Yes	No	Some
Judgment liability	Yes	Yes	Yes	No	No
Residual control	Yes	Yes	Yes	Yes	Yes

Based on Honoré, 'Ownership'; Kay, 'Stakeholder', table 12.1.

company, and provided the foundations of the modern legal doctrine of separate personality, whereby there is complete separation of company and members.[68] The shareholder owns outright and can dispose of his shares, but it is the directors who own the company in terms of possession, management and transmission of the physical assets.

What happens when a sole proprietorship or partnership converts into a private company? Essentially the outright owner splits ownership rights between himself as shareholder and himself as director. In law these directors are mere agents of the company, just well-paid employees who can be hired and fired like any other contractual party. By definition they cannot be principals, since it is the legal personality of the company to which they are contracted and which commands them, even though in practice the directors possess a significant number of the characteristics of ownership. On the other hand, the shareholders, who hold residual perpetual control over the company, have few powers to determine what the company actually does.

What advantage do owners get in moving from partnership to company? Crucially, the shareholder avoids two of the potential costs of outright ownership – judgment liability and duty not to do harm. As

---

[68] P. Ireland, 'Capitalism without the capitalist: the joint stock company share and the emergence of the modern doctrine of separate corporate personality', *Journal of Legal History*, 17 (1996), 41–73.

Jefferys, Cottrell and others have argued, from 1856 limited liability protected the general assets of a shareholder from compensatory claims made against the company – the shareholder's liability was restricted to the capital (paid and unpaid) denominated in the share. But, as noted above, limited liability for sleeping partners and all partners was also available from 1867 and 1907 respectively, but was barely used. Furthermore, the take-up of limited liability incorporation was slow until the mid-1880s, so the ability to avoid judgment liability cannot be the whole story.

There is a second advantage that owners can derive from shifting from partnership to incorporated company. Incorporation blurs the lines of responsibility for harm caused to third parties – both legal harms (torts) and social harms such as cutting wages or laying off workers. In a wholly owned business or partnership, it is clear that the owners are directly responsible for decisions and actions of the business. In a corporation, it is neither the directors nor the shareholders who are responsible for actions – it is the corporation itself. Although directors may take the key decisions, they cannot be personally responsible for the action of the company. Indeed, nineteenth-century company law was so lax that it was difficult to make directors responsible for anything. The slew of fraudulent companies – particularly overseas mining companies – formed in the 1880s prompted the introduction of the Directors Liability Act in 1890. This attempted to prevent gross misrepresentation in prospectuses by removing the need to prove deliberate fraud on the part of directors – something found to be almost impossible at law. However, directors could still escape any personal liability if they could show they had reasonable grounds for believing statements made on their authority, or if such statements were based on the advice of experts.[69] Nineteenth-century company directors were almost fully 'teflon-coated'.

By converting from partnership to corporate status, owners could retain all the power of control, without carrying the full responsibility of ownership. They could shirk both the legal liabilities of ownership and the moral responsibilities of control and authority that rested directly on partners and sole proprietors. The law of incorporation and limited liability allowed business owners to avoid (or minimise) the downside risk of liability for debts, torts and actions deemed by society to be unfair or unjust, without requiring them to forego any element of

---

[69] N. Lindley, *A Treatise on the Law of Companies Considered as a Branch of the Law of Partnership* (London, 1891), 1–12; R. R. Formoy, *The Historical Foundation of Modern Company Law* (London, 1923), 108–14.

control, or any of the upside gains from this business activity. The law gave business proprietors a one-way bet, and not surprisingly they took it in their thousands. In historical terms, this can be thought of as the final removal of the vestiges of a 'moral economy' in which property owners were expected to take some responsibility for the welfare consequences of their actions.[70] The nineteenth-century legal foundations of the classical capitalist firm reflected a modern form of 'non-responsible' capitalism.[71] In economic terms, the complex and ambiguous nature of ownership, once split between shareholders and directors, ensured that contracts between a corporation and its agents would be incomplete. The enhanced incompleteness arising from the transition from partnerships to the classical capitalist firm gave additional power to those parties to the contractual nexus who had privileged access to information and decision-making.[72]

There remain two conundrums. If incorporation provided business proprietors with a one-way bet, why did it take them thirty years to realise the advantages provided by the 1856 Act? And if incorporation was so attractive to principals and proprietors, why did partnerships remain the common organisational form in some economic sectors, particularly the professions? Part of the reason for slow take-up must have been the inherent uncertainty that judicial prerogative introduces into any common law system. Although writers of legal manuals quickly spotted the opportunity provided by the 1856 Act for sole proprietors to relieve themselves of a broad range of legal, financial and moral responsibilities, the absolute legal position remained ambiguous until Salomon's House of Lords appeal in 1896. Also important, however, were contemporaneous changes in the political and social context within which business operated. Atiyah has characterised the period from 1870 as a time of 'the decline of freedom of contract', where governments increasingly resorted to legislation to reinforce or protect the interests of weaker contractual parties.[73] The Food and Drug Act (1875) imposed costs on retailers and producers who supplied tainted goods, and in the 1880s the Local Government Board pressurised councils to enforce the legislation by appointing public analysts.[74] The Employer's Liability Act (1880)

---

[70] E. P. Thompson, 'The moral economy reviewed' in Idem, *Customs in Common* (Harmondsworth, 1993), 259–351.

[71] For an illuminating discussion of how 'non-responsbile' corporate forms have affected corporate behaviour in modern America see Lawrence Mitchell, *Corporate Irresponsibility: America's Newest Export* (New Haven, 2001).

[72] O. D. Hart, 'Incomplete contracts and the theory of the firm' in O. E. Williamson and S. G. Winter (eds.), *The Nature of the Firm* (Oxford, 1991), 138–58.

[73] Atiyah, *Rise and Fall*, part III.

[74] A. S. Wohl, *Endangered Lives* (London, 1983), 54.

gave injured workmen the right to sue their employer for negligence; the Bills of Sale Act (1882) gave borrowers and credit purchasers significant protection against aggressive lenders. At the same time the political organisation of the labour movement increased the rhetorical power of workers and, as shown in Chapter 2, increased their bargaining power in the labour market, and inaugurated a shift in public opinion away from employer interests (shown most clearly in the widespread middle-class support for the dockers' strike of 1889). In these circumstances, sole proprietors and partners could distance both their assets and their reputations from external assault by adopting the incorporated legal form, and placing the barrier of complex ownership and indistinct responsibility between themselves and their employees and customers.

The continuation of the partnership form in the professions requires a different explanation, since there is no particular reason to expect doctors, lawyers, architects and accountants to be less exposed to contractual and tortious claims than would the typical business proprietor. But just at the moment when businessmen were rushing for the protection of incorporation, the state granted massive powers of self-regulation and social closure to professional bodies, which effectively placed issues of contract performance in the hands of peer-controlled review bodies. Lawyers had long protected their reputations and pockets through the rules and customs of the Inns of Court and, for solicitors from the 1830s, the Law Society, although it was the Solicitors' Act of 1888 which finally gave the Law Society full regulatory power.[75] From 1858 doctors were licensed and regulated by the General Medical Council, accountants received similar privileges when the Institute of Chartered Accountants received a royal charter in 1880, something that was achieved by actuaries in 1884. The Royal College of Veterinary Surgeons was given a statutory duty to examine and regulate standards in 1881, and the Royal Institute of British Architects likewise in 1887.[76] The establishment of these professional bodies – which protected professional activity from external scrutiny – occurred at just the same time in the nineteenth century that company law was granting similar privileges to businessmen to distance themselves as individuals from the consequences of their commercial actions.

Incorporation in Victorian Britain was a preferred, and often necessary, route for large businesses that needed access to substantial amounts of

---

[75] B. Abel-Smith and R. Stevens, *Lawyers and the Courts: A Sociological Study of the English Legal System, 1750–1965* (London, 1967), 188–9.

[76] A. M. Carr-Saunders and P. A. Wilson, *The Professions* (Oxford, 1933).

external capital. But these large-scale enterprises with publicly traded shares, though economically important, were few in number. The overwhelming majority of companies were small, had low capitalisation, and made no public offering of their shares; for them, incorporation involved a technical change of ownership and governance, but no change in the activities, control or finance of the company. Partners chose to incorporate because by doing so they could separate the characteristics of ownership between themselves as shareholders and themselves as directors, thereby retaining substantial control of property without having to suffer the encumbrance of individual legal and moral responsibility. In an environment in which the legal and social obligations placed on business proprietors were increasing, this was a sensible strategy which served to reduce the private costs for capital owners of commercial activity. It is clear that the implementation of the law of limited liability was not a direct functional response to a broadly perceived and directly articulated need of the business community. It is also clear that the 'normalisation' of limited liability in the last two decades of the nineteenth century had little impact on the mode of operation of most businesses. What remains to be seen is whether 'companification' and limited liability produced positive economic returns for society as a whole; it is to this complex question that we turn in the next chapter.

6   Corporate performance

At the beginning of the nineteenth century the incorporation of business was prohibited by the Bubble Act; companies could be formed only by grant of royal charter or letters patent, and incorporation was restricted to large-scale enterprises deemed to be in the public interest. By the century's end, the limited liability company had become the dominant form of business organisation in Great Britain. This radical transformation of business structures coincided with the sustained growth and structural change in the British economy that turned it into the 'workshop of the world', and it is possible that there was some link between these two developments. A strong causal relationship might be one in which economic development created pressure for organisational change, with the new organisational forms themselves promoting further economic growth by increasing the efficiency of business operation. This is the underlying model that institutional economists have commonly applied when considering the rise of what has been called the 'classical capitalist firm' – that is, a company with shareholders, managers and workers.[1] The rise to dominance of the corporation is seen to reflect the relative efficiency of that form of business organisation over any alternative. In a competitive economy, organisational forms that are less responsive, less adaptable and less profitable will be crowded out by their more efficient competitors in an economic process of natural selection which will serve to reduce social costs and increase overall welfare.

The elegance of the theory of institutional change does not sit comfortably with the complexity of the historical record. The previous two chapters have shown that the emergence of the limited liability corporation was not a direct consequence of consistent pressure from business and commercial quarters, or because of any consensus among political economists that corporations were more efficient than partnerships,

[1] A. Alchian and H. Demsetz, 'Production, information costs, and economic organisation', *American Economic Review*, 57 (1972), 777–95.

or because of any broad political sentiment that general incorporation would be good for the economy. Furthermore, the widespread take-up of the incorporated business form lagged by almost three decades the date of enactment of the key enabling legislation, and when it was adopted it had little or no impact on the mode of operation of most businesses. Before the First World War the overwhelming majority of limited liability enterprises were formed by the simple conversion of partnerships into private companies in which a very small number of shareholders retained complete ownership and control of the business. Most of these private companies were small-scale affairs, like the boot-making business of Aron Salomon, but fully one-third of the largest hundred British manufacturing companies in 1906 were privately owned, and had not made any public issue of shares.[2]

The facility that incorporation gave to business proprietors to partition their ownership rights between themselves as shareholders and themselves as directors reduced the private costs of ownership by relieving them of the judgment liability and duty not to do harm inherent in partnership or sole proprietorship. But it cannot be assumed that the one-way bet offered to proprietors by limited liability incorporation produced any broader social benefits, or that it made any significant contribution to the overall success of the British economy in the latter years of Victoria's reign. The 'natural selection' process that may work to select optimal institutions in an entirely neutral market environment will not produce the same results if the market is skewed by rules – whether legislative or customary – that offer privileges to one particular institutional form. As Edward Cox noted in the immediate aftermath of the 1856 Joint Stock Companies Act, the extension of the privilege of limited liability to corporations, but not to partnerships, skewed the market by giving traders a clear incentive to convert their business into a company.[3]

Given that the 'rush to incorporation' from the 1880s cannot be taken as proof of any intrinsic superiority of corporations over partnerships in terms of operational efficiency, it is necessary to turn to other evidence to attempt to assess the contribution of general incorporation to British economic success in the nineteenth century. Few options are available, because the data do not exist to conduct a matched comparison of the performance of incorporated and non-incorporated firms across the entire Victorian economy. But there is one narrow sector in which different organisational forms directly competed with each other – life

---

[2] Shaw, 'Large manufacturing employers of 1907', 46.
[3] Cox, *Joint Stock Companies*, xviii–xix.

insurance. The competition was between incorporated insurers owned by shareholders and mutual insurers owned by policyholders, and the track record of these different firms provides some insight into the impact of incorporation on economic performance.

In 1806 the social arithmetician Sir Frederick Eden, as part of his campaign to obtain a charter of incorporation for the Globe Insurance Company, argued strongly that life insurance should be organised on the basis of joint stock incorporation. Joint stock companies, he wrote, offered greater security than mutual insurers because they are based upon subscribed capital which cannot be depleted by individual action, unlike the personal guarantees which lie behind mutual firms.[4] Twenty years later Charles Babbage, inventor of the calculating engine, advanced the opposite view: 'a large capital at the commencement is quite unnecessary' because life insurance is 'a business in which the receipts are paid long before any demands take place, and where, consequently there can occur no losses from bad debts'.[5] Similar disagreements about how best to organise the delivery of life insurance were rehearsed throughout the nineteenth century.[6] Every argument about the security provided by the reserve of shareholder capital was matched by counter-argument that such security was illusory and unenforceable. Each claim about the way joint-stock directors were incentivised by their dividend income to maximise the performance of the company was parried by arguments that proprietary companies exploited policyholders by retaining excessive profits for their shareholders.[7] And underpinning this unresolved debate was the evident coexistence of both organisational types, selling identical insurance products in an apparently competitive market.

The modern theory of the firm has systematised many of the arguments which Eden, Babbage and others advanced about the relationship

---

[4] Sir Frederick Eden, *On the Policy and Expediency of Granting Insurance Charters* (London, 1806), 6–7.

[5] Charles Babbage, *A Comparative View of the Various Institutions for the Assurance of Lives* (London, 1826), 21–2.

[6] There had been an earlier discussion in the eighteenth century about the relative merits of mutual organisation of fire insurance. See Robin Pearson, 'Mutuality tested: the rise and fall of mutual fire insurance offices in eighteenth-century London', *Business History*, 44 (2002), 1–28.

[7] For examples of a positive view of proprietary companies, see, G. M. Dent, *A Dialogue Showing How to Select a Life Office* (Manchester, 1888), 20; Equity and Law Life Assurance Society, *Prospectus for 1891*, 7. For negative views, see, for example, Alexander Colvin, *Actuarial Figments Exploded: A Letter to the Right Hon. J.W. Henley, M.P., in Defence of Life Assurance Offices* (London, 1852), 13; William Swiney, *A Letter to the Rt. Hon. Benjamin D'Israeli Respecting Certain Life Assurance Companies* (London, 1852), 6; C. J. Bunyon, *On the Liquidation of an Insolvent Life Office* (London, 1870), 5.

between corporate ownership and performance. In particular, agency costs are now seen to provide a coherent explanation for the structure of organisations, with those firms which most adequately resolve or contain the conflicting interests of different agents being the ones that maximise organisational efficiency, and thus which are likely to achieve long-run commercial success. In insurance one can think of there being three principal stakeholders – managers, owners and policyholders. The joint stock company is generally viewed as being more effective in controlling conflicts between owners and managers, because the market for corporate control provides owners with a mechanism for monitoring and constraining managerial opportunism. The mutual, on the other hand, is seen as being better able to control the conflict between policyholders and owners, because the mutual form merges these two stakeholder groups into one. The relative success of different organisational forms thus depends on their ability to control different sets of agency costs, which will vary with product types. These modern theoretical and empirical insights can be used to revisit issues which agitated nineteenth-century commentators on insurance, and to address two interrelated questions: how did the nineteenth-century performance of mutual and incorporated life insurance companies compare; and who gained what from the different organisational forms? The answers can then be used to draw some more general conclusions about the contribution of incorporation to the British economy in the nineteenth century.

There were two types of life insurance in nineteenth-century Britain, as well as two types of provider. Ordinary life insurance – the original form – began by selling whole life policies on the basis of annual (sometimes quarterly) premiums. The premiums were fairly large – £10 per annum, for example – and thus ordinary life insurance can be viewed as having a mainly middle-class customer base. This market was initiated by the formation of the Amicable Assurance Society in 1706 and the incorporation of the Royal Exchange and London Assurance in 1720, but the principle of long-term (rather than annual) insurance contracts based on actuarially determined premiums derives from the foundation of the Equitable in 1762 as a mutual insurance society. By the end of the eighteenth century there were 6 life offices in London, and 15 more by 1820. A further 71 new life offices were formed between the end of the Napoleonic wars and the passing of the Companies Act in 1844.[8] The introduction of general incorporation produced something of an

---

[8] Clive Trebilcock, *Phoenix Assurance and the Development of British Insurance. Volume 1: 1782–1870* (Cambridge, 1985), 531, 570–1.

Table 6.1. *Date of formation and organisational form of 66
ordinary life insurance companies operating throughout
the period 1892–1902*

Period	Proprietary	Mutual
Pre-1800	3	1
1800–1819	6	3
1820–39	19	10
1840–59	7	4
1859–92	11	2
Earliest	Royal Exchange (1720)	Equitable (1762)
Latest	Legal and General (1892)	Colonial Mutual (1873)

Source: Statist, *All About Assurance* (London, 1904); C. Spensley,
Twelve Hundred Facts about 'Ordinary' Life Assurance Offices (Bradford,
1901).

insurance bubble. By 1852 there were, according to the secretary of the
Institute of Actuaries, around 180 life assurance organisations in the
UK, though in the opinion of Robert Christie, Manager of the Scottish
Equitable, many of these life offices were 'rotten; and are in effect,
though perhaps not in design, fraudulent'.[9] Although 180 life assurance
companies were formed in the two decades following the Companies
Act, 144 of these had ceased to exist by 1864. Mortality was generally
swift: 42 of these 144 ceased trading within a year of foundation, and
97 within five years (although the great majority disappeared through
amalgamation – only three failed to transfer policyholders' interests
before the implementation of a Chancery winding-up order).[10]

The majority of the new life offices were joint-stock companies,
but some mutuals continued to be formed, and they had a greater life
expectancy.[11] By 1902 there existed 66 ordinary life offices which had
been in continuous operation for at least ten years, 20 of which were
mutuals. Table 6.1 shows the time profile of formation; annual premium income for these life offices in 1902 was almost £23m, representing a total sum insured of £955m.

[9] Robert Christie, *Letter to the Right Hon. Joseph W. Henley, M.P., Regarding Life
Assurance Institutions* (Edinburgh, 1852), 5.
[10] A Member of the Institute of Actuaries, *The Government Annuities Bill: A Letter to the
Rt. Hon. W.E. Gladstone* (London, 1864).
[11] This greater longevity of mutuals should not be interpreted as an indicator of greater
efficiency or competitiveness; it may simply have resulted from the absence of a market for corporate control of mutual insurers.

Table 6.2. *Date of formation and organisational form of 24 largest industrial life insurance offices operating throughout the period 1892–1902*

Period	Proprietary	Friendly Society
Pre-1850	1	4
1850–59	0	2
1860–69	7	5
1870–89	2	1
1890–99	2	0
Earliest	Prudential (1848)	Blackburn Philanthropic (1839)
Latest	Pioneer (1891)	General Friendly Society (1884)

Source: *Post Magazine Almanack*, 1908; Spensley, *Twelve Hundred Facts*; *Insurance Mail Yearbook*, 1908; Statist, *All About Assurance*.

The second type of life insurance was called 'industrial life insurance'. This evolved out of local self-help burial clubs, but was developed from the 1840s in an organised way. It was based on small premiums, paid weekly – often collected from households by itinerant collectors – and with benefits designed to contribute to funeral costs; thus it was principally a working-class business. It was much more expensive to operate than ordinary life assurance because of the costs of collection. Over the period 1884–1904 the ratio of expenses to premium income for ordinary life offices was 14 per cent, compared to 43 per cent for industrial life companies.[12] The majority of industrial assurance providers were friendly societies – i.e. mutuals. The first was the Preston Shelley Society (1831), followed by Blackburn Philanthropic (1839) and Liverpool Victoria (1843). The Prudential (1848) was in the vanguard of proprietary companies that chose to enter this working-class insurance market. Many small friendly societies operated burial insurance on a local level, within ten miles of their registered office, but by 1907 there were just 37 mutual friendly societies operating a business across a wider area, together with 18 incorporated industrial assurance companies.[13] The dates of formation, and organisational form, of the 24 industrial assurance offices transacting business in 1906 with an annual premium income of over £5,000 are given in Table 6.2.

It is clear that incorporated and mutual forms of life insurance offices co-existed throughout the nineteenth century in both the ordinary and

[12] Statist, *All About Assurance*, 71–2.
[13] *Insurance Mail Yearbook* (London, 1908), 33, 108.

industrial parts of the market. It is also apparent that no single institutional form dominated the start-up of new providers. This is perplexing, at least from the perspective of economic theory, since diversity of economic form rests uneasily with the standardising effects of competitive market pressures. In the agency theory view of the firm, agents – such as managers and workers – are forever trying to shirk on the bargain they have struck with the principals – the owners – of the firm.[14] Shirking or opportunism can be reduced by careful monitoring, and monitoring is best achieved in joint-stock firms via shareholder power. Shareholder blocks can pool their voting rights to pressure or evict management, and if shareholders do not do this, the take-over market will ultimately ensure that managerial opportunism is driven out. However, the democratic nature of the mutual – one member, one vote – makes it difficult to organise members in order to put pressure on managers to perform in the members' interests, and the long-term nature of an insurance contract ties members to the organisation – so voice and exit are both high-cost strategies for monitoring or pressurising management. In consequence we should, in the words of Alchian and Demsetz, 'find greater shirking in non-profit, mutually owned enterprises'.[15]

Managerial shirking in mutual insurers must ultimately be to the disadvantage of policyholders; so how is it that joint stock companies did not rapidly out-compete mutuals? Henry Hansmann has proposed an answer based on the uncertainty involved in long-term contracting.[16] Life insurance contracts are long-term, and typically are based on heavily front-loaded policy payments which lock-in the customers. This creates substantial scope for insurers to behave opportunistically, for instance by distributing profit at the expense of accumulating adequate reserves. The mutual organisational form overcomes this problem by making the customers the owners of the firm. Since the policyholders and owners are the same people, they cannot suffer from inappropriate profit distribution – they win either way. Hansmann believes it was the superiority of mutuals in writing credible long-term contracts that accounted for their domination of the US insurance market in the first half of the nineteenth century. He sees the development of protective legislation for policyholders as the key to the rise of joint-stock insurance companies, particularly since the Second World War.

---

[14] Alchian and Demsetz, 'Production', 777–95; Michael Jensen and William Meckling, 'Theory of the firm: managerial behavior, agency costs and capital structure', *Journal of Financial Economics*, 3 (1976), 305–60.

[15] Alchian and Demsetz, 'Production', 790.

[16] Hansmann, *Ownership of Enterprise*, ch. 14.

Hansmann's account raises two important points. First, the ability of mutuals to make credible commitments to long-term contracts is a non-price advantage, which should not conceal the presumed operational benefits of the closer monitoring of joint-stock managers. Second, the regulatory regime can have a profound effect on the relative advantages of mutual and joint-stock insurers, as can the tax regime. However, in the context of life insurance in nineteenth-century Britain, Hansmann's interpretation is not wholly relevant. Whereas in the US mutuals completely dominated the insurance market before 1850, in Britain, as we have seen, the two forms not only co-existed but continued to be created throughout the nineteenth century. Furthermore, there was little regulatory distinction between the rights of policyholders in mutual or joint-stock firms in the Victorian period – indeed there was precious little regulation at all. Although the legal basis of friendly society and insurance company registration was different, the practical impact was negligible.[17] As one commentator on life assurance complained in 1887, Britain lacked the degree of public scrutiny of life insurers that was the responsibility of each state insurance department in the US.[18] In Britain the by-word was *caveat emptor*, but even the most careful and diligent of purchasers could be misled by the published accounts. As *The Economist* remarked in 1886, 'it is a sad, but notorious fact, that there has not been a single one of the Life Assurance Offices that have failed in recent years that have not on the very eve of their bankruptcy found Fellows of the Institute of Actuaries prepared to certify their solvency'.[19]

Incorporated insurers responded to the challenge of making credible long-term commitments to policyholders by introducing, from mid century, 'with-profits' or 'bonus' policies. These allowed ordinary life insurance policyholders to receive a specified share of any surplus assets identified at the quinquennial valuation. The board of management of the Standard Life company believed that this distribution of profit to policyholders allowed the company 'to be nearly as possible a Mutual Association without all the drawbacks to which Mutual Assurance is liable'.[20] The size of the quinquennial bonus became a key factor in the competition both between and within the incorporated and mutual groups of ordinary life assurance providers. Some of the older

---

[17] *Insurance Mail Yearbook*, 118–21.
[18] T. L. Terloc, *Life Assurance: As It Is, and As It Should Be* (Birmingham, 1887), 17.
[19] *The Economist*, December 1886, quoted in Terloc, *Life Assurance*, 17.
[20] J. H. Treble, 'The Record of the Standard Life Assurance Company in the life assurance market of the United Kingdom, 1850–64' in O.M. Westall (ed.), *The Historian and the Business of Insurance* (Manchester, 1984), 101.

companies, such as the Royal Exchange, which were slow to adopt the 'with-profits' form, experienced a pronounced fall in market share.[21]

These characteristics of the British life insurance market suggest that there may have been no clear advantage of one type of organisational form over another, and might indicate that the broader economic benefits of incorporation were, at best, muted in this particular sector of the economy. But casual comparison of mutual and incorporated insurers is not an adequate way of determining the relative efficiency of alternative organisational forms. To do this, it is necessary to interrogate detailed data and conduct formal tests of performance. Three separate tests of the relative performance of incorporated and mutual insurers have been undertaken (the formal specification and results of these tests are reported in an appendix to this chapter).

The first test examines the expenses of running incorporated and mutual insurance businesses. Once factors such as size and vintage of each insurer are taken into account, it might be expected that incorporated insurers operated with lower expenses than mutuals, because the owners (shareholders) had a clear incentive to pressurise management to control costs in order to maximise dividend payments. An analysis of detailed revenue and expenses data from the end of the nineteenth century (1892–1901) for 66 ordinary life offices and 22 industrial life offices shows the opposite. Expenses were higher (and, by implication, efficiency was lower) for incorporated insurers. This effect is very weak, and is possibly a statistical artefact, for ordinary life insurers, but is stronger and significant for the industrial insurance business.

However, a higher level of expenses in incorporated insurance offices does not necessarily mean they offered a worse deal to policyholders than did mutuals. To examine this proposition it is necessary directly to compare the financial returns to policyholders from identical insurance policies. In the industrial insurance market there was no identifiable difference – the premiums were a standard penny per week, and the policy values were practically identical across all insurers. The same is true for without-profits ordinary life assurance for the same reason: in 1898 the editor of the *Insurers Review* noted that competition in the without-profits market had so levelled down the premiums that the differences between providers were negligible.[22] But in the with-profits market, there was considerable variation within and between the mutual and incorporated groups of insurers. The data show unambiguously that the pay-out value of with-profit life insurance policies sold by mutuals was

---

[21] Supple, *Royal Exchange Assurance*, 130–45, 169–84.
[22] A. J. Wilson, *Plain Advice About Life Insurance* (London, 1898), 31.

8 per cent higher than equivalent policies sold by incorporated insurers. A third test corroborates this apparent advantage of mutual over incorporated insurers. Data drawn from the quinquennial valuations of 19 mutual and 45 incorporated insurers in 1897 shows that the achieved rate of return on investments for the mutuals averaged 4 per cent per annum, compared with 3.85 per cent for the incorporated providers.

Together these three tests provide no support at all for the argument that mutual insurers will be less efficient – in the sense of having higher operating costs, lower policy values, or less assiduous management – than incorporated insurers. In industrial assurance, mutuals exhibited lower operating expenses, and in ordinary assurance, mutuals distributed more profit to policyholders, in part because they achieved a higher rate of return on their investment portfolio. In this unique market segment in which the relative performance of incorporated and unincorporated businesses can be compared, it appears that joint-stock incorporation was associated with higher costs and lower efficiency. However, in no case do the characteristics of the different insurers account for more than a minority of the inter-firm variance in either expenses or policy values – there appears to be a vast amount of 'noise' in this market, which suggests that these quantitative tests, though indicative, may fail to identify the true scale and nature of performance differences between mutual and incorporated insurers. In particular, quantitative tests cannot identify the causes of any performance differences which, according to agency theory, will have their roots in the different incentive, monitoring and control mechanisms faced by management working under different ownership structures. To identify what managers really did, it is necessary to move beyond the published accounts of the insurance firms, and to look at the details of managerial behaviour.

Managerial behaviour is seldom directly observable. Few managers have the time, even if they have the inclination, to produce written accounts of the motivation that underpins their decisions and actions. Furthermore, many actions are the result of verbal instructions, and so no documentary trail of causation can ever be established. These issues are compounded in any historical inquiry by the usually fragmentary nature of business history records. But there is one nineteenth-century life assurance office for which abundant evidence of managerial behaviour exists: the Royal Liver Assurance Company, which was second only to the Prudential in the scale and extent of its industrial assurance business.[23]

[23] Among industrial insurers in 1888 the capital reserves of the Royal Liver, at £1.008 million, were second only to the giant Prudential, which had reserves of £6.272

A case of Liver disease

The Royal Liver Assurance Company was founded in Liverpool in 1850 by a sea-captain called Lawrence, who headed a secession from an earlier burial society, the Philanthropic.[24] In 1861 Lawrence was himself ousted from office in the Royal Liver and was replaced on the board of management by his opponents headed by Henry Liversage and James Atherton. Liversage and Atherton were the prime movers and shakers in the Royal Liver over the following twenty-five years, holding the posts of Joint Secretaries of the Society from 1875, and some of their family details allow their personal entrepreneurial success to be tracked. The 1861 census finds both men recorded as collectors, and the local street directory clearly recorded Atherton as a collector for the Royal Liver.[25] They lived three streets apart in terraced houses in the Everton district of Liverpool, and though not an affluent area of the city, both men had some middle-class pretensions. Atherton's nearest neighbours declared their occupations to be broker and book-keeper, while Liversage lived next to a book-keeper, a shopman and a water collector. These were occupations on the bottom rung of white-collar employment, and indicative of an income slightly above that of a skilled manual worker. The household structure recorded in the census also reveals the trappings of lower-middle-class respectability. Atherton, aged 26, lived in a crowded house with his 24-year-old wife, their three children, his brother, his wife's brother and sister, and a 16-year-old domestic servant. Liversage, aged 38, shared his house with his wife, three children and an 18-year-old servant.

By 1867 both families had moved to more salubrious parts of town, and Liversage was describing himself in the street directory as a gentleman, an epithet adopted by Atherton the following year. By the time of the 1871 census Atherton had moved to the southern suburban fringes of Birkenhead, and Liversage had also moved up-market, acquiring as neighbours an agent, a wool-broker and a gentleman. Ten years later, Atherton was employing two residential domestic servants

---

million. In terms of annual policy income the Royal Liver came third behind the Prudential and the Refuge Insurance companies. Details from Statist, *All About Insurance*. The *Statist* was a monthly journal published in London 1878–1967 as a rival journal to *The Economist*. The book *All About Insurance* is a compendium of articles originally published in the monthly editions of the *Statist*.

[24] This is probably the same society as the Liverpool-based Loyal Philanthropic which, in 1880, had a membership of 42,544.

[25] Details in this section are derived from manuscript census returns for Liverpool for 1861, 1871 and 1881, and from successive editions of *Gore's Directory for Liverpool*.

to care for himself, wife and six children, while Liversage, now a widower, also employed two servants to keep house for himself and his two daughters. Both men marked their ever-rising status by endowing their houses with fancy names – Atherton's changed from 66 Greenway Road to 'Tranmere Hall', while Liversage, reflecting a patriotic pride in Florence Nightingale's work during the Crimean War, changed 8 Somerset Place to 'Scutari Villa', where his near neighbours included two clergymen, a schoolmaster, a marine insurance broker, an ironfounder and two ladies of independent means.

In 1885 Liversage moved to the leafy glades of Sefton Park; by 1888 he had left Liverpool, and Atherton had moved to a large secluded house in parkland south of Birkenhead, where he died in 1907. The probate records show the value of his estate at death was £12,840, or something over 200 times the annual income of an unskilled manual worker. Liversage, who died in the seaside resort of Skegness in 1894 (although by then normally resident in Middlesex), left an estate valued at just over £6,000.[26] Through their personal effort and initiative Liversage and Atherton had been able to acquire assets over their working life capable of sustaining a very comfortable middle-class lifestyle. How did they manage to make such a success out of the Royal Liver? To answer that question it is necessary to look at the internal management of the organisation.

Because of its status as a mutual Friendly Society, the Royal Liver was subject to certain democratic pressures from policy-holding *members* that could not be brought to bear on industrial assurance companies by policy-holding *customers*. The 1875 Friendly Society Act empowered the Registrar to appoint inspectors to investigate the internal management of any society on receipt of an application signed by at least 500 members. In 1885 a 'syndicate' of disaffected Royal Liver members, led by Edward Taunton, a former chief clerk of the society who had been dismissed for reasons of 'lack of loyalty', gathered the appropriate number of signatures, and applied for an investigation on the grounds that the Committee of Management, headed by the two joint secretaries, had been guilty of: gross mismanagement and extravagance due to the self-payment of enormous salaries and travelling expenses; falsification of balance sheets; and packing and otherwise manipulating general meetings of the Society. The government inspector, E. Lyulph Stanley, held a public enquiry into these allegations in Liverpool over fourteen days from 12 January to 10 February 1886.[27] The enquiry revealed a

---

[26] Copies of the will and probate records of Liversage and Atherton are held at the Principal Probate Registry, London.
[27] Details are taken from *Report on the Royal Liver Friendly Society*, PP 1886 lxi.

mixed record of management performance, in which the secretaries were shown consistently to have taken decisions which enhanced their remuneration and consolidated their power base. To understand how they achieved this it is first necessary to review the manner in which the industrial assurance system operated.

Industrial assurance was marketed door to door by agents of the various companies and societies, who earned a commission on the small sums (usually 1 penny per week for each insured person) which they collected. The agency problem – of how to align the interest of the agents with that of the company/society – was solved by a combined carrot–and-stick approach, which was adopted in a more-or-less uniform manner by all industrial life offices in the mid-Victorian period. Agents retained about 25 per cent of the monies they collected on recurrent business, and a higher proportion on new business (typically all the premiums paid in the first thirteen weeks). The agent made up a 'collecting book' listing details of all current policyholders, and was responsible for collecting weekly subscriptions and remitting the appropriate share to head office, together with a weekly record of lapses and arrears. When a new member was enrolled, a proposal form had to be filled in by the agent and returned to head office, which would then issue the insured person with an insurance certificate. Any claim on the policy required presentation of a death certificate to the agent; this was then forwarded by the agent of the head office and matched with a duplicate of the policyholder's certificate; payment would then be made via the agent (though in practice agents often advanced payment to the families of deceased members before they received authorisation from head office).

Fraud by agents on the society/company was limited by the system of reporting and record keeping. Payment of claims to an agent required both an official notification of death signed by a coroner or qualified medical practitioner and a cross-check of personal details (name, date of birth, address, policy value) with the duplicate policy document. This system necessitated a vast central record-keeping operation in head office, and a similarly vast office building (the massive twin-towered bulk of the Royal Liver's headquarters on the Liverpool pier head is the dominant architectural icon of that city). Any agent who presented an unusually large number of death claims to head office could expect a visitation from a salaried 'travelling inspector' who would seek local corroboration of the claims.

Fraud by agents on the policyholder was easier, since the agent could pretend to propose a new member, but never return the form to head office, thus keeping the full premium payment. However, this behaviour was limited both by the difficulty of maintaining the pretence of insurance cover for any individual in the absence of an insurance certificate, and by creating property rights for agents in their 'collection book'. A large and well-performing collection book could provide an easy income for an agent. Recurrent commission on penny-a-week policies from 200 households of average size would generate an annual income of over £60. Additional income from new business could further enhance an agent's income. The Royal Liver, in common with other life offices, allowed agents to sell their 'books' for a lump-sum transfer fee, the value of which was determined both by the size of the book and its performance – the lower the lapse (i.e. depreciation) rate, the higher the value. An agent's property right in his book was not legally enforceable, since the policyholder's contract was with the insurance office, and the office could nominate anyone it wished to act as collector for any particular policy. However, these customary rights well suited the societies/companies, since they gave head office considerable power over the agents: recalcitrant or dishonest agents could forfeit both their source of income and the capital accumulated in their collecting book if they fell foul of the managing committee.

This organisational relationship between agents and head office, and the nature of society membership, created a classic problem of collective action. In the words of the official inspector, Stanley:

in a society like the Royal Liver, there are only two parties who have any real power, the Head Office and the collectors. The members are scattered throughout the country. They have no cohesion, no power of knowing each other, and too small an interest to take the trouble to master the facts and vote. A general meeting called in Liverpool, with perhaps 1,500 persons present, of whom 600 or 700 will be officials, and their families and friends, is an absurd mode of governing a society with 1,100,000 members, £360,000 a year of premium income, and more than £800,000 of invested capital.'[28]

Moreover, within the Royal Liver, head office power was monopolised by Liversage and Atherton. Stanley considered them 'the real and effective managers and masters' of the society, while the other six members of the management committee 'appear to be cyphers' who were paid large salaries to do very little. This management structure allowed the two secretaries consistently to feather their own nest.

The 1875 Friendly Societies Act required all management committee members of friendly collecting societies to renounce all interests in the collection books. Atherton and Liversage, who had maintained control of large collection books since the early 1860s, were forced to divest themselves of this lucrative asset. This they did by transferring their

[28] Report on the Royal Liver, 9.

interest to other family members (in the one case a daughter, in the other a brother-in-law), but they then asked the society for additional compensation. Their salaries had been set at £20 per week, but for the loss of their collection books the management committee proposed that the secretaries should each earn 2.5 per cent commission on all new life assurance business. A change of rules of this magnitude had to be agreed by a general meeting of the society, at which all members were eligible to attend and vote. But when the meeting was held in 1876 it was packed with collectors who had been instructed to attend, it was chaired by William Atherton, father of one of the Secretaries, and it carried the proposed change of rules overwhelmingly.

Atherton and Liversage subsequently hid the commission paid directly to them by requiring the auditor to include it under general management expenses in the annual reports of the society. By 1881 their commission income, at £2,277 each per annum, was more than twice their official annual salary. By the time of the public enquiry, they had each boosted their total annual remuneration package to a few pounds short of £6,000 – about 10 per cent of total operating costs. They achieved this by rapidly expanding the new business of the Society, and thus their commission earnings. They employed a large number of special canvassers and travelling agents whose sole responsibility it was to drum up new business; but this was an expensive tactic in what was already a fairly crowded market, and the result was that the overall expenses of management, which had been under 40 per cent of premium income in the early 1870s, rose to over 47 per cent by the end of the decade. In order to conceal this lavish expenditure, the secretaries claimed that the higher costs were directly attributable to new reporting and valuation criteria imposed by the government on all friendly societies.

Stanley found the accusation of extravagance of management sustained by the evidence. He also agreed that the secretaries had deliberately manipulated the records and accounts of the society, and that they had used their power over the collectors to pack meetings and intimidate opponents. However, it proved impossible to bring any formal charges against the secretaries. They were consistently uncooperative, and used some practices all too familiar in modern cases of corporate malfeasance. One accusation was that they misappropriated society funds in order to bribe certain newspapers to print complimentary reports of the society and its officers.[29] However, as soon as the public enquiry commenced,

---

[29] Almost certainly one such newspaper was the *Liverpool Review*, which, over the six months from October 1885, printed a series of extravagantly flattering accounts of the society and the achievements of its two secretaries.

Liversage reported that the society's newspaper files for the previous five years had 'mysteriously' disappeared.[30] Another charge was that the secretaries and/or solicitors to the society had received illegal commissions from the trustees of the Maryport and Whitehaven Dock in order to secure a £10,000 loan from the society. The society's solicitors were Mssrs Hannan and Pugh (Pugh was Atherton's son-in-law, and Atherton's son was also a junior legal partner in the firm), but on the final day of the enquiry Hannan absconded to America, taking with him incriminating evidence contained in the Society's letter-book. The society's senior counsel then made a statement advising the secretaries, on a narrow point of law, to ignore Stanley's summons to attend the enquiry, and Atherton, Liversage and the Royal Liver clerks promptly withdrew. Stanley reluctantly terminated his enquiry, concluding that the withdrawal of the secretaries was 'the result of a knowledge that the conduct of the officers was incapable of further defence, and of a fear that the longer the inquiry lasted, the more extensive would be the revelations'.[31]

Stanley's enquiry into the internal management of the Royal Liver makes clear that a considerable part of the personal financial gain enjoyed by Atherton and Liversage was derived from action that was self-seeking, and possibly illegal. A guiding principle of their management strategy had been to increase their personal remuneration, and that of other members of their families. What appeared to be, from the evidence of their personal and family histories, an example of solid Victorian enterprise in the financial services sector, can now be seen as a clear case of venality: managerial opportunism writ large. But the Secretaries and their supporters responded by claiming that this sort of behaviour was commonplace, and that if there was a tendency towards illegality it was, nevertheless, a victimless crime.

A rationale and defence of Atherton and Liversage was printed in the always-supportive *Liverpool Review* a week after the publication of Stanley's report; it is worth quoting at length:

Mr Stanley seems to think it is a revelation – as most of his newspaper friends do – that the Secretaries and Committee of the Royal Liver Friendly Society have considered their own interests rather than the welfare of the members. Unfortunately, human nature being what it is, we did not need an official enquiry to tell us this ... Now, unless the inspector has failed in his duties, and has glossed over grave irregularities, the late Secretaries are not much to be blamed after all. They did well for themselves – a little too well no doubt. But they also did fairly well for the members who paid them. As far as the facts are

[30] *Liverpool Mercury*, 16 January 1886.   [31] *Report on the Royal Liver*, 21.

Table 6.3. *Membership, assets, and expenditure of largest friendly collecting societies in 1880*

	[1]	[2]	[3]	[4]	[5]	[6]
	Members	Assets (£)	[2]/[1]	Total expenditure (£)	Management expenditure (£)	[5]/[4] (%)
Royal Liver	932,912	668,953	0.71	280,596	137,691	49
Liverpool Victoria	568,102	282,123	0.50	160,125	91,820	57
Royal London	211,579	59,762	0.28	70,760	40,963	58
United Assurance	181,093	11,345	0.06	53,365	23,923	45

Source: *Report of the Chief Registrar of Friendly Societies for 1880*. Part IIB, app. I.

at present known – and we have no reason to believe there is anything in the background – the Royal Liver Friendly Society, under the condemned management, was the best, or one of the best, of its kind in the kingdom. Though its secretaries have of late years absorbed enormous salaries, it has insured members at as low a rate as any of its rivals ... Therefore the much-abused Secretaries have given the members who appointed and paid them as good value as they could have obtained elsewhere – and as good value as they are likely to receive in the future.[32]

Data relating to other mutual industrial assurance societies indicates that this claim was broadly true. Table 6.3 compares the cost of management and asset base in the Royal Liver with that of its three largest competitor friendly collecting societies. The Royal Liver had the highest asset per member, and had an expenditure ratio considerably below that of the Liverpool Victoria and the Royal London. The year 1880 probably represents the worst period for management expenses within the Royal Liver; by 1887 its expenses ratio was 40 per cent, slightly better than the 41.5 per cent achieved by the market leader, the Prudential Assurance Company.[33]

It is clear that the high expenses ratio in the Royal Liver was driven by the desire of the two secretaries to extract rents from the organisation, and this is *prima facie* evidence of managerial shirking and inefficiency.

[32] *Liverpool Review*, 13 March 1886, 9.
[33] *Select Committee on the Friendly Societies Act*, appendix 1. PP. 1889 x, 295.

Yet similar managerial costs were being charged by the other major players in the industrial assurance market. This was true not just of other mutuals, but also of incorporated insurers, including the most dynamic and innovative of the joint-stock industrial life insurers, the Prudential.

Established in 1848 as an unlimited company, by 1867 the Prudential had a paid-up capital of £5,839, which had risen by 1881 to £24,920 (by virtue of scrip issues), with shares held by fewer than 100 individuals. By 1893, and now a limited liability company, the Prudential still had only 170 shareholders, and of the 24 shareholders owning 1,000 shares or more, all but two were directors or members of their families. Profits apportioned to shareholders over the period 1867–1894 amounted to more than £2.1 million.[34] As with the Royal Liver, the Prudential was characterised by very large payments to senior managers and their relatives. Henry Harben, who joined the Prudential as a clerk in 1851, ascended through the ranks to become secretary and director (1874), deputy chairman (1878), chairman (1905) and president (1907), and was rewarded and incentivised by means of large share allocations as well as a substantial salary. Together with his son (who also became a director in 1879) and daughter, Harben owned 13,000 shares in the Prudential by 1893, something over 5 per cent of total issued stock.[35] The defence offered by the *Liverpool Review* for the behaviour of Atherton and Liversage – 'they did well for themselves ... but they also did fairly well for the members who paid them' – could equally apply to Harben. The key difference was that personal aggrandisement by senior managers and directors could be achieved in a legally and socially more acceptable manner in joint-stock companies than in mutuals. Rather than Harben have his managerial activities and remuneration investigated by a government inspector, he instead received a knighthood in 1897 for his services to the insurance industry. His estate at death in 1911 was valued at almost £400,000.[36]

Agency theory can give a good account of how managerial opportunism can become embedded in a mutual firm, but the quantitative evidence presented above indicates that joint-stock providers were certainly no more efficient, and were most likely less efficient, than mutuals. In the Royal Liver there is detailed and unambiguous evidence of managerial opportunism, but the overall performance of this insurer, in terms of expenses charged and benefits paid, was well above the sector

[34] Laurie Dennett, *A Sense of Security: 150 years of Prudential* (Cambridge, 1998), 122.
[35] *Ibid.*, 121.
[36] *Oxford Dictionary of National Biography* (Oxford, 2004).

average. This might indicate that Liversage and Atherton produced super-efficiencies within the Royal Liver which then allowed them to extract surplus without raising costs to customers. On the other hand, it may indicate that the senior management of many or most of the other players in this market were extracting a similar or greater level of rent. No comprehensive data exists which would allow this proposition to be tested, but in the case of the market leader, the Prudential, it seems that the most senior figure, Harben, who was both manager and director, received a substantially larger total remuneration package than did Liversage and Atherton. There is no doubt that this was legitimate reward, in the sense that it was fully sanctioned by the board of directors. However, there was no opportunity for 500 disgruntled policyholders to petition for an inquiry into Harben's remuneration, because in a joint-stock insurer the policyholders are simply paying customers with no stake in ownership or governance. It was only the shareholders who could take action, but shareholder power in the nineteenth century was very weak, and the corporate take-over market virtually non-existent, so the countervailing power that is assumed by agency theory did not exist: joint-stock directors had as much or more scope for opportunism as did the managers of mutuals.

The picture presented in this chapter is one of enduring and successful rent-seeking by managers and directors in the life insurance industry. This occurred even though Victorian life insurance firms operated in a highly competitive market characterised by the co-existence of many providers, which raises the question of why managerial and directorial opportunism was not rapidly competed out of existence? The likely answer is that despite the competition, despite the advertising and publicity, it was enormously difficult for customers to obtain clear information about the relative merits of different products and providers (much the same can be said of the financial services industry in the early twenty-first century). Life insurance products are complex, and the financial performance of life offices was, and still is, difficult to evaluate. In consequence consumers faced a smokescreen of claim and counter-claim. Joseph Allen, author of a guide to the selection of life insurance policies, wrote the following assessment in 1888:

Some Offices draw particular attention to the fact that they are 'Mutual' Offices, and proceed to show the advantages which a person will gain by insuring with them in preference to the 'Proprietary' Offices. On the other hand, the Proprietary Offices draw special attention to the fact that they are *not* Mutual Offices, and proceed to point out the advantages which a person will gain by insuring with them rather than with Mutual Offices; others boast of the advantage they possess by being *old*, others say they are better for being *young*. Some bid us notice that they have never amalgamated their business with that of any other Office; whilst others say they have effected amalgamations to the advantage of all concerned. Some make prominent allusion to the number of new Policies issued year by year, others to their large figures of Insurances in force, Funds invested, Shareholders' Capital, Claims paid, etc. etc. Whilst some are congratulating themselves upon the liberal rate of Interest realised upon their Investments, we find others rejoicing that their funds are mainly invested in 3 per cent. Government Securities. Some wish us to observe at what a small percentage of Outlay they are working their business, whilst others allege that they are pursuing a wise policy in spending liberally for the purpose of extending their sphere of operations. Some wish us particularly to observe that they do not accept second class, or unhealthy lives, whilst others are equally anxious that we should know they *do* accept such lives. Some point to their low Rates of Premiums for insurance, others to the large Amounts accruing to the Insured in the shape of Bonuses.[37]

The message sent to prospective customers in the marketplace was massively confused; furthermore, the messengers – the insurance agents, canvassers and salesmen – had no incentive at all to simplify it. As early as 1811 a review of life insurance company activity explicitly identified 'the disgraceful practice of bribing solicitors, agents and others' to push the policies of a particular company, a lament echoed by Babbage in almost the same language in 1826.[38]

This case study of the Victorian life insurance market cannot provide a direct test of the relative efficiency and productivity of joint-stock and partnership forms of organisation, which is what is needed to determine whether the rise of incorporation in the last third of the nineteenth century was driven by fundamental economic advantage (as is widely – if often implicitly – assumed in institutional economics). Representative matched comparisons of partnership and joint-stock business performance in nineteenth-century Britain are impossible to construct. However, a matched comparison of joint-stock and mutual life insurers is possible, and it reveals no evidence of greater efficiency or productivity among joint-stock providers; in general the performance of the mutuals seems to be better. Yet internal evidence from two market leaders, the Royal Liver and the Prudential, demonstrates or implies the presence of substantial rent-seeking behaviour on the part of the principal managers. This suggests two conclusions: first, selection of organisational form was not driven by efficiency considerations; second, the pressure of

---

[37] Joseph Allen, *Where Shall I Get the Most for My Money?* (London, 1880), 5–6.
[38] F. Baily, *An Account of the Several Life Assurance Companies Established in London* (London, 1811), 29; Babbage, *Comparative View*, 133–4.

market competition was insufficient to drive out inefficiency or impose organisational change.

The public corporation is widely viewed as the most important, and the most dynamic, institution of modern capitalism. It can agglomerate capital, harness human effort and enterprise on a vast scale, spread risk, and distribute benefit. But the public corporation is not, in any sense, a natural economic institution. It depends for its existence on a legal construct – the 'corporate personality' – and a large set of enabling rules and privileges. Prior to the mid-nineteenth century these privileges were jealously guarded by the State, but by 1900 incorporation had become a readily accessible organisational form available to any individual or group of individuals for more or less any purpose. The economic significance of the shareholder-owned, professionally managed corporation in the twentieth century has led many scholars – not just economists – to presume that there is a direct facilitative relationship between incorporation and economic success. The economic hegemon of the nineteenth-century – Britain – and the twentieth-century hegemon – the USA – were pioneers in the development of a legal regime which promoted and protected the interests of corporations.

Furthermore, it is common for economists to view the rise of the corporation, with its distinctive governance structure, as a natural economic outcome arising from specialisation and economies of scale: corporations could operate on a larger scale than partnerships or sole proprietorships, shareholders could specialise in risk bearing but, because of the divisibility and tradability of the share, could diversify these risks, and firms could hire (and fire) specialised professional managers. These interpretations of corporate advantage can be traced from Smith and Mill; they form the core tenets of the modern institutional economics of the firm, and underpin much recent analysis of the economics of corporate governance.

Yet the chapters in this section have shown that there was no inevitability about the emergence of general incorporation in nineteenth-century Britain. It was certainly not the case that the law responded in a functional manner to pressing practical needs of a rapidly growing economy. There was no coherent and unified economic interest pressing for general incorporation in 1844 or general limited liability in 1856. Nor was there a pronounced political interest either for or against this legislation; the timing and content was, to some considerable degree, accidental. Furthermore, the important role of judicial interpretation in the British common law system meant that the practical significance of this corporate legislation fully emerged only after four decades of case law, during which the moral precepts of judges, the political power of interest groups, and the intellectual arguments of economists, lawyers, politicians and essayists all played a formative role.

This section has also shown that the presumed economic advantages of incorporation were by no means self-evident in nineteenth-century Britain. Fully one-third of Britain's largest hundred companies in 1907 eschewed some of the major economic benefits of incorporation – injection of capital from external shareholders, open tradability of shares – by operating as private companies. Furthermore, in the one economic sector – life insurance – in which direct comparison can be made between incorporated and unincorporated firms, there is no evidence that incorporation was associated with higher levels of internal efficiency or lower product prices. However, once incorporation became generally available to businessmen, and once the advantages became clear to proprietors, they seized the opportunity to convert from partnership status, because this allowed them to retain personal control over their firm while distancing themselves from some of the legal and moral responsibilities of ownership. There is no evidence of dishonest intent on the part of most partnerships which converted to incorporation; the issue was one of prudence. The legislature and the courts, through a long and haphazard process, had created an opportunity for businessmen to protect their assets and their reputations at almost no cost to themselves. It was this personal benefit, rather than an increase in social welfare through improved economic efficiency, that accounted for the rise of the incorporation in Victorian Britain.

Appendix to Chapter 6

There are two primary hypotheses in the modern insurance literature about the performance of joint-stock and mutual firms. The *efficient structure hypothesis* holds that these two types of firm are sorted into those market segments in which they hold a comparative advantage in terms of agency and production costs; thus they should operate with approximately equal levels of efficiency when the product mix is controlled for. The *expense preference hypothesis* holds that mutuals fail to minimise costs or maximise revenues due to unresolved agency conflicts.[39] As noted above, there does not appear to have been any sorting of mutuals and proprietary companies by product type in the Victorian

---

[39] J. D. Cummins, M. Rubio-Misas, and H. Zi, 'The effect of organizational structure on efficiency: evidence from the Spanish insurance industry', *Journal of Banking and Finance*, 28 (2004), 3115.

insurance market, so the idea that different internal cost and agency structures helped to shape the industry seems untenable. The expense preference hypothesis, on the other hand, can be tested only by looking in some detail at the internal performance of different firms. In the modern life insurance literature a standard approach to assess the impact of ownership form on life office performance is to relate the expenses ratio to characteristics of the firm. This is a direct test of agency theory: if mutual ownership permits more managerial opportunism, then the expenses ratios should be higher in mutual than in proprietary insurers. Analysis of modern American life insurance companies has revealed little systematic difference between mutual and joint-stock insurers in expenses or in other indicators of performance, although the strict nature of the modern regulatory regime makes the proposition difficult to test.[40] The absence of complex life insurance and tax regulation in late-Victorian Britain allows for a much more straightforward test of the expense preference hypothesis.

Data have been collected for the period 1892–1902, and the expenses ratio in 1902 has been regressed on the following firm characteristics:

LY: natural logarithm of premium income
1/AGE: reciprocal of the number of years the firm has been in existence
GROW: growth rate of premium income over previous decade
RESERVE: ratio of investment income to premium income
FORM: dummy variable, 1 if proprietary, 0 if mutual

Premium income is intended to capture scale effects, since there are well-known economies of scale in head office operations within insurance companies. However, scale economies are not linear with respect to size, hence the natural logarithm is used here; the expected coefficient is negative, since larger businesses should be able to operate with lower expenses ratios. Expenses may also be a function of the age of the firm. Relatively new firms may have to spend heavily on sales promotion and advertising to gain a foothold in the market, so older firms may exhibit a lower expenses ratio. Again the relationship is expected to be non-linear, with vintage mattering much more for younger than for older firms, so here age is entered as a reciprocal, with the expected sign being positive. Expenses are likely to be high if a firm has adopted

[40] Mary Anne Boose, 'Agency theory and alternative predictions for life insurers: an empirical test', *Journal of Risk and Insurance*, 57 (1990), 499–518; Steven Pottier and David W. Sommer, 'Agency theory and life insurer ownership structure', *Journal of Risk and Insurance*, 64 (1997), 529–43; J. D. Cummins, M. A. Weiss and H. Zi, 'Organizational form and efficiency: an analysis of stock and mutual property-liability insurers', *Management Science*, 45 (1999), 1254–69.

Table A6.1. *Regression of 1902 expenses ratio*
on firm characteristics

[1] Ordinary Life Assurance (n=66)

LY	1/AGE	GROW	RESERVE	FORM	R-bar-2	F
−1.371	42.1	−1.54	−11.9	1.07	.25	5.32
(2.67)	(1.13)	(1.96)	(2.77)	(1.02)		

[2] Industrial Life Assurance (n=21)

LY	1/AGE	GROW	RESERVE	FORM	R-bar-2	F
−8.32	−.908	−3.42	−285.8	22.3	.39	3.62
(2.87)	(1.66)	(0.30)	(2.42)	(1.92)		

(t-statistics in parentheses)

a strategy of growth, so the growth rate of premium income over the past decade is expected to be positively associated with the expenses ratio. Large reserves generate a high ratio of asset income to premium income, and represent a history of careful financial management. The relationship between reserves and expenses is therefore expected to be negative. Finally, the organisational form of the firm may affect the expenses ratio. If there is managerial opportunism in mutuals, then the coefficient on form will be negative; but if the drive for profits in proprietary firms drives up expenses, the coefficient will be positive.

Table A6.1 shows that scale effects matter for both ordinary and industrial insurers – the larger the premium income, the lower the expenses ratio. Vintage effects were not significant for either type of insurer. Growth was insignificant for industrial insurers, but for ordinary insurers was marginally significant and negative, thus indicating that, contrary to expectations, rapid growth of premium income in the previous decade had not been bought at the cost of an increase in the expenses ratio. Reserves have the expected negative sign, showing that past capital accumulation was linked to a low current expenses ratio. The key variable, of course, is FORM, which is positive for both types of insurer. This indicates that mutuals were more effective at minimising the expenses ratio than were for-profit insurers, and so runs counter to the agency theory view that mutuals will exhibit lower levels of operational efficiency because of the opportunity for managerial feather-bedding. However, it should be noted that this effect is not statistically significant for ordinary life insurance, is only marginally significant ($p = .074$) for industrial assurance, and that the explanatory power of the equations is low. It can be concluded that there is some – albeit weak – evidence in these results for an efficiency advantage of the mutual over the joint-stock form of organisation of life insurance provision.

The expenses ratio may not capture the way in which the competitive advantage of different organisational forms is revealed to customers. Expenses may be driven up by managerial opportunism, but they may also be raised by employing staff with higher skill levels, who provide policyholders with a better service (non-price competition might, for instance, revolve around issues such as the ease of making a claim, and the promptness of payment). This type of non-price competition is difficult to evaluate, but it is possible to measure direct product competition by comparing the returns on different types of insurance policy. Is it the case that mutuals offered less to their policyholders per £ of premium payment than did proprietary companies?

This proposition can be tested for ordinary life assurance companies, since they sold a broad array of different types of product, including both non-profit and with-profit policies. (The typical penny-a-week industrial assurance policy made limited use of actuarial scales and did not include a share of profits, so there is practically no variance in the cost and returns offered to policyholders.) The returns to two types of policy have been examined, drawing on data assembled in 1904:

i. a whole-life without profits policy with an annual premium of £10, taken out by a male aged 30;
ii. a whole-life with profits policy with an annual premium of £10, taken out by a male aged 30, assuming death at age 65, and based on the past bonus performance of each insurance office.[41]

The expected returns to these two policy types have been regressed on a range of provider characteristics:

1/AGE: reciprocal of the number of years the firm has been in existence
X1902: the expenses ratio in 1902
LON: dummy variable, 1 if in London, 0 if elsewhere
FORM: dummy variable, 1 if proprietary, 0 if mutual

If the market is competitive, new entrants will need to offer purchasers some sort of bonus to compensate them for the additional perceived risk for the lack of company pedigree. It might be expected, therefore, that newer companies will offer higher returns to premiums than will established companies, so the expected sign on the vintage variable is

---

[41] Statist, *All About Assurance*, 48–9; 52–3.

Table A6.2. *Regression of policy returns
on firm characteristics*

[3] Whole-life non profit (n=52)

1/AGE	X1902	LON	FORM	R-bar-2	F
−287	.165	1.91	−1.09	.03	0.65
(1.54)	(0.28)	(0.36)	(0.19)		

[4] Whole-life with profit (n=57)

1/AGE	X1902	LON	FORM	R-bar-2	F
1178	−6.55	41.1	−50.0	.34	8.29
(2.29)	(3.45)	(2.79)	(3.02)		

(t-statistics in parentheses)

positive. Companies with high expenses are unlikely to be able to offer high returns, so the expected sign on the expenses ratio is negative. A dummy variable has been introduced for companies based in London, to take account of the fact that the greater concentration of life insurance offices may create competitive pressures which force companies to offer better deals to their policyholders.

Equation 3 in Table A6.2 shows no relationship at all between the returns to non-profit policies and the characteristics of providers. This is not surprising; in 1898 the editor of the *Investors' Review* noted that competition in the without-profits market had so levelled-down the premiums that differences between companies were negligible.[42] Equation 4, however, shows a clear link between with-profits policy values and type of provider. All coefficients are statistically significant, and the first three confirm that new entrants offered higher returns than established insurers, that companies with high expenses ratios shared less profit with policyholders, and that the metropolitan insurance market was more competitive than the provincial. But crucially, the coefficient on FORM is negative, indicating that proprietary companies offered with-profit policies with a significantly lower return than those offered by mutuals. The mean value of the pay-out on these polices was £624, so on average proprietary companies offered returns 8 per cent (£50) lower than mutuals. Equation 4 suggests that the payment of dividends to shareholders was not fully compensated for by any greater internal efficiency that proprietary companies achieved over

---

[42] Wilson, *Plain Advice About Life Insurance*, 31.

mutuals – hence mutuals could offer with-profits policyholders a better deal than proprietary companies. This inference is supported by direct evidence of the investment performance of insurance companies. Data drawn from the quinquennial valuations of nineteen mutual and forty-five proprietary insurers in 1897 reveals that the achieved rate of return on investments for the mutuals averaged 4.00 per cent per annum, compared with 3.85 per cent for the proprietary companies.[43]

[43] Data from G. M Dent, *How to Select a Life Office* (3rd edn, London, n.d. [1897]), Table 1. The 0.15% p.a. difference in rate of return is statistically significant at the 5% level.

Part III

Information

> Capital consists in a great part of knowledge and organization: and of this some part is private property and other part is not. Knowledge is our most powerful engine of production; it enables us to subdue Nature and force her to satisfy our wants. Organization aids knowledge; it has many forms, *e.g.* that of a single business, that of various businesses in the same trade, that of various trades relatively to one another, and that of the State providing security for all and help for many. The distinction between public and private property in knowledge and organization is of great and growing importance: in some respects of more importance than that between public and private property in material things; and partly for that reason it seems best sometimes to reckon Organization apart as a distinct agent of production.
>
> Alfred Marshall, *Principles of Economics* (1890)[1]

Alfred Marshall's insight about the economic significance of knowledge and information reflected the huge transformation in the knowledge economy that occurred in the second half of the nineteenth century. The telegraph and the telephone unified hitherto distant and discrete markets, thereby creating the informational consistency required for Smithian competition. Daily financial newspapers which carried the latest price information, and ticker-tape machines in stockbroker's offices throughout the country, democratised information that once had been the preserve of a small clique of dealers in Exchange Alley and Capel Court in the City of London.

Common access to the same market information is a necessary condition for the achievement of efficient allocation and a unique market-clearing price, but informational symmetry was easier for Marshall and other late-nineteenth-century neo-classical economists to describe than for the late-nineteenth-century economy to achieve in practice. Even in that most transparent of markets, the Stock Exchange, where purchase and sale prices for shares were publicly quoted and daily listed in the financial press, there existed multiple layers of information and knowledge about the current conditions and future prospects of each publicly listed company, only some of which were accessible to the public at

---

[1] Marshall, *Principles*, Book IV, ch. 1.

large. The chapters in this section consider the way in which 'companification' placed new requirements for public information on the hitherto private world of businesses and their directors. Private listed companies could, and usually did, confine almost all financial and commercial information to their handful of shareholders and directors. However, for the minority of limited companies that had made a public call for capital through the offer of shares, there existed among the shareholder-owners a clear and legitimate expectation that they would be supplied with relevant and accurate information about commercial performance and prospects. Between 1856 and 1900 this expectation received no endorsement from legislation, and the shareholding public received only that information which directors deigned to supply; in Marshall's terms, the balance was very definitely in favour of private rather than public knowledge. This created a suspicion, at least during the periodic investment crises of the later nineteenth century, that public companies were run more for the benefit of their promoters and directors than their shareholders.

7   Shareholders, directors and promoters

The mid-Victorian market was characterised by political economists as a largely neutral, natural, self-regulating mechanism in which competitive pressures between a multiplicity of buyers and sellers produced efficient outcomes. In the seventy-five years between the publication of Adam Smith's *Wealth of Nations* and the Great Exhibition of 1851, Britain had shed almost all the legacy of mercantilist economic interventionism, and had simultaneously become the 'workshop of the world'. Competitive exchange was widely believed to be the engine of economic prosperity and national prowess, and for some, at least, it also formed the basis of a modern social morality. The shift in social and economic relationships from status to contract identified by Henry Maine was believed to have replaced semi-feudal structures with an opportunity for everyone to define their economic and social worth through free competition in the market.[1] An *Economist* editorial in 1856 on 'The Higgling of the Market' concisely encapsulated this position: 'Mutual higgling, then, in perfect freedom seems the proper means of determining the rights and duties of all.'[2]

The capacity of economically aware readers of *The Economist* to higgle in perfect freedom was not shared by the majority of the population. As we have seen in previous chapters, the credit and labour markets were structured by law and custom in ways which significantly constrained the capacity of workers to higgle in the same manner as their more affluent peers. Even among the business community there was a major asymmetry between the rights and duties of proprietors and partners compared with directors and shareholders.

In the great majority of companies formed after 1844 this asymmetry worked to the advantage of the original owners as they divided their proprietorial rights into shareholder ownership and directorial control. Yet in a small number of cases, initially in the transport, utilities and financial sectors, and subsequently in commerce and manufacturing,

[1] See above, Chapter 2.   [2] *The Economist*, 9 August 1856, 868.

shareholdings were widely dispersed through public sale. This dispersion of share ownership set the market new challenges. How could a company's many shareholders properly evaluate the worth of their claim to ownership when they had little or no direct contact with or knowledge of the company? How could they negotiate a fair price for their shares with distant purchasers who might be similarly ill-informed? How could the rights of minority shareholders be protected against attempted appropriation by a hostile majority? How could knowledge and information about the market economy be appropriately distributed to the growing number of large- and small-scale owners, investors, directors and other financial intermediaries?

The formal response to these challenges was slow and minimalist. The position of minority shareholders attracted little legislative attention in Victorian Britain.[3] The potential for appropriation certainly existed; whereas in a partnership any change to the structure of ownership or control had to be agreed to by all partners, in a company it could generally be determined by a majority of shareholder votes. In practice, many private companies with closely held shares constrained the scope for opportunistic appropriation through formal clauses in the articles of association requiring something other than simple majority decisions, and they inculcated mutual cooperation and loyalty through the same informal means that partnerships used to align the interests of the several partners – for instance through developing interlocking social, professional and familial networks between the handful of shareholders.

In companies with widely dispersed shareholdings, on the other hand, exit could be a more attractive strategy than loyalty in the face of potential appropriation, though exit opportunities depended on there being an active market for the shares. In 1867 when the first *Daily Stock and Share List* was published it contained 835 securities; by 1914 there were 4,500.[4] It has been estimated that the number of people holding tradable financial securities in Britain rose from around 250,000 in 1870 to around 1 million in 1914 (from 0.8 to 2.2 per cent of the population). In 1870 company shares were held by only a minority of these personal investors; most of their assets were in the form of government and corporate bonds. By 1900 perhaps half the investing public held

---

[3] By contrast in the USA a number of legislative restrictions on the concentration of shareholdings protected the interests of minority shareholders. According to Mark Roe, this reflected a popular mistrust in America of concentrated financial power. This pressure developed during the late-nineteenth-century merger wave, but much of the relevant legislation was introduced after 1918. See Mark Roe, *Strong Managers, Weak Owners: The Political Roots of American Corporate Finance* (Princeton, 1994).

[4] J. R. Edwards, *A History of Financial Accounting* (London, 1980), 105.

shares, even though industrial and commercial securities accounted for no more than 15 per cent of the total nominal value of all securities quoted on the London Stock Exchange.[5] Furthermore, shareholdings became more diversified over time, with the average investor holding seven or eight different securities by the end of the century. The opportunity to trade shares at will, and the diversification of individual shareholder portfolios, together reduced the risk and the cost for minority shareholders of appropriation.

It has also been suggested that the risk of appropriation in Britain was significantly less than in the USA because the distribution of shareholder voting rights in Britain was more democratic. The norm in any modern corporation is for voting rights to be allocated in proportion to the scale of shareholding, on the basis of one vote per share. This 'plutocratic' distribution of shareholder rights was the norm in the USA by 1880, but in Britain the model articles of association that formed the default corporate structure for companies formed between 1845 and 1900 included a graduated voting scale: one vote per share for the first 10 shares, one vote for every five shares between 11 and 100, and one vote for every ten shares above 101. A sample of fifty-five corporate charters from the period 1845–65 examined by Colleen Dunlavy indicates that two-thirds of companies in this period adopted a graduated voting scale, although by 1900 the norm had become one vote per share.[6]

The idea that nineteenth-century British companies were democratic institutions or 'little republics' in which shareholders came together in order collectively to agree on the policies and activities of the business has been explored by Timothy Alborn. His analysis of what he calls 'joint-stock politics' reveals the extent to which the principles and language of representative democracy suffused both the internal discussions and external relationships of joint-stock companies.[7] He argues that the new joint-stock corporations of Victorian Britain 'blurred the boundaries between politics and the market', with shareholders in the early joint-stock banking companies taking an active role in corporate governance, in much the same manner as they participated in the

[5] Michie, *The London Stock Exchange*, 71–2; E. V. Morgan and W. A. Thomas, *The Stock Exchange: Its History and Functions* (London, 1962), table V.
[6] Colleen Dunlavy, 'From citizens to plutocrats: nineteenth-century shareholder voting rights and theories of incorporation' in K. Lipartito and D. Sicilia (eds.), *Constructing Corporate America: History, Politics, Culture* (Oxford, 2004), 66–93.
[7] Alborn, *Conceiving Companies*. The phrase 'little republics' was used by Robert Lowe when introducing the 1856 Companies Act to parliament.

subscriber democracies of middle-class voluntary organisations. He also sees the democratic corporation to have had a short heyday; the speculative mania of 1836–7, and the later railway mania, made apparent some of the costs of shareholder interference in management, and the diversity of interests between small-scale shareholders and directors.

Alborn's argument draws more on what companies and shareholders said than on what they actually did. Pearson and others have focused instead on the internal constitutions and decisions of early joint-stock companies. In the insurance sector, Pearson finds that 'the principle of the pro-active shareholder, insuring as well as investing for the "cause" of his firm, and involved in the busy schedule of his local committee, was negated by frequently rubbing up against the opposite ethos of boardroom secrecy and the centralizing control of management'.[8] Much the same was true for companies engaged in the coastal shipping trade, where there was a clear move away from shareholder participation from the 1830s.[9] Pearson concludes that even at its height in the early nineteenth century, shareholder power was severely limited: 'Despite the rights enshrined in company constitutions, discontented shareholders were usually outmanoeuvred by managers and directors.'[10] In fact companies legislation and relevant common law principles provided almost no explicit protection to minority shareholders in Britain prior to the middle of the twentieth century.[11]

The practice of corporate decision-making frequently paid only lip-service to the principles of corporate legislation. At the general meetings of companies, votes were usually taken by a show of hands, and the democratic ambit of the meeting was determined as much by the geographical dispersion of shareholders as by formal voting rules. Prior to the 1880s the shares of those few industrial and commercial enterprises that issued securities to the public were traded mainly on the provincial stock exchange closest to the company's home. Thereafter the fashion for 'companification' was increasingly focused on the London Stock Exchange, on which the paid-up value of domestic industrial and commercial securities rose from 1 per cent to almost 10 per cent of the total

---

[8] Robin Pearson, 'Shareholder democracies? English stock companies and the politics of corporate governance during the Industrial Revolution', *English Historical Review*, cxvii (2002), 840–66, 862.

[9] Mark Freeman, Robin Pearson and James Taylor, 'Technological change and the governance of joint-stock enterprise in the early nineteenth century: the case of coastal shipping', *Business History*, (2007), 573–94.

[10] Pearson, 'Shareholder Democracies?', 866.

[11] B. Cheffins, 'History and the global corporate governance revolution: the UK perspective', *Business History*, 43 (2001), 87–118.

between 1883 and 1903.[12] By the 1880s shares in the larger publicly traded companies were more usually viewed as financial instruments that produced a dividend income than as part-ownership of a real entity that required direct personal engagement.

The public quiescence in Britain on the subject of minority share-holdings and shareholder voter rights reflected the fact that in a corporation many of the rights and duties of ownership are exercised by directors rather than shareholders. The role and responsibilities of company directors was the subject of heated public discussion. The political economist William Newmarch, drawing on his extensive commercial and corporate experience as secretary of the Globe Insurance Company and chief officer at the bank of Glyn, Mills and Co., explained to a parliamentary committee in 1877 that:

The difference between a joint stock company ... and a private partnership is this, that the private partnership consists of two, three, four, five or half-a-dozen persons who are in constant communication with each other, and who have the means, therefore, of confidential discussion regarding the whole affairs of the concern; whereas in the case of a joint stock company it is a collection of miscellaneous persons, not in communication with each other at all, or only so in a very imperfect manner; and the business of the company must be necessarily in the hands of a small number of persons called directors. The object is to keep the general body of the shareholders reasonably informed of what is actually being done by the people who administer the affairs of the company.[13]

But what was a reasonable amount or type of information? Directors had a huge degree of discretion over what to reveal to shareholders, creditors or the public at large. The 1844 Joint Stock Companies Act required companies to keep books of account and to produce a 'full and fair' balance sheet to each ordinary meeting. Auditors were to be appointed to report on the accounts, and the audited balance sheet was to be filed with the Registrar of Joint Stock Companies. The Report of the Select Committee on Joint Stock Companies, which was a direct precursor to the Act, fully displays a Gladstonian belief in information and publicity as the source of good governance and efficient markets: 'Periodical accounts, if honestly made and fairly audited, cannot fail to excite attention to the real state of a concern; and by means of improved remedies, parties to mismanagement may be made more amenable for acts of fraud and illegality.'[14] Yet these apparently unambiguous

---

[12] Michie, *Stock Exchange*, 94.
[13] *House of Commons Select Committee on the Companies Acts 1862 and 1867*, PP 1877 VIII, q. 724.
[14] *First Report of the Select Committee on Joint Stock Companies*, PP 1844 vii, p. v.

disclosure requirements were negated by a number of loopholes in the legislation: the form and content of the accounts were not defined, nor were the valuation principles, nor the duties of the auditors. Directors who wished to issue transparent accounts and balance sheets to their shareholders could do so, but those who wished to conceal information were able to produce worthless documents deliberately designed to meet the reporting requirements of the Act while revealing nothing of the true financial state of the business.[15]

These purposive but flawed reporting provisions were superseded in 1856 by an entirely *laissez-faire* approach to company accounting. Between the Joint Stock Act of that year and the Companies Act of 1900 there existed no compulsory accounting or audit requirement for registered companies, excepting banks and insurance companies which were subject to separate corporate legislation. On the other hand, the model articles of association appended to the 1856 Act laid out a detailed set of accounting and auditing rules which companies could adopt if they so wished. Hannah has recently suggested that the reporting vacuum created by the 1856 legislation was filled through voluntary compliance with professional auditing practices, at least among the larger industrial and commercial companies. He notes that the new requirements from 1900 to audit and present accounts to shareholders, from 1907 to file balance sheets (for public perusal) with the Registrar of Companies, and from 1929 to publish profit statements 'affected only a small rump of recalcitrant London-listed companies'.[16]

In Hannah's view, the market largely overcame the deficiency of legislation by ensuring that adequate information was disseminated in a voluntary and flexible way. Bryer proposes a different, distinctly Marxist, interpretation. He notes that Companies Bills requiring the publication and regulation of the accounts of limited companies were introduced to parliament in 1884, 1888, 1890 and 1892, but none were passed into legislation. The oft-rehearsed objection to public disclosure of accounts was that it would expose the financial position of companies to their competitors, thereby disadvantaging them in the market.[17] Bryer suggests it had rather more to do with fear that increasingly militant

[15] H. C. Edey and Prot Panitpakdi, 'British company accounting and the law, 1844–1900', in A. C. Littleton and B. S. Yamey (eds.), *Studies in the History of Accounting* (Homewood, IL, 1956), 356–79.
[16] Leslie Hannah, 'Pioneering modern corporate governance: a view from London in 1900', *Enterprise and Society*, 8 (2007), 642–86, at 656.
[17] R. A. Bryer, 'The late nineteenth-century revolution in financial reporting: accounting for the rise of investor or managerial capitalism?', *Accounting, Organizations and Society*, 18 (1993), 649–90, at 677.

organised labour would use any statement of profit as a justification for higher wages. What emerged after 1900, he suggests, was a doctrine of accounting conservatism that deliberately understated profit.

Hannah and Bryer are both correct up to a point. Voluntary reporting served to provide information to shareholders and financial markets, while the ambiguity of accounting conventions allowed directors very wide discretion about how to report the financial standing of a company. It was not until 1883 that the first detailed principles for depreciation accounting were published, and the first book on depreciation written by a chartered accountant did not appear until 1897.[18] Accountants and auditors thus had tremendous latitude over how to report the assets and liabilities of any company, and how to integrate the trading and capital accounts of a business into a consolidated balance sheet. Legislative control over accounting standards was exercised only in those few sectors – railways, banking, insurance – where there existed a long-standing presumption of public interest in the operation of these businesses. In 1868 the Regulation of Railways Act specified detailed and standardised forms of account for railway companies after investigations into the operations of several railway companies revealed widespread laxity in accounting practices. The failure of the City of Glasgow Bank in 1878 led to the introduction in the following year of compulsory annual audit for limited liability banks. Life insurance companies were also required to publish annual accounts and periodic actuarial valuations of their assets and liabilities.[19] In the rest of the economy, however, companies were left to do as they pleased, on the grounds that the State had no need and no right to interfere in the contractual relationships freely entered into between shareholders and the corporation.

The *laissez-faire* approach to company reporting severely compromised the capacity of minority and remote shareholders to monitor corporate performance. This was of no great concern to owners of private companies where shares were tightly held by family members, senior managers and an occasional external investor. In the genuinely public companies, however, the mass of shareholders were kept largely ignorant of the real performance of the company. Even the declaration of a dividend was no guarantee that the company's financial position was sound. The default articles of association attached to the 1862

[18] *Ibid.*, 657, 663.
[19] Christopher Napier and Christopher Noke, 'Accounting and law; an historical overview of an uneasy relationship', in M. Bromwich and A. Hopwood (eds.), *Accounting and the law* (Hemel Hempstead, 1992), 30–54, at 38.

Companies Act, and widely adopted by companies formed after this date, explicitly declared that: 'No dividend shall be payable except out of the profits arising from the business of the company.' Yet directors were simultaneously permitted to set aside profits in a reserve fund with the explicit purpose of meeting contingencies, equalising dividends over several years, or repairing and maintaining capital equipment.[20] It was therefore quite legitimate for a company to pay a dividend to shareholders when the trading operations were generating a loss. Furthermore, the laxity surrounding depreciation accounting and asset valuation gave carte blanche to directors to pay dividends out of capital if they could claim that there had been a significant appreciation in the book value of assets.

Until the 1880s non-managing shareholders had only two protections against deliberate misrepresentation of corporate performance – the professional standards of accountants and auditors, and the integrity and competence of directors. From the 1880s a third line of defence emerged – public revelation of a company's affairs in the financial press. None of these protections was absolute; in fact, as we will see, they could be used as much to conceal the truth as to publicise it.

The accounting profession played an important role in bringing rigour and transparency to company financial reporting in the second half of the nineteenth century. The first societies and institutes of accountants were formed in Scotland in the 1850s, with organisation of the profession in England not commencing until the 1870s. The Institute of Chartered Accountants of England and Wales had 599 members when it was incorporated by royal charter in 1880, and almost 1,700 members a decade later. Members were governed by a code of ethics, but the Institute was reluctant to take a position on technical matters of principle such as depreciation, and it thereby effectively endorsed a laxity of accounting standards. Further leeway was provided by a multiplicity of competing professional bodies – for example the Society of Accountants and Auditors (1885), the London Association of Accountants (1904), the Central Association of Accountants (1905) – with different membership qualifications.[21] Although there is no doubt that general accounting standards rose significantly over this period, there was plenty of scope for less virtuous practitioners to hide behind the veil of professional integrity.

[20] 1862 Companies Act, Table A, sections 73, 74.
[21] W. Habgood (ed.), *Chartered Accountants in England and Wales: A Guide to Historical Records* (Manchester, 1994), 10–16: E. Jones, *Accountancy and the British Economy 1840–1980: The Evolution of Ernst and Whinney* (London, 1981), ch. 2.

Furthermore, virtue could be costly. Accountants and auditors, although nominally appointed by the company, in practice were appointed by the very directors whose prudence and propriety they were in part required to evaluate. An unaccommodating approach to the preparation of annual accounts and audit statements could result in loss of business as directors switched allegiance to more compliant accountancy practitioners. The description of the audit relationship proffered by Horace Samuel in 1933 could have been applied throughout the Victorian period, and in many respects applies still today: 'though an auditor may be a watch-dog, he is yet a watch-dog who, in order to discharge his duties, may be compelled to bite the hand that feeds him'.[22]

While accountants and auditors worked in the background, it was directors who had the formal legal responsibility to manage the business of each company and to report on the activities and accounts to shareholders at the annual general meeting. The integrity and competence of the directors was, therefore, the most direct safeguard available to shareholders. But directorial integrity and competence are difficult attributes to evaluate and track over time, and it is therefore not at all surprising that publicly accessible indicators of high social status were commonly used as a proxy for directorial integrity. This fact was widely recognised by company promoters, who typically sought out the great and the good to serve on the board of any new company. The practice operated throughout the nineteenth century and into the twentieth with little variation. As early as 1826 Charles Babbage was castigating the trade in respectability associated with company directorships:

The readiness with which gentlemen, of respectability, wealth, and intelligence, allow their names to be attached to companies, with whose principles they are but little acquainted, is much to be regretted. The public have been accustomed, and with some degree of reason, to infer the respectability of an undertaking from that of the names under whose sanction it is introduced, and to trust that the facts, stated in the prospectus, have been examined into, and are vouched for by the officers of the society.[23]

More than fifty years later the same behaviours and beliefs were still prevalent. New companies would try to enlist the services of someone already on the board of a business of good standing: 'He will be made chairman, and if he happens to be an Earl, or Sir Somebody, this is all in favour of the new enterprise. If a Right Honourable, a Mayor, a Justice of the Peace, C.C., C.E., F.R.S., or any other combination

[22] H. B. Samuel, *Shareholders' Money* (London, 1933); H. A. Shannon, 'Review of H. B. Samuel, "Shareholders' Money"', *Economica*, November 1933, 507–9.
[23] Babbage, *Comparative view*, 53–4.

of initials that can be got, by all means secure his services, but do not overlook the necessity of attracting a Captain to the board.'[24]

These 'guinea-pig' directors, as they came to be known, typically paid infrequent attention to the affairs of the companies for which they were responsible. There was nothing shy or accidental about this casual approach to fiduciary obligations. In 1899 Arthur Balfour, leader of the House of Commons and Chancellor of the Exchequer, defended the retention of directorships by cabinet ministers on the grounds that they did not need to attend board meetings. The Home Secretary, Sir Matthew White Ridley, for example, was a railway director, but did not attend the board and received only £150 a year as token payment. According to Balfour, the company 'said they would be grateful if [Ridley] would consent to remain a member of the board'.[25] Such well-remunerated gratitude was of long standing. By the end of the railway mania of 1845, over 150 MPs had 'made a traffic on their personal responsibility' by becoming railway directors, thereby gaining entitlements to advantageous share allocations as well as directors' fees.[26] The bond between board room and parliament grew ever stronger throughout the nineteenth century: in 1866, 216 MPs were company directors, and by 1898 this had risen to 293, representing 44 per cent of the House of Commons.[27] A remarkable sociological analysis of membership of the House of Commons published in 1868 noted that 'the railways, which have hardly any voters at the polling booth ... have 179 railway directors in the House of Commons, who represent only shareholders, not railway travellers. The banks have 78 bankers and bank directors in the House, the insurance offices 53'.[28] Some of these parliamentary directors no doubt executed their responsibilities to shareholders with exemplary care and diligence, but many were, in the cutting words of an inter-war commentator, nothing more than 'financial gigolos'.[29] A guide for investors and shareholders published in 1894 estimated that 'the annual tribute of the British public for the directorial services of all companies making returns under the Acts' was around £6.5 million, 'and it certainly cannot be said they get value for their money'.[30]

[24] Jaycee, *Public Companies: From the Cradle to the Grave* (London, 1883), 16.
[25] *The Times*, 24 Feb 1899, 15.
[26] D. M. Evans, *The Commercial Crisis of 1847–8* (London, 1848), 5, 19n.
[27] *The Joint-Stock Companies Directory, 1866* (London, 1866), 961–1266; *Directory of Directors for 1898* (London, 1898), *passim*.
[28] B. Cracroft, *Essays, Political and Miscellaneous* (London, 1868), 118. The essay 'Analysis of the House of Commons in 1867' (95–113) was originally published in the *Saturday Review*.
[29] Samuel, *Shareholders Money*, quoted in Shannon, 'Review', 507.
[30] J. D. Walker and Watson, *Investor's and Shareholder's Guide* (Edinburgh, 1894), 143.

Even when directors assiduously performed their duty to effect good governance in the best interest of shareholders, they faced a huge challenge in communicating with the company's owners where these were numerous and geographically dispersed. The comments (reported above in Chapter 6) of the government inspector, Stanley, in relation to the governance of the Royal Liver insurance society – 'the members are scattered throughout the county. They have no cohesion, no power of knowing each other, and too small an interest to take the trouble to master the facts and vote' – applied equally to joint-stock companies with dispersed shareholdings. Furthermore, even when shareholders did attend the annual meeting and read the annual report and accounts, they were served only a periodic snapshot of commercial fortune, and had little opportunity otherwise to question directors about how their company was faring as business conditions changed. What a shareholder could do, however, which a mutual society member could not, was sell their stake in the company if they were unhappy with the course set by directors and managers.

Decisions about whether or when to buy or sell shares were driven by the information that individual shareholders had about price. As early as 1844 a daily list of railway share prices was being published in London, and by that date most of the major daily newspapers were carrying commercial and financial reports, including information on a limited number of share prices. Periodical publications such as the *Banker's Magazine* (1844) and *Investors' Chronicle* (1860) catered to the interests of finance professionals, but it was not until 1884 that London's first financial daily, the *Financial News*, was launched, followed four years later by the *Financial Times*.[31] The *Financial News*, borrowing from American journalistic style, brought an accessible and vibrant form of investigative reporting to financial affairs, which hitherto had been characterised by dull and dry listings of facts. This new style of financial journalism appealed to the growing (though still small) band of private investors, as well as to finance professionals, and provided an opportunity for the direct marketing of new investment prospects. In the satirical social commentary *Diary of a Nobody* (1892), Lupin, the son of the lower-middle-class clerk, Mr Pooter, 'was riveted to the *Financial News* as if he had been born a capitalist'.[32]

Better, and more, information about companies, their performance and their share price, provided on a daily basis, was a necessary condition for the development of an efficient and broadly based share market,

---

[31] Morgan and Thomas, *The Stock Exchange*, 165. The *Financial News* merged with the *Financial Times* in 1945.
[32] George and Weedon Grossmith, *The Diary of a Nobody* (Bristol, 1892).

and it seems certain that this provided impetus to the expansion of share ownership in the last two decades of the nineteenth century. However, not all information was quite what it seemed.

The sword of truth and the curse of Thanet

On 14 January 1887 the Rae-Transvaal Gold Mining Company was registered at Companies' House with limited liability status. This was one of many prospecting companies floated during the 'Kaffir' speculation of 1886–7, and at first sight appeared to be no better or worse placed than any of its many competitors. However, in the judgement of the *Financial News*, this new company displayed 'every element of success' and was 'likely to prove a good speculation'. So confident was the *Financial News* of the prospects for the Rae-Transvaal that it offered no less than thirty-three recommendations for these shares between 18 January and 29 April 1887. Yet the performance of the company was lamentable: it spent only £138 on prospecting equipment and managed to sink a shaft to a depth of just 30 feet, it produced not an ounce of gold, never made a profit, and was liquidated on 22 May 1888. Shareholders lost everything; creditors received payments of less than 6d. in the £.[33]

The fortunes of this company, and the fate of the shareholders, were far from exceptional. The intriguing part is the way in which the company was formed, floated and promoted by Harry H. Marks. In late 1886 Marks purchased a bankrupt 6,154-acre Transvaal farm for £10,300, and immediately sold it on for a notional £50,000 to a company he formed for the purpose, using a dummy (a stockbroker's clerk) to sign the appropriate deeds and checks in exchange for £200. Marks was paid with about 23,000 of the company's £1 shares. He then set about drawing up a prospectus for the company prior to registration and public flotation. The enthusiasm of the *Financial News* encouraged members of the public to apply for almost 8,000 shares, but this still left over 19,000 shares unallocated, so Marks generated a slew of bogus applications from, among others, his brother-in-law and his brother-in-law's mistress. To encourage further public support for the issue he ensured that the shares were quoted at a false premium in the *Financial News*; this created an active market which allowed him and his dummy shareholders to offload their holdings at a profit. A total of 45,500 shares were foisted on the public, all at a price above their £1 par value.

---

[33] The details of the Rae-Transvaal company are taken from Henry Hess, *'The Critic' Black Book*, appendix volume (London, 1901–2), 179–85.

labouchère's precedents.

The Rae-Transvaal was just one of many dubious deals carried out by Marks. He was deeply implicated in at least one other gold-prospecting fraud, appears to have received bribes in excess of £17,000 from the corrupt financial empire of E. T. Hooley, and was described as 'a scoundrel on his own admission' and 'a dishonest rogue' by a judge in a libel case in 1903.[34] But Marks was no ordinary company fraudster. He was, in addition, founder, chief proprietor and managing editor of the *Financial News*, member of the London County Council from 1889–91 and 1895–7, and Conservative MP for Tower Hamlets 1895–1900 and for Thanet 1904–10. Born in 1855 to the prominent Jewish theologian David Woolf Marks, Harry cut his journalistic teeth in the USA before returning to England in 1883. Under his editorship the *Financial News* fearlessly wielded the sword of truth to expose other people's fraud and corruption. Marks was responsible for revealing the financial misdeeds within the Metropolitan Board of Works, and it was largely for this reason that he secured election as one of the first cohorts of LCC councillors.[35] But he was not content with the rewards of an editor's salary, and he used his position to 'puff' companies in exchange for payment. He was not alone: according to the seasoned financial journalist Charles Duguid, 'the writer of the money article, from the highest to the lowest, is subject to the constant temptation of those financiers who would have him withhold his criticism or praise their wares'.[36] In the case of the Rae-Transvaal, however, Marks went much further, and conducted a massive fraud on the public.

From at least 1890 Marks' fraudulent activity was sufficiently well known to lead to public accusations and a number of (unsuccessful) suits by Marks for libel.[37] By 1903 Henry Hess was writing openly about the Rae-Transvaal scam that 'it has become a standing wonder to all who know the particulars, how Marks and those who subsequently joined him in the venture, escaped penal servitude'.[38] But this invective was not sufficient to prevent Marks re-entering parliament in 1904, having retired in 1900 because of ill health. He retained his Thanet seat in 1906, much to the dismay of a dissident group of local Conservatives who in November of that year wrote to the Speaker of

---

[34] Hess, *Black Book*, 159–62; Dilwyn Porter, '"A trusted guide of the investing public": Harry Marks and the *Financial News*, 1884–1916' in R. P. T. Davenport-Hines (ed.), *Speculators and Patriots: Essays in Business Biography* (London, 1986), 8, 10; *Times*, 26 Nov. 1906.

[35] *Men and Women of the Time* 15th edn (London, 1899), 722–3. Marks' articles exposing MBW corruption were reprinted in *The Metropolitan Board of Works: A Brief Account of the Disclosures which Have Led to the Appointment of a Royal Commission* (London, 1888).

[36] C. Duguid, *How to Read the Money Article* (London, 1901), 103.

[37] Porter, 'Harry Marks', 8. [38] Hess, *Black Book*, 179.

the Commons itemising Marks' past record and arguing that he was 'unfit to be a member of the House'. They followed this up with a pamphlet, circulated to every sitting MP, detailing a number of court cases from 1890 to 1904 in which the fraudulent actions of Marks had been exposed.[39] There was, however, never any attempt to prosecute him for market-rigging, or to unseat him from parliament. At his death in 1916 he owned a country estate of 200 acres in Kent where he was a JP, had a London residence in Cavendish Square, and was a member of the Carlton, Royal Cinque Ports and Royal Temple Yacht Clubs.

A century later, in an uncanny case of historical repetition, Marks' successor as MP for Thanet was also a journalist, and one who similarly laid claim to 'the sword of truth and the trusty shield of British fair play' in order to 'fight against falsehood and those who peddle it' in a series of libel suits against newspapers and broadcasters. This was the junior finance minister, Jonathan Aitken. Like Marks he lost the libel cases when his denial of corrupt behaviour was shown to be false; unlike Marks, he was charged with perjury and in 1999 was jailed for eighteen months.[40]

Harry Marks was unscrupulous as a member of parliament and as a company promoter. He was far from being alone: George Hudson (the 'Railway King'), 'Baron' Albert Grant, Jabez 'Teddy' Balfour and Harry Seymour Foster all shared the dubious honour of being sometime elected members of the House of Commons and serial company promoters, in which role they made (and in most cases lost) a fortune for themselves, and for their many investors.[41] The excoriation of company promoters became common sport in Victorian Britain, particularly after a spectacular corporate collapse. None was more spectacular than the failure of the bank of Overend, Gurney and Company, Limited, in May 1866, less then ten months after the conversion of the private bank into a public limited company.[42] The prospectus offered by the directors assured the investing public that 'the company could not fail to ensure a highly remunerative return to the shareholders'. What the prospectus did not reveal was that two separate deeds were

---

[39] *The Times*, 26 November 1906, 11 November 1907. In addition to his commercial frauds, Marks was also publicly accused of extensive electoral bribery and malpractice. See J. C. Haig, 'The case of Thanet, illustrating the methods of Mr H. H. Marks' in C. R. Buxton, *Electioneering Up-to-Date* (London, 1906), 77–90.

[40] Jonathan Aitken, *Pride and Perjury* (London, 2000).

[41] For a description of a number of deliberately fraudulent promotions see G. Robb, *White-Collar Crime in Modern England: Financial Fraud and Business Morality, 1845–1929* (Cambridge, 1992), ch. 5.

[42] G. Elliott, *The Mystery of Overend and Gurney: Adventures in the Victorian Financial Underworld* (London, 2006).

executed for the transfer of the business from the firm to the Company, one of which – detailing a financial deficiency of over £3 million – was concealed from the shareholders.[43] The ensuing legal wrangles – of Byzantine complexity – hinged on whether the promotion of the new joint-stock company by the directors had been fraudulent, and this issue of fraud and concealment stood at the heart of Victorian anguish over company promotion.

The Times noted that 'Messrs Gurney and Birkbeck, the partners in the firm of Overend, Gurney and Co., concealed nothing from Messrs Gurney, Birkbeck and their colleagues, the Directors in Overend, Gurney and Co. Limited', so there was no fraud by the partnership on the company.[44] Although the partnership faced potential losses of over £3 million on investments of dubious worth, these investments were entered in the firm's accounts as bona fide debts. Ultimately a charge of conspiracy to defraud the public was brought against the directors, and although the judge found their behaviour was characterised by 'grave error', they were duly found not guilty. It was determined that although the business was in a precarious financial state when it was floated as a public company, it was not worthless, the directors did not believe it was insolvent, they did not misrepresent its solvency to the public (largely because they refrained from representing anything at all about the financial standing of the business in the prospectus), and they did not intend to defraud the public. Instead, they hoped that an injection of capital would allow them to trade out of their financial difficulties and re-establish positive cash flow and profit.[45] However, a subsequent claim for civil damages against the directors for misrepresentation led to a different conclusion in 1873, with the House of Lords implicitly recognising that an original allottee of shares in Overend, Gurney and Co., who had retained these shares, would have been entitled to recover damages against the directors who issued the prospectus, because the prospectus was a deceit. On the other hand, anyone who had subsequently purchased the shares in the market had no claim against the directors, because they were not party to the original flotation. A fine distinction, and in the end an idle one, because six years after the original collapse of the company the statute of limitations barred any further action by original allottees.[46]

[43] A. Barrister, *Overend, Gurney & Co. (Limited): A Plain Statement of the Case* (London, 1867), 16–17.
[44] *The Times*, 14 December 1869, 7.
[45] Anon, *Responsibilities of Directors and Promoters* (London, 1873), 45–51. This is a collection of articles on the Overend and Gurney collapse originally printed in *The Investors' Guardian Newspaper* between 1865 and 1873.
[46] *Ibid.*, 72–3.

The case of Overend, Gurney and Co. was seen by the firm's share-holders as a whitewashing of directors and their responsibilities, but it had broader impact on attitudes to investment and risk because the collapse of the bank ushered in a more general loss of confidence in the financial sector and created what today would be called a 'credit crunch'. Far from the 1862 Companies Act creating a more stable investment environment, it seemed to have produced a boom in company promo-tion (one of a series of cycles evident in the company registration data reported in Figure 4.1), and in the ensuing credit and commercial crisis of 1866 companies both legitimate and fanciful fared ill. With share prices falling, and some companies going to the wall, investors were reluctant to purchase partly paid-up shares, for fear they might have to throw good money after bad if the business collapsed. For inveter-ate opponents of limited liability, this was the inevitable nemesis. The banker Lord Overstone felt these untradeable shares were 'little else but gambling symbols used not for the purpose of promoting industry, but to facilitate practices which had about as much relation to honest indus-try as the exchange of cards over the gaming table'.[47] Yet the Select Committee appointed the following year to examine the working of the limited liability acts was fundamentally supportive of the principle and the practice of limited liability joint-stock companies.[48] Perhaps this was not surprising, given the entrenched position of so many MPs in the boardrooms of the country's joint-stock enterprises.

Beyond the inner sanctum of the boardroom, however, there was considerable disquiet, and much soul-searching, about the opera-tions of joint-stock companies, and the supporting cast of directors, promoters, brokers, jobbers and financial scribblers. This was not a new phenomenon; just as the flow of company registrations went in cycles, so did contemporary indictments of Mammonism. In the 1850s Thackeray (*The Newcomers*), Dickens (*Little Dorrit*) and Trollope (*The Three Clerks*) all critically engaged with the contemporary enthusiasm for financial speculation, and the moral challenges faced by charac-ters in search of a fast profit. Mary Poovey has argued that these and other fictional representations were 'part of a discursive system in which Britons constructed ideas about finance and money alongside the system of finance itself'.[49] Typically these fictional representations both explained something of the inner workings of financial institu-tions, thereby serving to demystify that which was remote and arcane,

[47] *HCDeb* 7 June 1866, col. 2028.   [48] Taylor, *Creating Capitalism*, ch. 5.
[49] M. Poovey (ed.), *The Financial System in Nineteenth-Century Britain* (Oxford, 2003), 5.

and largely exonerated these institutions of any fundamental flaw by focussing on the personal traits and moral failings of the key characters. A series of fictional accounts of Stock Exchange speculation that followed the commercial crisis of 1866 did much the same; they 'conveyed the idea that money-hungry shareholders were as much to blame as directors for the unsoundness of the companies of the mid-1860s'.[50]

There was, nevertheless, a genuine concern that the structures of financial markets, and particularly of the Stock Exchange, led, and even forced, decent men to behave dishonourably. As early as 1816 an anonymous pamphleteer remarked that although individual traders on the Stock Exchange 'generally speaking are respectable members of society', nevertheless the collective body of the Stock Exchange 'exists by manoeuvres and deceptions'.[51] The particular focus of this, and many other, complaints was that the majority of Stock Exchange trades were driven not by 'real' transactions, but by the trade in options, or 'time bargains'. Time bargains created price movements that were unnatural, and which thereby could disadvantage honest investors. More importantly, time bargains were immoral, because they were nothing more than a gamble: 'This practice, which is really nothing else than a wager concerning the price of Stock, is contrary to law; yet it is allowed to be carried on to such an alarming extent, that almost the whole city of London, and many at distant parts, have become gamblers.'[52]

The law in question was Barnard's Act, which, from enactment in 1734 to repeal in 1868, made illegal 'the frequent and mischievous practice' of dealing in time bargains – future contracts in which settlement was determined not by exchange of stock, but by exchange of money between the contracting parties, depending on whether the price had risen or fallen in the intervening period. But from the outset this law was a dead letter; dealers in stocks and shares habitually settled accounts with each other periodically (fortnightly once the Stock Exchange was established in 1801) rather than daily, and so necessarily carried 'short' or 'long' positions for some days. Furthermore, many dealers deliberately entered into 'put' (sell) or 'call' (buy) options covering longer periods in order to speculate on price movements, though in 1821 the Stock Exchange limited the length of options to fourteen days, in order to limit systemic risk in the market (an interesting case

[50] Taylor, *Creating Capitalism*, 201.
[51] A Practical Jobber, *The System of Stock-Jobbing Explained*, London, 1816, 12.
[52] *Ibid.*, 15.

of a private institution publicly regulating an activity that was formally illegal).[53]

The critique of time bargains arose in part from a general evangelical assault on gambling which held that it undermined morals and weakened the habits of industry. This pressure contributed to the abolition of public lotteries in 1826.[54] Time bargains were also held to create incentives for corrupt behaviour, because the lapse in time between initiation and execution of the contract provided an opportunity to distort the 'true' market price. This became apparent in bizarrely theatrical circumstances towards the end of the Napoleonic War.

The Stock Exchange 'hoax'

In the early hours of Monday 21 February 1814, a man wearing a staff officer's red military tunic adorned with gold star and medal hammered on the door of the Ship Inn at Dover. The stranger demanded pen, ink, paper, a post-chaise and four, together with an express horse and rider to take a message to Admiral Foley at the Deal garrison. The message was that Napoleon had been slain by Cossacks; the allied forces had saved Paris from destruction and entered the city; the white cockade (symbol of the Bourbons) was everywhere displayed; peace was imminent. The signature was that of Lieutenant-Colonel R. du Bourg, Aide-de-Camp to Lord Cathcart, ambassador to the Court of Russia and British military commissioner at the Czar's headquarters. Foley attempted to transmit this news to the Admiralty in London by means of semaphore telegraph, but a heavy mist made this impractical. Meanwhile Colonel du Bourg was proceeding to London in his chaise and four, dispensing the good news at each coaching inn, where payment for new horses was made from a large stock of gold napoleons (although the coachman at Dover, suspicious of dubious foreign coins, demanded and received payment in Bank of England one pound notes). By about 9 a.m. du Bourg had arrived at Marsh Gate, on the south side of Blackfriars bridge, where he transferred into a hackney carriage and made off in the direction of Grosvenor Square. Around midday, striking confirmation of the news of peace was brought by another chaise and four, decorated with laurels and containing three French officers wearing white cockades, which drove over London bridge, down Lombard Street, along Cheapside, and over

---

[53] C. Duguid, *The Story of the Stock Exchange* (London, 1901), 48–50; Michie, *London Stock Exchange*, 47–50.
[54] Searle, *Morality*, 230–3.

Blackfriars bridge. Throughout their passage, the occupants distributed small leaflets inscribed with 'Vive le Roi! Vivent les Bourbons!'

The rumour of victory and peace proved to be false, and at first sight the events of 21 February appear to be farce rather than fraud. But for a short time, at least, the news of Napoleon's defeat was believed. Newspapers had been awash with speculation and rumour since late January when Napoleon had ventured out of Paris. Reports of initial success for the allied forces filtered back to London; unsubstantiated news of Napoleon's death appeared in the *Courier* on 10 February. Four days later it was clear that this was nothing but false hope; by 18 February *The Times* acknowledged that Napoleon had secured an impressive victory over Blucher. The country was eager for good news; rumour piled on rumour.[55]

Nowhere did such rumours have a larger impact than on the Stock Exchange. Hopes and expectations had been driving up the value of government stock since the beginning of February. Consols were priced at 66½ on Monday 7th, and within a week reached 72, before falling back to 70 on Saturday 19th. Over the same period, Omnium (a mixture of government stock and public annuities) rose from 19⅛ to 28¾ before falling to 26¾.[56] When the exchange opened at 10 a.m. on Monday 21st, prices rose rapidly on strength of the news from Dover, with Omnium reaching 30¼. The absence of official verification created some disquiet, and prices were sliding around midday until confirmation appeared in the form of the three French officers and their handbills. Omnium touched 32, but after a messenger returned from government offices in the afternoon to report that the whole affair had been a fraud, prices sank back to their level of Saturday.

Trading on the exchange on Monday 21st had been heavy, though not much more so than over the previous two weeks of extremely volatile prices. Nevertheless the blatant and deliberate way in which the false rumour had been generated led the Committee of the Stock Exchange to instigate an inquiry. This investigation revealed that three people together accounted for sales on Monday 21st of over £1.1 million of Consols and Omnium, 'most of which had been purchased in the course of the week preceding'.[57] These three people were Thomas, Lord

[55] Information about the personation of du Bourg, and other details of the fraud, are taken from J. B. Atlay, *The Trial of Lord Cochrane before Lord Ellenborough* (London, 1897), 3–14.

[56] *Ibid.*, 13.

[57] Stock Exchange, *Report of the Sub-Committee of the Stock Exchange Relative to the Late Fraud* (London, 1814), 15.

Cochrane, naval hero, radical member of parliament for Westminster and eldest son of the ninth Earl of Dundonald; his uncle the Hon. Andrew Cochrane-Johnstone, also an MP, and sometime army colonel and Governor of Domenica; and Richard Butt, former naval pay clerk, successful Stock Exchange speculator, and financial adviser to Lord Cochrane. The Stock Exchange investigation also found that du Bourg's hackney coach had taken him to 13 Green Street, Grosvenor Square, the recently established residence of Lord Cochrane. Furthermore, it was found that four of the one pound notes generously paid out by du Bourg on his journey from Dover had been paid to Butt by his stockbroker on the previous Saturday afternoon.

The Stock Exchange was variously praised and abused for publishing the result of its enquiry, which had no legal standing and which did not take evidence under oath. In the Commons the Whig Francis Horner congratulated the Stock Exchange on tracing the fraud to its source, and in *The Satirist* George Cruickshank viciously lampooned the conspirators. Meanwhile William Cobbett, ever keen to support a fellow radical, fulminated that:

under no wild democracy, under no military despotism, under no hypocritical and cunning oligarchy, under no hellish tyranny upheld by superstition, was there ever committed an act more unjust and more foul than what has, within these three weeks, been committed, in the city of London, through the means of the Press, against the three gentlemen.[58]

However, publication of this report pressurised Lord Cochrane into voluntarily swearing an affidavit about his movements on 21 February. He acknowledged that he knew well, and had breakfasted with, Cochrane-Johnstone and Butt, that he had traded down all his Omnium, and that a uniformed officer had visited his house. His defence, however, was that he had left general orders with his broker to sell whenever the price rose to one point over the purchase price, and had issued no direct, personal instructions to trade on the 21st. Furthermore the officer who visited him was a Captain Random de Berenger, a distant acquaintance, who had earlier contacted Cochrane about joining him on a forthcoming naval mission.

De Berenger was a designer, inventor, rifleman, pyrotechnician and insolvent debtor of Prussian birth, currently living under the rules of the King's Bench (as was, it subsequently emerged, one of the three men who purported to be a French officer). He was arrested in Leith

---

[58] *HCDeb* 20 May 1814 col. 987; *Cobbett's Weekly Political Register*, 26 March 1814 (vol. xxv, no. 13), col. 385.

in early April while trying to buy a passage out of the country, and in his possession were found a number of gold napoleons, together with bank notes that traced back to Cochrane-Johnstone and Butt: De Berenger and du Bourg were one and the same person.[59] With evidence in place, the Stock Exchange brought a prosecution against both major and minor players in the fraud. The case was heard before Lord Ellenborough in June 1814; the key charge was that Lord Cochrane, Cochrane-Johnstone and Butt had conspired, by disseminating false information, to raise the price of government funds 'with a wicked and fraudulent intention' to 'cheat and defraud' the King's subjects.[60] The motive was made plain by the chief prosecuting counsel, the Quaker Adolphus Gurney (of the banking family later associated with the 1866 collapse of Overend, Gurney and Co., Ltd.). For several months prior to the fraud the three principal conspirators had been speculating heavily on the Stock Exchange,[61] invariably as 'bulls' – that is, they bought in the expectation of the price rising, so they could sell out at a profit. They traded very large quantities, but needed very little cash to do so, because, as long as equal amounts were bought and sold, the only money that changed hands at the end of the fortnightly Stock Exchange accounting period was the difference between the buying and selling price, plus the broker's $1/8$ per cent commission. The account open at the time of the fraud (or 'hoax' as Lord Cochrane whimsically chose to call it) had begun on 8 February and was due to close on the 23rd.[62] Cochrane et al. were speculating heavily on an increase in price. According to Adolphus Gurney, 'their purchases vastly exceeded their sales ... they had gone on plunging deeper and deeper until they were out of their depth'.[63] They had contracted to buy more than £1 million of stock, in anticipation of selling at a profit before 23 February. But news from France on the 14th kept prices flat, while on the 18th confirmation of Napoleon's victory depressed prices. An attempt to offload £1 million of stock on to a declining market would have sent prices spiralling; the trio of conspirators faced 'an immense loss, perhaps irrecoverable ruin', according to de Berenger.[64] The fraud was designed not

[59] Atlay, *Trial*, 50.
[60] W. B. Gurney, *The Trial of Charles Random de Berenger, Taken in Shorthand* (London, 1814), 7.
[61] Cochrane first traded on the exchange in November 1813. See Anon., *The Trial of Lord Cochrane* (London, 1814), 32.
[62] Anon., *The Calumnious Aspersions Contained in the Report of the Sub-Committee of the Stock-Exchange Exposed and Refuted* (London, 1814), 32.
[63] Gurney, *Trial*, 40.
[64] Charles Random de Berenger, *The Noble Stock Jobber* (London, 1816), 64.

to make them vast sums (though their net profits, seized by the Stock Exchange Committee and subsequently donated to various charities, totalled more than £10,000), but to prevent even larger losses.[65]

Despite the efforts of a strong defence team which included the future Lord Chancellor Henry Brougham, the future Chief Justice of Common Pleas, William Best (Lord Wynford), and 'by far the most successful advocate of his day' and future attorney general, James Scarlett (Lord Abinger),[66] the special jury of City men found for the prosecution.[67] The chief conspirators were each sentenced to twelve month's imprisonment in the Marshalsea, a fine of £1,000, and an hour in the pillory outside the Royal Exchange.[68] The case is remarkable for more than just its extraordinary genesis and the ensuing lordly dispute between three generations of Dundonalds and Ellenboroughs over the probity of court proceedings and the validity of the verdict.[69] The personal history of Lord Cochrane, the legal basis of the case, and the public and parliamentary reaction to the verdict, all shed light on the nature of commercial morality in the early nineteenth century.

Cochrane had achieved both fame and fortune as a courageous and imaginative naval captain. He had been awarded the Order of the Bath for his heroic assault on the French fleet in the Aix roads in 1809, but had attracted the unbending hostility of the naval establishment by using his privilege as an MP to accuse his commander, Lord Gambier, of incompetence.[70] He was briefly MP for the rotten borough of Honiton

---

[65] Atlay, *Trial*, 239. Cochrane-Johnstone in particular could not afford to lose, as he was already in financial difficulty and evading arrest only by means of his privileges as an MP.

[66] *DNB*, xvii, 891.

[67] Special juries, made up of City merchants, were used widely in the late eighteenth and early nineteenth centuries to hear commercial cases. Bentham criticised special juries, believing that in some cases judges selected jurors according to their political leanings. See James Oldham, 'Special juries in England: nineteenth-century usage and reform', *Journal of Legal History*, 8 (1987), 148–66.

[68] Anon, *The Case of Thomas Lord Cochrane* (Edinburgh, 1814), 60. After parliamentary discussion it was agreed to revoke the sentence of pillory.

[69] Cochrane's grandson petitioned parliament in 1877 to have the trial verdict set aside, and in 1890 republished, with amendment, Cochrane's autobiography, but did not alter a number of accusations levelled against the trial judge. Ellenborough's nephew and grandson replied personally in print and at length, as well as commissioning Atlay to write an account of the case. The last of these ripostes appeared a full century after the trial. See: Thomas, 10th earl of Dundonald, *Autobiography of a Seaman* and Thomas, 11th earl of Dundonald and H. R. Fox Bourne, *Life of Thomas, 10th Earl of Dundonald, Completing the Autobiography of a Seaman* (2 vols., London, 1869), reprinted in one volume in 1890; Henry Spencer Law, *Reviews of the 'Autobiography of a Seaman'* (London, 1877); Lord Ellenborough (Edward Downes Law), *The Guilt of Lord Cochrane* (London, 1914).

[70] C. Lloyd, *Lord Cochrane* (London, 1947), 81–104.

in 1806, before winning one of the Westminster seats in 1807, where his fellow MP was the radical Sir Francis Burdett. With support from *Cobbett's Political Register*, Cochrane launched a number of parliamentary attacks on the gross inefficiency of admiralty administration and on the scale and extent of sinecures paid, under the guise of pensions, to many parliamentarians. He took an unambiguous personal stand against privilege and 'old corruption'; indeed, at an initially unsuccessful attempt to secure the seat of Honiton, he promised the electors that 'I shall never accept any sinecure or pension, or any grant of the public money; and that I will never ask or receive any such for any person whatever that may be in any way dependent on me.'[71] Cochrane's public profile, both as naval hero and as anti-corruption campaigner made his fall from grace all the more poignant. He had claimed the moral high ground for himself, but, in the words of Mr Justice Leblanc in the preamble to the sentence, was found guilty of 'a crime, which, in its progress, was denoted by every unseemly characteristic; it was tainted with meanness, mendacity, and avarice'. Furthermore, Cochrane 'had not even the palliative of poverty as an apology for the sin'.[72]

Cochrane claimed that both the verdict and the sentence were politically motivated, and that Ellenborough conducted the case with overt bias and political spite. This claim was accepted by Burdett and other radicals, who commenced an active campaign to rescue Cochrane's reputation. The details of the case, however, hardly reveal a concerted Tory attack on radicalism. The prosecution was brought not by the government, but by the Stock Exchange, and the evidence of Cochrane's intimate knowledge of the 'hoax' was overwhelming. Cochrane does not appear to have viewed Stock Exchange speculation, or even the manipulation of stock prices through rumour-mongering, as morally wrong.[73] Although he was unrestrained in his critique of public corruption, and forthright in his renunciation of all public favours (something which his subsequent career proved to be a rhetorical flourish rather than a principled stand), he behaved in the market as he did in war, adopting morally dubious policies in the belief that the ends justified the means.[74]

---

[71] *The Case*, 2. On 'old corruption' in general see Philip Harling, *The Waning of 'Old Corruption'* (Oxford, 1996).

[72] *The Case*, 60.

[73] See the disquisition on Cochrane's motives in the anonymous *Letter to the Electors of Westminster on the Case of Lord Cochrane* (London, 1814), 9–10.

[74] Part of Cochrane's dispute with Gambier over the naval action in the Aix roads arose because Cochrane wanted to use fire ships against the French fleet, which Gambier thought improper. Cochrane also developed in 1812 a 'top secret' scheme for chemical warfare (using sulphur gas to poison garrison towns), and relentlessly pressed

The legal basis of the prosecution case also reveals a good deal about contemporary perceptions of commercial probity. Cochrane et al. were charged with conspiracy to defraud the king's subjects by deliberately manipulating stock prices. Yet, as Cobbett noted before the trial, 'Whether it be a *legal* offence to spread false reports for the purpose of gaining in the funds, remains to be shewn; but if it be a legal offence, it is one which the newspaper people have been accusing each other almost every week, for twenty years past.'[75] It was not just newspapers that generated false rumours; individuals did this too. Nathan Rothschild used the rumour-mill to manipulate prices; when he possessed advance news (often from his private Paris–London pigeon-post) calculated to make the funds rise, he would sell heavily, knowing that others would follow his lead, thereby allowing him to buy in at a much reduced price before the good news arrived and prices rose.[76] There were many ways of creating false rumours; Cochrane's scheme was more theatrical than most, but it seems certain that the Committee of the Stock Exchange tolerated many less blatant manipulations.

However, the prosecution managed to demonstrate that Cochrane's hoax was not a victimless crime. On the day of the fraud the Accountant General had purchased over £15,000 of Consols at inflated prices on behalf of the official trustee, who managed assets for public charitable trusts, orphans and other dependants. Had this purchase been made at the price prevailing on the preceding Saturday, the same quantity of Consols could have been had for some £340 less. The case demonstrates that both within the Stock Exchange fraternity and among jurors in the King's Bench court there existed a clear conception of commercial probity. Concealing privileged information from the public, as Nathan Rothschild often did when he traded on the market, was legitimate, but knowingly creating and supplying false information was not.

The official response to Cochrane's crime was damning. He lost income, political position and social status as he was struck off the navy list, expelled from the Commons, and ejected from the Order of the Bath with ritualistic humiliation: his heraldic banner was torn down from the Chapel of Henry VII in Westminster Abbey and ignominiously kicked down the steps. The public response, however, was very

his ideas on the British government over the next four decades. In response to criticisms that such methods were immoral, he argued that such a plan might save lives by ending conflict more quickly than conventional warfare. Lloyd, *Lord Cochrane*, 105–113.
[75] *Cobbett's Weekly Political Register*, 18 June 1814 (vol. xxv, no 25), col. 771.
[76] David Morier Evans, *The City: or, The Physiology of London Business* (London, 1845), 51–3; John Francis, *Chronicles and Characters of the Stock Exchange* (London, 1855), 300.

different: within a few days of his expulsion from the House he was returned again by the electors of Westminster.[77] He was forthright in pursuing his personal grievances and claims for recompense, and in 1816 brought forward in the House a charge of 'partiality, misrepresentation, injustice and oppression' against Lord Chief Justice Ellenborough, the motion being lost by 89 votes to 0. From 1818 until the 1830s he served with the navies of Chile, Peru, Brazil and Greece, but he maintained a long-running campaign to have his sentence quashed, making lengthy representations to government in 1825 and 1830. His perseverance paid off. In May 1832 he was granted a free pardon and reinstated to his rank of rear-admiral and placed on half pay. In 1841 he was granted a naval pension for meritorious service, in 1847 was restored to the Order of the Bath, and in 1848–51 was appointed Commander-in-Chief of the North American and West Indian station. Not content with this, in 1856 he wrote to Palmerston requesting the restoration of his banner to Henry VII's chapel, repayment of his £1,000 fine, and restoration of half pay for the period 1814–32. This latter claim he bequeathed to his heirs, who in 1877 successfully petitioned for a Select Committee to investigate the claim. This Committee noted that his treatment since 1832 amounted to 'nothing less than a public recognition by those Governments of his innocence', and in the following year the grandson received an ex gratia payment of £5,000 in respect of the 'distinguished services' of his grandfather.[78]

From being the best-known fraudster of his day, Cochrane managed gradually to re-write his personal history and re-invent himself. Although he regained his formal rank and honours, he never became fully accepted by the mid-Victorian elite. He was buried in 1860 in the nave of Westminster Abbey, but no cabinet minister or officer of the state attended the funeral, though his old friend Lord Brougham did.[79] Yet in popular standing Cochrane was a hero rather than a fraud, and his heroism grew over time, finally being lionised in one of G. A.Henty's historical tales.[80] In 1814 he had erred against the laws and morals of the day, but over time the public perception of his crime diminished. To some extent his naval exploits may have atoned for his sins, but attitudes towards commercial morality were changing.

---

[77] For details see A. Aspinall, 'The Westminster election of 1814', *English Historical Review*, xl (1925), 562–9.

[78] Atlay, *Trial*, 241–54, 283–91, 369–77.

[79] J. W. Fortescue, *Dundonald* (London, 1895), 201.

[80] G. A. Henty, *With Cochrane the Dauntless* (London, 1897). Henty makes no reference to the Stock Exchange fraud, but the incident is used as the centrepiece of a more recent novel of naval heroism. See Patrick O'Brian, *The Reverse of the Medal* (London, 1986).

Cochrane's defence was that no crime had been committed. Everyone who traded on the Exchange on 21 February did so voluntarily, and they did so facing the same set of information (this was true of Cochrane's broker, who traded in accordance with explicit price-point instructions he had been given several days beforehand). The conditions on the Stock Exchange were those of perfect Smithian competition – willing buyers, willing sellers, equal access to information and no government interference. Furthermore, the flamboyant actions of de Berenger and the other hoaxers created political rather than financial rumour, and this rumour had an impact on stock prices only because of the credulity or gullibility of other traders who were speculating or gambling on price movements. It was the pursuit of a quick profit by other dealers, rather than anything done by Cochrane, that caused the price of Omnium to rise and then fall. In 1814 a jury of City men found this defence to be inadequate, perhaps because at this date, even within commercial circles, the workings of the Stock Exchange were seen by many as something mysterious and suspicious. Successive cycles of speculative fervour, which emerged in each and every decade throughout the nineteenth century, expanded the social and financial reach of the stock market, and made commonplace that which had been arcane. By the 1840s the financial commentator David Morier Evans felt able to write, with some equanimity, that the majority of stock market trades were 'purely of a gambling nature',[81] and by the 1850s there existed a ready supply of advice to readers of a new genre of investment manuals. One such guidebook, purportedly penned by 'a late MP', was addressed to:

The active, the intelligent, the far-seeing men of the world, of quick eye and energetic grasp of mind; to these we say, the field of enterprise is open to you in the FUNDS, wherein millions of pounds are lost and won *almost daily*, in the RAILWAY SHARE MARKET, a source of gain which has enriched thousands, BANKING SHARES, MINING SHARES, LAND SPECULATION, etc., all these various modes of making money we mean to discuss *seriatim*.[82]

In the 1870s a Royal Commission, established to investigate the practices of the Stock Exchange after many investors lost considerable sums they had committed to foreign loans floated on the exchange, drew a distinction between appropriate and excessive levels of options trading:

It is an undoubted fact that the great facilities afforded by the Stock Exchange for the unlimited purchase or sale of all sorts of securities, coupled with the

---

[81] Evans, *The City*, 37.
[82] Anon. (a late MP), *How to Make Money; or Hints to Speculators* (Birmingham, 1857), 5.

system of making bargains for the 'account', that is, for a future day, open a wide door to mere gambling as well as to legitimate speculation. And where this has been carried to excess or undertaken by people of limited means, frequently with ruinous results to creditors, the blame by many persons is thrown upon the Stock Exchange.[83]

Just as novelists tended to account for financial scandals and defalcations by reference to the character flaws of individuals, this Royal Commission whitewashed the Stock Exchange as an institution, explaining away perceived problems by reference to the excessive desire or limited means of investors. There was a fine line between Victorian perceptions of gambling (immoral, sinful and, depending on the context, illegal) and speculation (robust, reliable and required for the good functioning of any market). Where the dividing line was drawn depended on the circumstances of the observer, and the circumstances of the observed; as the author of an anti-gambling tract published by the Society for the Promotion of Christian Knowledge conceded in 1897, 'it will always be difficult to say where it is exactly that legitimate speculation ends and gambling begins'.[84]

Attempts by religious moralists to define and delineate illegitimate speculation foundered in a sea of inconsistent or illogical definitions. According to the Archdeacon of Westmoreland, 'legitimate speculation submits to no uncertainty except such as is inevitable; it courts no risk', whereas illegitimate speculation or gambling 'traffics in uncertainties. Risk and chance are its chief commodities.'[85] But in practice, as noted in Chapter 2, there never was a risk-free transaction, except in the stylised market of classical economics where buyers and sellers transacted instantly and effortlessly, without the messy encumbrance of contracts which needed to be enforced. All trade was, to some extent, speculative – a gamble on whether market prices would rise or fall, on whether the counter-party would honour the contract. By 1911, when Francis Hirst, editor of *The Economist*, wrote a guide to the Stock Exchange, speculative behaviour was recognised as being ubiquitous: 'even in an old and conservative country like England the average investor is a speculator in the sense that he not only wishes his investment to yield him interest but also hopes and expects that he will some day be able to sell out at a profit. Such an aspiration is perfectly natural and legitimate'.[86]

[83] *Report of the Royal Commission on the Stock Exchange*, PP 1878 XIX, 20.
[84] A. T. Barnett, *Why are Betting and Gambling Wrong?* (London, 1897), 20.
[85] Archdeacon Diggle, *Speculation and Gambling* (London, 1899), 6–7.
[86] F. W. Hirst, *The Stock Exchange* (London, 1911), 164.

Over the course of the nineteenth century the activity of dealing on the Stock Exchange was normalised, legitimised and moralised. Actions that were pejoratively termed 'gambling' in the 1810s were described as 'speculation' by mid-century, and as 'investment' by the century's end.[87] The practice of buying and selling stocks and shares originated with a narrow group of financial insiders, but a series of speculative booms in foreign loans and railway shares in the 1820s, 30s and 40s extended the clientele of the stock market, though it was still primarily confined to a select group of upper-middle-class men of substance. The second half of the century witnessed a rapid expansion of direct share-holding, with the number of private investors rising to reach over 2 per cent of the British population by 1913. This growth was fuelled by the development of financial journalism, by the establishment of a large number of retail stock-brokers in every major city who, from the 1850s, were directly linked to the London Stock Exchange by telegraph, and by a somewhat sceptical popularisation of speculative behaviour through the works of a large number of novelists, playwrights and essayists.

These developments produced a gradual democratisation of share-holding. That which once had been the preserve of the rich and well-connected became an opportunity open to anyone who could pay the entry price. This price was not always what it seemed – something that the 'class of small people' who had invested in the Royal British Bank discovered in 1856 when shareholders were called on to cover the lia-bilities of the failed business. The butlers, household servants, clerks, shopkeepers, artists and publicans who comprised some of the Bank's 280 shareholder had undoubtedly been unwise to make an investment in this unlimited company. Even after the introduction of general lim-ited liability there remained considerable financial exposure attached to the unpaid portion of a company share, until companies began to issue fully paid-up low denomination shares valued at £1 or less.[88] By the 1890s the entry price to the shareholders' club was well within the reach of lower-middle-class households with money to save.

The reduction in the entry price helped fuel an expansion of direct shareholding and the growth of the popular financial press. In turn the wider discourse around stocks, shares and 'companification' came to be reflected in popular culture. For fraudulent company promoters like Harry Marks this democratisation of shareholding provided new

[87] For a discussion of this terminological change see David C. Itzkowitz, 'Fair enter-prise or extravagant speculation: investment, speculation and gambling in Victorian England', *Victorian Studies*, 45 (2002), 121–47.
[88] Jefferys, 'Denomination and character of shares'.

opportunities to extract money from gullible investors. But the majority of capital invested on the stock market was placed in legitimate publicly traded, credit-worthy companies through the offices of honest financial professionals. The increased scale of investment activity created greater liquidity in the share market, which was of benefit to all investors. The greatest benefit, however, was derived by the corporate insiders – the directors and senior managers, the brokers and financial journalists – who could use their privileged access to information to play the market. For them, insider dealing, far from being seen as inappropriate, was simply a perk of the job.

8   Mammon's conceit

In 1906 a group of sixteen leading 'City men' formed the 'Bribery and Secret Commissions Prevention League, Incorporated' to challenge those immoral and illegal commercial practices which they believed to be ubiquitous. *The Times* reported that this action 'represents, and will increasingly represent, the moral sense of the commercial community and the attitude of all that is best in the business world towards a canker that has eaten deeply into the commercial integrity of which this country is justly proud'.[1] Members of the Prevention League actively pursued prosecutions under the 1906 Prevention of Corruption Act, which extended to commercial transactions some of the provisions of the 1889 Public Bodies Corrupt Practices Act, which itself was the legislative response to the bribery and corruption in the Metropolitan Board of Works that had been exposed earlier by Harry Marks in the *Financial News*.[2]

It might be thought that this campaign for moral rectitude in commercial affairs would have targeted the company promoters who knowingly foisted worthless shares on the public, or the financial journalists who 'puffed' companies in return for side payments, or the absentee directors who took money for nothing, or the accountants and auditors who casually certified the financial integrity of companies just weeks before they succumbed to insolvency. But those who were tried and convicted under the Prevention of Corruption Act were of an altogether different character. There was the greengrocer's book-keeper who offered pheasants to the Clerk of the Board of Guardians in order to obtain a supply contract – instead he received a sentence of one month's hard labour. There was the 67-year-old actor who attempted to bribe a football captain to lose a match (five months' imprisonment); the picture theatre proprietor who gave bribes to obtain the use of cinema films

---

[1] Allen Potter, 'Attitude groups', *Political Quarterly*, 29 (1958), 72–82; *The Times* quoted in W. B. Leonard, *Bribery* (London, 1919), 19.

[2] Marks, *Metropolitan Board of Works*.

(six months' imprisonment); the tailor's traveller who offered a porter 3d. per name for a list of hotel visitors (£5 fine plus £10 10s. costs).[3]

It was the small people, untouched by professional accreditation, standards or standing who were to be tamed by this legislation. For the major corporate players, on the other hand, strength of character, rather than force of law or shareholder pressure, was held to be sufficient to sustain probity. For Alfred Marshall it was 'strong proof of the marvellous growth in recent times of a spirit of honesty and uprightness in commercial matters, that the leading officers of great public companies yield as little as they do to the vast temptations to fraud which lie in their way'.[4] And although Marshall was, to a large degree, correct to emphasise the importance of internalised controls in determining behavioural standards in the corporate world, it was also the case that standards and expectations had changed over the course of Victoria's reign. The repetitive cycle of stock market boom and bust, of bank failure, of corporate defalcation, of company puffing, of secure returns that were never realised, of high hopes dashed, had, by the century's end, created a somewhat weary familiarity with the principles of corporate morality.

It was a familiarity that, despite the weariness, was generally not unwelcome. By the 1890s corporate capitalism was part and parcel of the lives of most middle-class households – through investment in publicly traded shares, through employment in public companies, through the daily process of buying and selling goods and services. The railway and insurance company clerks no less than the directors, the widows living off dividend income no less than the bankers and brokers, were direct and beneficial players in this market. For most people, most of the time, the market behaved in a predictable manner and market actors behaved honestly and judiciously. If some of the aspirations and assertions about the benefits of the late-Victorian market were a little overblown, then this could be an opportunity for some self-deprecatory satire – as with Gilbert and Sullivan's *Utopia*.

Yet by the century's end there was also a degree of cynicism about the morality of market relationships. The concern was not that the majority of businessmen and bankers were dishonest – they were not. Rather it was that it seemed increasingly difficult to distinguish between honest and disreputable behaviour, and to hold those responsible for dishonesty to account. In the 1830s there had been little ambiguity about the accountability of businessmen or investors. Partners in an enterprise

---

[3] Albert Crew, *Bribes and Bribery in Business* (London, 1916), 40–52.
[4] Marshall, *Principles*, Book IV, ch. 12, s. 4.

shared to an unlimited extent the risks of failure and the rewards of success. Investors in an unlimited company underwrote all the liabilities of the firm. By the 1890s limited liability incorporation had interposed the 'corporate personality' of the company between shareholders and directors, between directors and managers, between the firm and its trading partners. But the corporate personality was not subject to either guilt or retribution, and could not be consigned to hell or to jail. Directors, in particular, repeatedly displayed an unwillingness to accept responsibility for corporate insolvency. When the Royal British Bank collapsed in 1856, this abdication of responsibility was so widely condemned that the government took it upon itself to prosecute the directors. The Commissioner for Bankruptcy at the time remarked that in public bodies such as joint-stock companies, 'the disgrace of error or even criminality of conduct belongs to so many that no-one is shamed of the part which belongs to himself ... responsibility becomes infinitesimal by division'.[5] By 1896, when the *Salomon* v. *Salomon and Co.* case was finally resolved by the House of Lords, the abdication of directorial responsibility had become a legally entrenched attribute of the corporate economy, regardless of whether the 'disgrace of error' belonged to many directors or to one only. The final and complete separation of the entity of the corporation from the individuals who populated that entity created a terrain of moral ambiguity in which corporate activity took place.

This moral ambiguity was unsettling for, but ultimately accepted by, Victorian society. In the 1870s, when Trollope was plotting the career of his predatory capitalist Melmotte, his readers expected a satisfyingly retributive denouement. They were served up the treat of suicide as Melmotte's speculative and partly fraudulent empire collapsed around him. Three decades later one of the most popular novels of 1899, *The Market-Place* by Harold Frederic – a 'very brilliant piece of work' according to *The Spectator* – offered a very different (im)moral tale. The principal character, Thorpe, lies and cheats his way to fortune by exploiting the avarice and gullibility of investors and by cornering the market, but rather than condemnation or prosecution, he ascends through high society. At the close of the novel he decides to become a philanthropist, but his motivation is not compassion for the plight of the poor, or shame at his own duplicitous past. Rather it is to accumulate yet more power, with the ultimate goal to 'rule England'.[6]

---

[5] *The Times*, 15 May 1857, 11.
[6] Harold Frederic, *The Market-Place* (London, 1899). For details of the popular response to this novel see Austin Briggs, *The Novels of Harold Frederic* (Ithaca, NY, 1969), 176–85.

Thorpe found ways of working the stock market to extract profit from the avarice of others without having to exhaust the capital of his personal reputation – a trick that ultimately eluded Melmotte. Yet in less dramatic ways this was the goal of many investors in the Victorian stock market. In mid century such ambition was deemed unseemly. In 1857 *The Economist* castigated the naivety of investors: 'The public, always unreasoning and generally unreasonable, want the security of Consols without submitting to the low interest – they want the high profits of speculating business without incurring the risk attending them, and without taking the labour and trouble of looking after them.'[7] By 1911, however, the editor of *The Economist*, Francis Hirst, described the speculative ambition of the average investor for capital gains as 'perfectly natural and legitimate'.[8]

The moral ambiguity of corporate capitalism in late-Victorian Britain was not a conscious construct. At no point in Victoria's reign did politicians, judges, businessmen, financiers or political economists devise a master plan in which the institutional building blocks of this capitalist system were sketched out. Nor was there much sense that institutional change was driven by a process of competitive evolution in which the more useful and effective laws and institutions crowded out the ineffective and redundant. Chapters 4 and 5 showed that general incorporation and limited liability were introduced almost by accident in 1844 and 1856 respectively, and received far from universal support from commercial and financial commentators. Corporate law was repeatedly refined after each large-scale crisis or fraud, but despite these refinements, corporations in Victorian Britain operated in conditions of almost complete lack of accountability and transparency. Chapter 2 showed that bankruptcy legislation fluctuated between *dirigiste* and *laissez-faire* approaches across the course of the century, but never managed significantly to reduce the cost of administration or increase the average dividend to creditors. Simultaneously, the process for recovering small debts from workers was massively simplified and streamlined, but was kept quite separate from bankruptcy proceedings, with the result that workers paid a much larger share of their debts than did traders.

In every case of institutional change and legal reform, a multiplicity of ideas and proposals were on offer, and the outcomes owed a good deal to chance, political whim, and the exercise of pressure group interests. It is difficult to demonstrate that these outcomes facilitated the operation of the Victorian market by reducing costs and increasing

[7] *The Economist*, 1 January 185, quoted in Taylor, 'Company fraud', 713.
[8] Hirst, *Stock Exchange*, 164

efficiency. In fact, in the case of limited liability incorporation in the life insurance market, the evidence presented in Chapter 6 suggests that, on balance, the limited companies operated with higher costs and lower returns to policyholders than did mutuals. It is also apparent that market agents found ways to accommodate significant changes to the rules and technologies that governed economic activity without fundamentally altering their behaviour. Chapter 3 demonstrated that neither the mechanisation of textile production, nor the repeal of Master and Servant legislation, led to any major change in age-related wage payments in the textile industry; employers were locked in to a path-dependent structure of remuneration which they had to work around but could not transform. Chapter 3 also revealed the massive bias in favour of employers that existed, up to 1875, in the structure of labour contracts, a bias that was unnoticed, or at least unacknowledged, by the great majority of economists and legal theorists who wrote expansively about the merits of a free and fair labour market.

The corporate economy of Victorian Britain was based on a set of legal institutions and behavioural norms that were created, developed, amended and extended throughout the nineteenth century. There were many decision points when new rules were introduced or new interpretations of existing rules implemented, and at every decision point a variety of options were available to the law makers, judges, businessmen, financiers and economists who had the primary responsibility for setting the parameters within which the corporate economy operated. In its performance this economy appeared to be quite resilient to change in specific institutional detail; markets are extremely adaptable. Individuals, partnerships and companies found ways of writing and enforcing necessary commercial and employment contracts regardless of the prevailing legal framework. To be sure, some of the legal work-arounds involved high costs – such as the use by unincorporated companies of trust law to undertake collective actions. On the other hand, the way in which general incorporation was implemented – with little transparency for shareholders or accountability for directors – also involved costs. The scale and incidence of the costs and benefits arising from different institutional manifestations of the corporate economy were seldom articulated in contemporary discussion, and have been given little consideration in subsequent historical and economic analysis.

There can be no doubt that in some cases institutional structures were deliberately formed to serve the interests of particular groups. For example, Kostal has demonstrated that much of the regulatory complexity surrounding the formation of railway companies was deliberately designed by lawyers to allow the legal profession to extract huge fees.[9] It was more common, however, to find a diversity of opinion among judges and legislators about any proposed innovation or amendment to the institutional structures of corporate capitalism. At the beginning of Victoria's reign this diversity of opinion extended to fundamental questions about the legal and moral legitimacy of the reified corporation which permitted individuals to hide behind the corporate veil. By the end of the nineteenth century the debate was largely confined to pragmatic issues about how corporate entities should be regulated. No doubt the intertwining of the corporate world with legislature and judiciary, particularly through the widespread take-up of company directorships by members of the House of Lords and House of Commons, contributed to the more accommodating stance to the corporate economy adopted by courts and parliament over the course of the nineteenth century. It was seldom the case, however, that corporate legislation followed a linear path advocated by a powerful and self-aware pressure group. Although the legal framework for debt recovery and for the enforcement of labour contracts clearly favoured the interests of traders and employers above those of workers, this was more because of implicit beliefs held by legislators and judges about working-class morality and behaviour than the outcome of pressure group action. The legal framework regulating companies – their formation, operation and winding-up – was less transparent in its biases, and the relative advantage for the various stakeholders – the owners, shareholders, directors and trading partners – waxed and waned over time. But there was never any dominant interest that managed to secure advantage on top of advantage. In fact, as the Royal Commission on Mercantile Laws made clear, it was quite common for members of commercial interest groups and associations to express completely divergent views about the preferred framework of corporate law.

The manner by which the institutions of the corporate economy were formed in nineteenth-century Britain must serve as a challenge to rationalistic evolutionary models of institutional formation, in which efficient structures dominate through a process of institutional competition. This model has underpinned much modern institutional economics, though it has more often been an implicit rather than an explicit assumption. Since the construction of the Anglo-American global economic order after the Second World War, and with increasing vigour since the collapse of the Soviet regime in the late 1980s, a largely unspoken assumption – perhaps a conceit – of neo-classical economics

---

[9] See Chapter 4 above, and Kostal, *Railway Capitalism*.

has been that the moral ambiguities of western corporate capitalism should be of little concern, because the structure delivers beneficent results, in terms of profits, economic growth and rising personal living standards. The global financial crisis that emerged in 2008 has given pause for thought as the moral basis of finance capitalism has been called into question in a manner not seen since the Victorian period. Many of the contentious issues of propriety and responsibility that were aired in the mid-nineteenth century – the role of directors and the value of the services they deliver to their companies, the rights of shareholders to be kept fully informed, the legitimacy of incentive payments, the capacity of 'time bargains' to destabilise financial markets, the need for and effectiveness of corporate regulation – have re-emerged as topics for urgent consideration.

If the structure of corporate capitalism that existed in 2008 is viewed not as a finely-honed, efficient, maximising set of rules and institutions that evolved through a process of competitive survival, but instead as a somewhat accidental but path-dependent outcome of complex historical processes, then it becomes evident that different decisions made at key turning points in the past could have generated different outcomes today. It is worth outlining some plausible historical counterfactuals, because they may shed some light on the issues of corporate governance and market regulation that are now uppermost in the mind of all western governments.

Imagine that instead of being repealed in 1868, Barnard's Act, which rendered illegal the 'mischievous practice' of dealing in 'time bargains', had been rigorously enforced, and then strengthened over time. The entire business of option contracts in commodity and stock markets would have been terminated. This would have imposed significant costs on some economic actors, and no doubt alternative institutional forms would have emerged to meet the market need for futures contracts. But there would then have been none of the hand-wringing about the insidious effect of naked short selling that emerged in the latter part of 2008.

Imagine that the critique made almost two centuries ago, in 1811, of the payment by insurance companies of up-front commissions to agents who sold their products had led to the same punitive legislative response that the 1906 Prevention of Corruption Act served up to small businessmen and traders who offered secret commissions. The entire structure of commission-based selling of financial products would have been undermined, and the financial services industry would undoubtedly have developed more slowly. On the other hand, if commissions had been rendered illegal, there would in all likelihood have been no sub-prime mortgage fiasco. The sale of these mortgages to clients who had little prospect of meeting long-term repayment obligations was driven by the opportunity to extract substantial up-front sales commissions, as was the packaging of these mortgages by investment banks into collateralised debt obligations.

Imagine that corporations formed with limited liability for shareholders and unlimited liability for directors – an almost entirely neglected element of the 1867 Joint Stock Companies Act – had become the norm through legislative fiat. This might, at first, have led to massive flight from directorial positions, but in due course an insurance market for directors' liability would have emerged. In order to evaluate the risk of insolvency, insurers would have needed to audit rigorously each company, and through the insurance contract could have placed prudential requirements on directors far in excess of those imposed by company legislation.

These, and many more, nineteenth-century developmental byways remind us that the market was – and still is in the early twenty-first century – a constructed, not a natural and neutral phenomenon. It can be shaped and reshaped by legislation, by judicial decision, by collective beliefs and moral understandings, by political pressures and economic incentives, by ideas, philosophies and enthusiasm. The form of the market can be deliberately designed or can emerge through happenchance, through the accidental confluence of multiple influences which produce unanticipated – sometimes unwanted – outcomes. Though the propensity to truck, barter and exchange may, as Adam Smith claimed, be innate, the *locus* for this activity, the market, is a human construct of intriguing complexity and constant change. The reluctance of economists from Smith, Marshall and beyond to recognise and embrace this messy complexity has done little to detract from the long-term rise of economics as a formalistic social science. But it has created an evaluative gap between professional economic science and popular experience of economic behaviour, in which trade and exchange is a relational activity, occurring within a specific legal, institutional and moral context. As today's commentators pick over the carcass of the global financial system, and pose questions that would have been familiar to their Victorian forebears – questions about self-interest and greed, about individual and corporate responsibility, about the need for and effectiveness of regulation, about commercial morality – we begin to realise how little we understand what we thought we knew about the market.

Bibliography

PARLIAMENTARY PAPERS

Report of the Select Committee on the Weavers' Petition, PP 1810–11 ii, 1.

Fifth Report of the Commissioners on the Courts of Common Law, PP 1833 (247).

Report on the Law of Partnership by Mr Bellenden Ker, reprinted as Appendix I of the *First Report of the Select Committee on Joint Stock Companies*, PP 1844 vii.

Select Committee on Investments for the Savings of the Middle and Working Classes, PP 1850 xix.

Select Committee on the Law of Partnership, PP 1851 xviii.

House of Lords Select Committee on the Bankruptcy Bill, PP 1852–3 xxii.

Royal Commission on the Assimilation of Mercantile Laws in the UK and Amendments in the Law of Partnership, as Regards the Question of Limited or Unlimited Responsibility, PP 1854 xxvii.

Select Committee on the State of the Laws as Regards Contracts of Service between Master and Servant, PP 1865 viii and 1866 xiii.

Return of the Questions Addressed by the Committee of County Court Judges to the Judges of Those Courts, on County Court Commitments, PP 1867 lvii.

Select Committee on Imprisonment for Debt, PP 1873 xv.

Select Committee on the Companies Acts 1862 and 1867, PP 1877 viii.

Report of the Royal Commission on the Stock Exchange, PP 1878 xix.

Report of the Chief Registrar of Friendly Societies for 1880. Part IIB, app. I pp 1883 lxviii.

Report on the Royal Liver Friendly Society, PP 1886 lxi.

Select Committee on the Friendly Societies Act, appendix 1. PP 1889 x.

House of Lords Select Committee on the Debtors Act, PP 1893–4 (HL) ix.

Report on Company Law Amendment Act, [Cd 3052], 1906 xcvii.

Annual Return Relating to Joint Stock Companies for 1906, PP 1907 lxxvi.

Select Committee on Debtors (Imprisonment) PP 1909 vii.

NEWSPAPERS AND PERIODICALS

Berkshire Chronicle
Cobbett's Weekly Political Register
County Courts Chronicle
The Economist
Financial News
Gore's Directory for Liverpool

Halifax Guardian
The Investors' Guardian
Investors' Review
Liverpool Mercury
Liverpool Review
The Times

BOOKS AND ARTICLES

A Member of the Institute of Actuaries, *The Government Annuities Bill: A letter to the Rt. Hon. W.E. Gladstone*, London, 1864.

A Practical Jobber. *The System of Stock-Jobbing Explained*, London, 1816.

Abel-Smith, B. and Stevens, R. *Lawyers and the Courts: A Sociological Study of the English Legal System, 1750–1965*, London, 1967.

Addison, C. G. *A Treatise on the Law of Contracts and Parties to Actions ex contractu*, London, 1845.

Aitken, J. *Pride and Perjury*, London, 2000.

Alborn, T. 'The moral of the failed bank: professional plots in the Victorian money market', *Victorian Studies*, **38**, 199–226, 1995.
 Conceiving Companies: Joint-Stock Politics in Victorian England, London, 1998.

Alchian, A. and Demsetz, H. 'Production, information costs, and economic organisation', *American Economic Review*, **57**, 777–95, 1972.

Allen, J. *Where Shall I Get the Most for My Money?*, London, 1880.

Amsler, C. E., Bartlett, R. L. and Bolton, C. J. 'Thoughts of some British economists on early limited liability and corporate legislation', *History of Political Economy*, **13**, 774–93, 1981.

Anderson, G. M. and Tollison, R. D. 'Adam Smith's analysis of joint-stock companies', *Journal of Political Economy*, **90**, 1237–56, 1982.

Anon. *The Calumnious Aspersions Contained in the Report of the Sub-Committee of the Stock-Exchange Exposed and Refuted*, London, 1814.

Anon. *The Case of Thomas Lord Cochrane*, Edinburgh, 1814.

Anon. *Letter to the Electors of Westminster on the Case of Lord Cochrane*, London, 1814.

Anon. *The Trial of Lord Cochrane*, London, 1814.

Anon. *How to Make Money; or Hints to Speculators*, Birmingham, 1857.

Anon. *Responsibilities of Directors and Promoters*, London, 1873.

Anson, Sir W. R. *Principles of the English Law of Contract*, Oxford, 1879.

Arthurs, H. W. '"Without the law": courts of local and special jurisdiction in nineteenth century England', *Journal of Legal History*, **5**, 130–49, 1984.

Aspinall, A. 'The Westminster election of 1814', *English Historical Review*, **xl**, 562–9, 1925.

Atiyah, P. S. *The Rise and Fall of Freedom of Contract*, Oxford, 1979.

Atlay, J. B. *The Trial of Lord Cochrane before Lord Ellenborough*, London, 1897.

Babbage, C. *A Comparative View of the Various Institutions for the Assurance of Lives*, London, 1826.

Baily, F. *An Account of the Several Life Assurance Companies Established in London*, London, 1811.

Bain, G. and Price, R. *Profiles of Union Growth*, Oxford, 1980.

Bakan, J. *The Corporation: The Pathological Pursuit of Profit and Power*, London, 2004.

Banks, J.A. 'The way they lived then: Anthony Trollope and the 1870s', *Victorian Studies*, **12**, 177–200, 1968.

Barber, B. 'Absolutization of the market: some notes on how we got from here to there'. In G. Dworkin, G. Bermant and P. G. Brown (eds.), *Markets and Morals*, Washington, DC, 15–31, 1977.

Barnett, A. T. *Why are Betting and Gambling Wrong?*, London, 1897.

Barrister, A. *Overend, Gurney & Co. (Limited): A Plain Statement of the Case*, London, 1867.

Barton, J. L. 'The enforcement of hard bargains', *Law Quarterly Review*, **103**, 1987.

Baskin, J. B. and Miranti, P. J. *A History of Corporate Finance*, Cambridge, 1997.

Bennett, A. 'The fire of London'. In his *The Loot of the Cities*, London, 1905.

Berg, M. 'What difference did women's work make to the Industrial Revolution?', *History Workshop*, **35**, 22–44, 1993.

Berle, A. A. and Means, G. C. *The Modern Corporation and Private Property*, New York, 1933.

Biagini, E. F. 1987, 'British trade unions and popular political economy, 1860–1880', *Historical Journal*, **30**, 811–40, 1987.

Liberty, Retrenchment and Reform: Popular Liberalism in the Age of Gladstone, 1860–1880, Cambridge, 1993.

Black, B. 'Age and earnings'. In M. B. Gregory and A. W. J. Thomson, *A Portrait of Pay, 1970–1982: An Analysis of the New Earnings Survey*, Oxford, 274–98, 1990.

Blackstone, Sir W. *Commentaries on the Laws of England*, Oxford, 1865–9.

Blaug, M. *Economic Theory in Retrospect*, London, 1964.

Boose, M.A. 'Agency theory and alternative predictions for life insurers: an empirical test', *Journal of Risk and Insurance*, **57**, 499–518, 1990.

Boot, H.M. and Maindonald, J.H. 'New estimates of age- and sex-specific earnings and the male-female earnings gap in the British cotton industry, 1833–1906', *Economic History Review*, **61**, 380–408, 2008.

Bourne, K. *Palmerston: The Early Years 1784–1841*, London, 1982.

Bower, T. *Maxwell: The Outsider*, London, 1988.

Maxwell: The Final Verdict, London, 1995.

Briggs, A. *The Novels of Harold Frederic*, Ithaca, NY, 1969.

Brooks, C. *Lawyers, Litigation and English Society since 1450*, London, 1998.

Bryer, R.A. 'The late nineteenth-century revolution in financial reporting: Accounting for the rise of investor or managerial capitalism?', *Accounting, Organizations and Society*, **18**, 649–90, 1993.

'The Mercantile Laws Commission of 1854 and the political economy of limited liability', *Economic History Review*, **50**, 37–56, 1997.

Bunyon, C.J. *On the Liquidation of an Insolvent Life Office*, London, 1870.

Burnette, J. 'An investigation of the female-male wage gap during the industrial revolution in Britain', *Economic History Review*, **50**, 257–81, 1997.

Gender, Work and Wages in Industrial Revolution Britain, Cambridge, 2008.

Cain, G. G. 'The economic analysis of labor market discrimination: a survey'. In O. Ashenfelter and R. Layard (eds.), *Handbook of Labor Economics,* vol. 1, Amsterdam, 693–785, 1986.

Cairnes, J. E. *Some Leading Principles of Political Economy,* London, 1874.

Capaldi, N. *John Stuart Mill: A Biography,* Cambridge, 2004.

Carr-Saunders, A. M. and Wilson, P. A. *The Professions,* Oxford, 1933.

Chadwick, E. 'Results of different principles of legislation and administration in Europe, of competition for the field, as compared with competition within the field, of service', *Journal of the Statistical Society of London,* **22,** 381–420, 1859.

Chandler, A. *The Visible Hand: The Managerial Revolution in American Business,* Cambridge, MA, 1977.

Cheffins, B. 'History and the global corporate governance revolution: the UK perspective', *Business History,* **43,** 87–118, 2001.

Chiozza Money, L. G. *Riches and Poverty,* London, 1906.

Christie, R. *Letter to the Right Hon. Joseph W. Henley, M.P., Regarding Life Assurance Institutions,* Edinburgh, 1852.

Clapham, J. H. *An Economic History of Modern Britain, vol. II: Free Trade and Steel,* Cambridge, 1926.

The Bank of England: A History, Cambridge, 1944.

Clements, R. V. 'British trade unions and popular political economy, 1850–1875', *Economic History review,* **14,** 93–104, 1961–2.

Cocks, R. C. J. *Sir Henry Maine,* Cambridge, 1988.

Cohen, J. 'The history of imprisonment for debt and its relation to the development of discharge in bankruptcy', *Journal of Legal History,* **3,** 153–71, 1982.

Colvin, A. *Actuarial Figments Exploded: A Letter to the Right Hon. J.W. Henley, M.P., in Defence of Life Assurance Offices,* London, 1852.

Conley, C. A. *The Unwritten Law: Criminal Justice in Victorian Kent,* New York, 1991.

Cooke, C. A. *Corporation, Trust and Company,* Manchester, 1950.

Corley, T. A. B. *Quaker Enterprise in Biscuits: Huntley and Palmers of Reading, 1822–1972,* London, 1972.

Cornish, W. R. and Clark, G. de N. *Law and Society in England, 1750–1950,* London, 1989.

Cottrell, P. L. *Industrial Finance, 1830–1914,* London, 1980.

Cox, E. W. *The New Law and Practice of Joint Stock Companies with and without Limited Liability,* 4th edn., London, 1857.

Cracroft, B. 'Analysis of the House of Commons in 1867'. In his *Essays, Political and Miscellaneous,* London, 1868.

Crew, A. *Bribes and Bribery in Business,* London, 1916.

Cummins, J. D., Rubio-Misas, J. D. and Zi, H. 'The effect of organizational structure on efficiency: evidence from the Spanish insurance industry', *Journal of Banking and Finance,* **28,** 3113–50, 2004.

Cummins, J. D., Weiss, M. A. and Zi, H. 'Organizational form and efficiency: an analysis of stock and mutual property-liability insurers', *Management Science,* **45,** 1245–69, 1999.

David, P. A. 'Clio and the economics of QWERTY', *American Economic Review,* **75,** 332–7, 1985.

'Path dependence, its critics and the quest for "historical economics"'. In
P. Garrouste and S. Ioannides (eds.), *Evolution and Path Dependence in
Economic Ideas*, Cheltenham, 15–40, 2001.

De Berenger, C. R. *The Noble Stock Jobber*, London, 1816.

Deakin, S. and Wilkinson, F. *The Law of the Labour Market*, Oxford, 2005.

Dennett, L. *A Sense of Security: 150 years of Prudential*, Cambridge, 1998.

Dent, G. M. *A Dialogue Showing How to Select a Life Office*, Manchester, 1888.
How to Select a Life Office, London, 1897.

Derry, T. K. 'The repeal of the apprenticeship clauses of the Statute of
Apprentices', *Economic History Review*, **3**, 67–87, 1931.

Dicey, A. V. *Lectures on the Relation between Law and Public Opinion During
England in the Nineteenth Century*, London, 1905.

Dickens, C. *Dombey and Son*, London, 1848.

Diggle, Archdeacon. *Speculation and Gambling*, London, 1899.

Directory of Directors for 1898, London, 1898.

Dod, C. R. *Electoral Facts from 1832 to 1853*, London, 1853.

Doeringer, P. and Piore, M. *Internal Labor Markets and Manpower Analysis*,
Lexington, MA, 1971.

Duguid, C. *How to Read the Money Article*, London, 1901.
The Story of the Stock Exchange, London, 1901.

Dunlavy, C. 'From citizens to plutocrats: nineteenth-century shareholder voting rights and theories of incorporation'. In K. Lipartito and D. Sicilia
(eds.), *Constructing Corporate America: History, Politics, Culture*, Oxford,
66–93, 2004.

Dutton, H. I. and King, J. E. *'Ten Per Cent and No Surrender': The Preston Strike,
1853–1854*, Cambridge, 1981.
'The limits of paternalism: the cotton tyrants of North Lancashire, 1836–
54', *Social History*, 7, 59–74, 1982.

Eastwood, D. 'Tories and markets, 1800–1850'. In M. Bevir and F. Trentmann
(eds.), *Markets in Historical contexts*, Cambridge, 70–89, 2004.

Eden, Sir F. *On the Policy and Expediency of Granting Insurance Charters*,
London, 1806.

Edey, H. C. and Panitpakdi, P. 'British company accounting and the law, 1844–
1900'. In A. C. Littleton and B. S. Yamey (eds.), *Studies in the History of
Accounting*, Homewood, IL, 1956.

Edgar, A. 'On the jurisdiction of Justices of the Peace in disputes between
employers and employed arising from breach of contract', *Transactions of
the National Association for the Promotion of Social Science, 1859*, London,
1860.

Edwards, J. R. *A History of Financial Accounting*, London, 1980.
'Companies, corporations and accounting change, 1835–1933: a comparative study', *Accounting and Business Research*, **23**, 59–73, 1992.

Elliott, G. *The Mystery of Overend and Gurney: Adventures in the Victorian
Financial Underworld*, London, 2006.

English, H. *A Complete View of the Joint Stock Companies formed during 1824 and
1825*, London, 1827.

Equity, and Law Life Assurance Society. *Prospectus*, London, 1891.

Essex-Crosby, A. 'Joint-stock companies in Great Britain 1890–1930',
M.Comm thesis, University of London, 1938.

Evans, D. M. *The City: or, The Physiology of London Business*, London, 1845.
  The Commercial Crisis of 1847–8, London, 1848.
  Facts, Failures and Frauds: Revelations Financial, Mercantile, Criminal,
    London, 1859.
Feinstein, C. H. 'The rise and fall of the Williamson curve', *Journal of Economic
    History*, **48**, 699–729, 1988.
  'New estimates of average earnings in the United Kingdom, 1880–1913',
    Economic History Review, **43**, 595–632, 1990.
Ferguson, R. B. 'The adjudication of commercial disputes and the legal system
    in modern England', *British Journal of Law and Society*, **7**, 141–57, 1980.
Finn, M. 'Being in debt in Dickens' London: fact, fictional representation and the
    nineteenth-century prison', *Journal of Victorian Culture*, **1**, 203–36, 1996.
  'Women, consumption and coverture in England, c. 1760–1960', *Historical
    Journal*, **39**, 703–22, 1996.
  'Scotch drapers and the politics of modernity: gender, class and national-
    ity in the Victorian tally trade'. In M. Daunton and M. Hilton (eds.),
    *The Politics of Consumption: Material Culture and Citizenship in Europe and
    America*, London, 89–107, 2001.
  'Victorian law, literature and history: three ships passing in the night',
    Journal of Victorian Culture, **7**, 134–46, 2002.
  The Character of Credit: Personal Debt in English Culture, 1740–1914, Cambridge,
    2003.
Floud, R. and Johnson, P. *The Cambridge Economic History of Modern Britain*, 3
    vols., Cambridge, 2004.
Floud, R. and McCloskey, D. *The Economic History of Britain since 1700*, 2 vols.,
    Cambridge, 1981.
  The Economic History of Britain Since 1700, 2nd edn., 3 vols., Cambridge,
    1994.
Foreman-Peck, J. and Millward, R. *Public and Private Ownership of British
    Industry, 1820–1990*, Oxford, 1994.
Formoy, R. R. *The Historical Foundation of Modern Company Law*, London, 1923.
Fortescue, J. W. *Dundonald*, London, 1895.
Fox, A. *A History of the National Union of Boot and Shoe Operatives, 1874–1957*,
    Oxford, 1958.
Francis, J. *Chronicles and Characters of the Stock Exchange*, London, 1855.
Frederic, H. *The Market-Place*, London, 1899.
Freeman, M., Pearson, R. and Taylor, J. 'Technological change and the gov-
    ernance of joint-stock enterprise in the early nineteenth century: the case
    of coastal shipping', *Business History*, **49**, 573–94, 2007.
Freifeld, M. 'Technological change and the "self-acting" mule: a study of skill
    and the sexual division of labour', *Social History*, **11**, 319–43, 1986.
Frow, E. and Katanka, M. *1868: Year of the Unions*, London, 1968.
Gambles, A. *Protection and Politics: Conservative Economic Discourse, 1815–1852*,
    Woodbridge, 1999.
Garnett, E. J. 'Aspects of the relationship between protestant ethics and economic
    activity in mid-Victorian England,' Oxford University D.Phil thesis, 1986.
Getzler, J. and Macnair, M. 'The firm as an entity before the Companies Acts'.
    In P. Brand, K. Costello and W. N. Osborough, *Adventures of the Law*,
    Dublin, 267–88, 2005.

Getzler, J. 'The role of security over future and circulating capital: evidence from the British economy *circa* 1850–1920'. In J. Getzler and J. Payne (eds.), *Company Charges: Spectrum and Beyond*, Oxford, 227–51, 2006.

Gilmore, C. and Willmott, H. 'Company law and financial reporting: a sociological history of the UK experience'. In M. Bromwich and A. Hopwood (eds.), *Accounting and the Law*, London, 159–190, 1992.

Gordon, R. 'Critical legal histories', *Stanford Law Review* **36**, 57–125, 1984.

Gore, C. *The Banker's Wife*, London, 1843.

Granovetter, M. 'Economic action and social structure: the problem of embeddedness', *American Journal of Sociology*, **91**, 481–510, 1985.

Grossmith, G. and W. *The Diary of a Nobody*, Bristol, 1892.

Guinnane, T., Harris, R., Lamoreaux, N. and Rosenthal, J-L. 'Putting the corporation in its place', *Enterprise and Society*, **8**, 687–729, 2007.

Gurney, W.B. *The Trial of Charles Random de Berenger, Taken in Shorthand*, London, 1814.

Habgood, W. *Chartered Accountants in England and Wales: A Guide to Historical Records*, Manchester, 1994.

Haig, J.C. 'The case of Thanet, illustrating the methods of Mr H. H. Marks'. In C. R. Buxton, *Electioneering Up-to-Date*, London, 1906.

Haines, J. *Maxwell*, London, 1988.

Hall, N.J. *Trollope: A Biography*, Oxford, 1991.

Hannah, L. *The Rise of the Corporate Economy*, 2nd edn., London, 1983.

'Pioneering modern corporate governance: a view from London in 1900', *Enterprise and Society*, **8**, 642–86, 2007.

Hansmann, H. *The Ownership of Enterprise*, Cambridge, MA, 1996.

Harling, P. *The Waning of 'Old Corruption'*, Oxford, 1996.

Harris, R. *Industrializing English Law: Entrepreneurship and Business Organisation 1720–1844*, Cambridge, 2000.

'The encounters of economic history and legal history', *Law and History Review*, **21**, 297–346, 2003.

Harrison, F. *Imprisonment for Breach of Contract, or, the Master and Servant Act*, Tracts for Trade unionists, no. 1, London, 1874.

Hart, O.D. 'Incomplete contracts and the theory of the firm'. In O.E. Williamson and S.G. Winter (eds.), *The Nature of the Firm*, Oxford, 138–58, 1991.

Hay, D. 'Property, authority and the criminal law'. In D. Hay, P. Linebaugh, J. Rule, E.P. Thompson and C. Winslow (eds.), *Albion's Fatal Tree*, Harmondsworth, 1977.

'Master and servant in England; using the law in the eighteenth and nineteenth centuries'. In W. Steinmetz (ed.), *Private Law and Social Inequality in the Industrial Age*, Oxford, 227–64, 2000.

Hedley, S. 'The "needs of commercial litigants" in nineteenth and twentieth century contract law', *Legal History*, **18**, 85–90, 1997.

Henty, G.A. *With Cochrane the Dauntless*, London, 1897.

Hess, H. *'The Critic' Black Book*, London, 1901–2.

Hilton, B. *The Age of Atonement: The Influence of Evangelicalism on Social and Economic Thought, 1785–1865*, Oxford, 1988.

Hilton, M. *Consumerism in Twentieth-Century Britain*, Cambridge, 2003.

Hirst, F. W. *The Stock Exchange*, London, 1911.

Hobsbawm, E. J. *Labouring Men*, London, 1964.

Holcombe, L. *Wives and Property: Reform of the Married Women's Property Law in Nineteenth-Century England*, Toronto, 1983.

Hollander, S. *The Economics of David Ricardo*, London, 1979.

Honoré, A. 'Ownership'. In A. G. Guest (ed.), *Oxford Essays in Jurisprudence* Oxford, 107–47, 1961.

Hoppen, K. T. *The Mid-Victorian Generation, 1846–1886*, Oxford, 1998.

Hoppit, J. 'The use and abuse of credit in eighteenth-century England'. In R. B. Outhwaite and N. McKendrick (eds.), *Business Life and Public Policy*, Cambridge, 64–78, 1986.

Risk and Failure in English Business, 1700–1800, Cambridge, 1987.

Howell, G. *A Handy-Book of Labour Laws*, London, 1867.

Huberman, M. *Escape from the Market*, Cambridge, 1996.

Hudson, P. *The Genesis of Industrial Capital: A Study of the West Riding Wool Textile Industry, c. 1750–1850*, Cambridge, 1986.

Humphries, J. '"…The most free from objection…": the sexual division of labour and women's work in nineteenth-century England', *Journal of Economic History*, **47**, 929–49, 1987.

Hunt, B. C. *The Development of the Business Corporation in England, 1800–1867*, Cambridge, MA, 1936.

Hunt, E. H. *Regional Wage Variation in Britain, 1850–1914*, Oxford, 1973.

British Labour History, 1815–1914, London, 1981.

'Industrialization and regional inequality: wages in Britain, 1760–1914', *Journal of Economic History*, **46**, 935–66, 1986.

Innes, J. 'Prisons for the poor: English Bridewells 1555–1800'. In F. Snyder and D. Hay (eds.), *Labour, Law and Crime: An Historical Perspective*, London, 42–122, 1987.

Insurance Mail Yearbook, London, 1908.

Ireland, P. 'The rise of the limited liability company', *International Journal of the Sociology of Law*, **12**, 239–60, 1984.

'Capitalism without the capitalist: the joint stock company share and the emergence of the modern doctrine of separate corporate personality', *Journal of Legal History*, **17**, 41–73, 1996.

Itzkowitz, D. C. 'Fair enterprise or extravagant speculation: investment, speculation and gambling in Victorian England', *Victorian Studies*, **45**, 121–47, 2002.

Jackson, R. V. 'The structure of pay in nineteenth-century Britain', *Economic History Review*, **40**, 561–70, 1987.

Jaycee, *Public Companies: From the Cradle to the Grave*, London, 1883.

Jefferys, J. B. 'Trends in Business Organisation in Great Britain since 1856', PhD thesis, University of London, 1938.

'The denomination and character of shares, 1855–1885', *Economic History Review*, **16**, 45–55, 1946.

Jensen, M. and Meckling, W. 'Theory of the firm: managerial behavior, agency costs and capital structure', *Journal of Financial Economics*, **3**, 305–60, 1976.

Johnson, P. *Saving and Spending: The Working-Class Economy in Britain 1870–1939*, Oxford, 1985.

'Class law in Victorian England', *Past and Present*, **141**, 147–69, 1993.

'Small debts and economic distress in England and Wales, 1857–1913', *Economic History Review*, **46**, 65–87, 1993.

'Age, gender and the wage in Britain, 1830–1930'. In P. Scholliers and L. Schwartz (eds.), *Experiencing Wages*, Oxford, 229–49, 2003.

'Market discipline'. In P. Mandler (ed.), *Liberty and Authority in Victorian England*, Oxford, 203–23, 2006.

Johnson, P. and Zaidi, A. 'Work over the life course'. In N. F. R. Crafts, I. Gazeley and A. Newell (eds.), *Work and Pay in Twentieth-Century Britain*, Oxford, 98–116, 2007.

Jones, E. *Accountancy and the British Economy 1840–1980: The Evolution of Ernst and Whinney*, London, 1981.

Jones, S. and Aiken, M. 'British companies legislation and social and political evolution during the nineteenth century' *British Accounting Review*, **27**, 61–82, 1995.

Jordan, E. 'The lady clerks at the Prudential: the beginning of vertical segretation by sex in clerical work in nineteenth-century Britain', *Gender and History*, **8**, 65–81, 1996.

Judd, D. *Palmerston*, London, 1975.

Katz, L. F. and Autor, D. H. 'Changes in the wage structure and earnings inequality'. In O. Ashenfelter and D. Card (eds.), *Handbook of Labor Economics*, vol. 3A, Amsterdam, 1463–555, 1999.

Kay, J. 'The Stakeholder Corporation'. In G. Kelly, D. Kelly and A. Gamble (eds.), *Stakeholder Capitalism*, Basingstoke, 125–141, 1997.

Kelman, M. *A Guide to Critical Legal Studies*, Cambridge, MA, 1990.

Kent, D. A. 'Small businessmen and their credit transactions in early nineteenth-century Britain', *Business History*, **36**, 47–64, 1994.

Kirk, N. *Labour and Society in Britain and America*, Aldershot, 1994.

Kostal, R. W. *Law and English Railway Capitalism, 1825–1875*, Oxford, 1994.

Koten, D. C. *The Post-Corporate World*, West Hartford, CT, 1998.

Krippner, G. R. 'The elusive market: embeddedness and the paradigm of economic sociology', *Theory and Society*, **30**, 775–810, 2001.

La Porta, R., Lopez-de-Silanes, F., Schleifer, A. and Vishny, R. 'Legal determinants of external finance', *Journal of Finance*, **52**, 1131–50, 1997.

'Law and finance', *Journal of Political Economy*, **106**, 1133–55, 1998.

Lamoreaux, N. R. 'Constructing firms: partnerships and alternative contractual arrangements in early nineteenth century American business', *Business and Economic History*, **24**, 43–71, 1995.

Lavington, F. *The English Capital Market*, London, 1929.

Law, E. D. *The Guilt of Lord Cochrane*, London, 1914.

Law, H. S. *Reviews of the 'Autobiography of a Seaman'*, London, 1877.

Lester, V. M. *Victorian Insolvency*, Oxford, 1995.

Leonard, W. B. *Bribery*, London, 1919.

Leventhal, F. M. *Respectable Radical: George Howell and Victorian Working Class Politics*, London, 1971.

Levi, L. 'On the abolition of imprisonment for debt', *Law Magazine and Review*, **3**, 1847.

'On joint stock companies', *Journal of the Statistical Society*, **33**, 1–41, 1870.

'The progress of joint stock companies with limited and unlimited liability in the United Kingdom, during the fifteen years 1869–84', *Journal of the Statistical Society of London*, **49**, 241–72, 1886.

Lieberman, D. 'Contract before "freedom of contract"'. In H. N. Scheiber (ed.), *The State and Freedom of Contract*, Stanford, 1998.

Liebowitz, S. and Margolis, S. 'The fable of the keys', *Journal of Law and Economics*, **33**, 1–25, 1990.

'Path dependence, lock-in, and history', *Journal of Law, Economics, and Organization*, **11**, 205–26, 1995.

Lindley, N. *A Treatise on the Law of Companies Considered as a Branch of the Law of Partnership*, London, 1891.

Lloyd, C. *Lord Cochrane*, London, 1947.

Lobban, M. *The Common Law and English Jurisprudence, 1760–1850*, Oxford, 1991.

Loftus, D. 'Capital and community: limited liability and attempts to democratize the market in mid nineteenth-century England', *Victorian Studies*, **45**, 93–120, 2002.

Longe, F. D. *A Refutation of the Wages Fund Theory of Modern Political Economy, as Enunciated by Mr Mill and Mr Fawcett*, London, 1866.

Lowe, R. *Speech on the Amendment of the Law of Partnership and Joint Stock Companies*, London, 1856.

Lown, J. *Women and Industrialization: Gender at Work in Nineteenth-Century England*, Cambridge, 1990.

MacDonagh, O. 'The Nineteenth Century Revolution in Government: A Reappraisal', *Historical Journal*, **1**, 52–67, 1958.

Mahoney, J. 'Path dependence in historical sociology', *Theory and Society*, **29**, 507–48, 2000.

Maine, Sir H. *Ancient Law*, London, 1861.

Maitland, F. W. *State, Trust and Corporation*, D. Runciman and M. Ryan (eds.), Cambridge, 2003.

Manchester, A. H. *A Modern Legal History of England and Wales*, London, 1980.

Mann, J. de L. *The Cloth Industry in the West of England from 1640 to 1880*, Oxford, 1971.

Marcet, J. *Conversation on Political Economy in which Elements of that Science are Familiarly Explained*, London, 1816.

Marks, H. *The Metropolitan Board of Works: A Brief Account of the Disclosures which Have Led to the Appointment of a Royal Commission*, London, 1888.

Marshall, A. *Principles of Economics*, London, 1890.

Industry and Trade: a Study of Industrial Technique and Business Organization, London, 1919.

Martin, R. M. *TUC: The Growth of a Pressure Group, 1868–1976*, Oxford, 1980.

Martineau, H. 'The Manchester Strike', *Illustrations of Political Economy*, London, 1832.

Matthew, H. C. G. *Gladstone 1809–1874*, Oxford, 1986.

McCulloch, J. R. *Considerations on Partnership with Limited Liability*, London, 1856.

McIvor, A. J. *Organised Capital: Employers' Associations and Industrial Relations in Northern England, 1880–1939*, Cambridge, 1996.

Men and Women of the Time, London, 1899.

Michie, R. *The London Stock Exchange: A History*, Oxford, 1999 and 2001.

Micklethwait, J. and Wooldridge, A. *The Company*, London, 2003.

Mill, J. *Elements of Political Economy*, London, 1821.

Mill, J. S. *Principles of Political Economy*, London, 1848.

'Thornton on Labour and its claims', *Fortnightly Review*, May, 517–8, 1869.

Mincer, J. *Schooling, Experience and Earnings*, New York, 1974.

Mitchell, L. *Corporate Irresponsibility: America's Newest Export*, New Haven, 2001.

Morgan, E. V. and Thomas, W. A. *The Stock Exchange: Its History and Functions*, London, 1962.

Morris, R. J. *Class, Sect and Party: The Making of the British Middle Class, Leeds 1820–1850*, London, 1990.

Muldrew, C. *The Economy of Obligation: The Culture of Credit and Social Relations in Early Modern England*, Basingstoke, 1998.

Mullen, R. *Anthony Trollope: A Victorian and His World*, London, 1990.

Napier, C. and Noke, C. 'Accounting and law; an historical overview of an uneasy relationship'. In M. Bromwich and A. Hopwood (eds.), *Accounting and the Law*, Hemel Hempstead, 30–54, 1992.

Nelson, R. R. and Winter, S. *An Evolutionary Theory of Economic Change*, Cambridge, MA, 1982.

North, D. 'Institutions and Economic Performance'. In U. Maki, B. Gustafsson and C. Knudson (eds.), *Rationality, Institutions and Economic Methodology*, London, 242–61, 1993.

O'Brian, P. *The Reverse of the Medal*, London, 1986.

O'Brien, D. P. *The Classical Economists*, Oxford, 1975.

Oldham, J. 'Special juries in England: nineteenth-century usage and reform'. *Journal of Legal History*, **8**, 148–66, 1987.

Orth, J. V. *Combination and Conspiracy: A Legal History of Trade Unionism 1721–1906*, Oxford, 1991.

Oxford Dictionary of National Biography, Oxford, 2004.

Parris, H. 'The nineteenth century revolution in government: a reappraisal reappraised', *Historical Journal*, **3**, 17–37, 1960.

Pearson, R. 'Mutuality tested: the rise and fall of mutual fire insurance offices in eighteenth-century London', *Business History*, **44**, 1–28, 2002.

'Shareholder democracies? English stock companies and the politics of corporate governance during the Industrial Revolution', *English Historical Review*, cxvii, 840–66, 2002.

Phelps Brown, E. H. and Hopkins, S. V. 'Seven centuries of building wages', *Economica*, **22**, 195–206, 1955.

Phelps Brown, E. H. 'The labour market'. In T. Wilson and A. S. Skinner, *The Market and the State*, Oxford, 1976.

Phillips, D. 'Black Country Magistracy 1835–60', *Midland History*, **3**, 161–90, 1975–6.

Phillips, G. and Whiteside, N. *Casual Labour: The Unemployment Question in the Port Transport Industry 1880–1970*, Oxford, 1985.

Pierson, P. 'Increasing returns, path dependence, and the study of politics', *American Political Science Review*, **94**, 251–67, 2000.

'Not just what, but *when*: timing and sequence in political processes', *Studies in American Political Development*, **14**, 72–92, 2000.

Polden, P. 'Judicial Selkirks: the county court judges and the press, 1847–80'. In C. W. Brooks and M. Lobban (eds.), *Communities and Courts in Britain 1150–1900*, London, 245–62, 1997.

A History of the County Court 1846–1971, Cambridge, 1999.

Pollock, F. *Principles of Contract at Law and in Equity*, London, 1876.

Poovey, M. 'Writing about finance in Victorian England: disclosure and secrecy in the culture of investment', *Victorian Studies*, **45**, 17–41, 2002.

The Financial System in Nineteenth-Century Britain, Oxford, 2003.

Porter, D. '"A trusted guide of the investing public": Harry Marks and the *Financial News*, 1884–1916'. In R. P. T. Davenport-Hines (ed.), *Speculators and Patriots: Essays in Business Biography*, London, 1986.

Posner, R. A. *Economic Analysis of Law*, Boston, 1972.

Potter, A. 'Attitude groups', *Political Quarterly*, **29**, 72–82, 1958.

Pottier, S. and Sommer, D. W. 'Agency theory and life insurer ownership structure', *Journal of Risk and Insurance*, **64**, 529–43, 1997.

Puffert, D. 'The standardization of track gauge on North American railways, 1830–1890', *Journal of Economic History*, **60**, 933–60, 2000.

Randall, A. 'Work, culture and resistance to machinery in the West of England woollen industry'. In P. Hudson (ed.), *Regions and Industries*, Cambridge, 175–200, 1989.

Reddy, W. M. *The Rise of Market Culture: the Textile Trade and French Society, 1750–1900*, Cambridge, 1984.

Redford, A. *Manchester Merchants and Foreign Trade: 1794–1858*, Manchester, 1934.

Reid, A. J. 'Old unionism reconsidered: the radicalism of Robert Knight, 1870–1900'. In E. F. Biagini and A. J. Reid (eds.), *Currents of Radicalism: Popular Radicalism, Organised Labour and Party Politics in Britain, 1850–1914*, Cambridge, 214–43, 1991.

Ricardo, D. *On the Principles of Political Economy and Taxation*, London, 1817.

Richardson, R. J. 'Exposure of the banking and funding system', *The English Chartist Circular: The Temperance Record for England and Wales* 1.23 (1841), 90–1.

Ridley, J. *The Young Disraeli*, London, 1995.

Robb, G. *White-Collar Crime in Modern England: Financial Fraud and Business Morality, 1845–1929*, Cambridge, 1992.

Roe, M. *Strong Managers, Weak Owners: The Political Roots of American Corporate Finance*, Princeton, 1994.

Rose, S. *Limited Livelihoods: Gender and Class in Nineteenth-Century England*, Berkeley, 1992.

Rosen, S. 'The theory of equalizing differences'. In O. Ashenfelter and R. Layard (eds.), *Handbook of Labor Economics*, vol. 1, Amsterdam, 641–92, 1987.

Royal British Bank. *Prospectus*, Goldsmiths' Library, London, 1849.

Rubin, G. R. 'The county courts and the tally trade, 1846–1914'. In G. Rubin and D. Sugarman (eds.), *Law, Economy and Society, 1750–1914*, Abingdon, 321–48, 1984.

  'Law, Poverty and Imprisonment for Debt, 1869–1914'. In G. R. Rubin and D. Sugarman (eds.), *Law, Economy and Society, 1750–1914*, Abingdon, 241–99, 1984.

Russell, N. *The Novelist and Mammon*, Oxford, 1986.

Rutherford, M. 'Predatory practices or reasonable values? American Institutionalists on the nature of market transactions'. In N. De Marchi and M. Morgan (eds.), *Higgling: Transactors and their Markets in the History of Economics*. Annual Supplement to vol. 26 of *History of Political Economy* (Durham, NC, 1994), 253–75, 1994.

Samuel, H. B. *Shareholders' Money*, London, 1933.

Saul, S. B. *The Myth of the Great Depression, 1873–96*, London, 1985.

Saville, J. 'Sleeping partnerships and limited liability, 1850–1856', *Economic History Review*, **8**, 418–33, 1956.

Scott, W. R. *The Constitution and Finance of English, Scottish and Irish Joint-Stock Companies to 1720*, Cambridge University Press, 1910–12.

Sealy, L. S. *Company Law and Commercial Reality*, London, 1984.

Searle, G. R. *Morality and the Market in Victorian Britain*, Oxford, 1998.

Senior, N. *An Outline of the Science of Political Economy*, London, 1836.

Shannon, H. A. 'The coming of general limited liability', *Economic History*, 2, 267–91, 1931, reprinted in E. M. Carus-Wilson (ed.), *Essays in Economic History*, London, 1954, 358–79.

  'The first five thousand limited companies and their duration', *Economic History*, **2**, 396–424, 1932.

  'The limited companies of 1866–83', *Economic History Review*, **4**, 290–316, 1933.

  'Review of H. B. Samuel, "Shareholders' Money"', *Economica*, November, 507–9, 1933.

Shannon, R. *The Age of Disraeli, 1868–1881: The Rise of Tory Democracy*, London, 1992.

Sharpe, P. 'Continuity and change: women's history and economic history in Britain', *Economic History Review*, **48**, 353–69, 1995.

Shaw, C. 'The large manufacturing employers of 1907', *Business History*, **25**, 42–59, 1983.

Sheldrake, J. *Municipal Socialism*, Aldershot, 1989.

Simon, D. 'Master and Servant'. In J. Saville (ed.), *Democracy and the Labour Movement Essays in honour of Dona Torr*, London, 160–200, 1954.

Simpson, A. W. B. *A History of the Common Law of Contract*, Oxford, 1975.

  Leading Cases in the Common Law, Oxford, 1995.

Smith, A. *An Inquiry into the Nature and Causes of the Wealth of Nations*. In R. H. Campbell and A. S. Skinner (eds.), Oxford, 1976 [1776].

Smith, H. 'The resurgent County Court in Victorian Britain', *American Journal of Legal History*, **13**, 126–38, 1969.

Snagge, Sir T. *The Evolution of the County Court*, London, 14, 1904.

Snyder, F. and Hay, D. (eds.), *Labour, Law and Crime*, London, 1987.

Southall, H. 'The origins of the depressed areas: unemployment, growth, and regional economic structure in Britain before 1914', *Economic History Review*, **41**, 236–58, 1988.

Southall, H. and Gilbert, D. 'A good time to wed?: marriage and economic distress in England and Wales, 1839–1914', *Economic History Review*, **49**, 35–57, 1996.

Spain, J. 'Trade unionists, Gladstonian Liberals and the labour law reforms of 1875'. In E. F. Biagiani and A. J. Reid (eds.), *Currents of Radicalism*, Cambridge, 109–33, 1991.

Spencer, H. *The Man versus The State*, Indianopolis, 1981 [1884].

Spensley, C. *Twelve Hundred Facts about 'Ordinary' Life Assurance Offices*, Bradford, 1901.

Statist, *All About Assurance*, London, 1904.

Steinfeld, R. *Coercion, Contract, and Free Labor in the Nineteenth Century*, Cambridge, 2001.

Steinmetz, W. 'Was there a de-juridification of individual employment relations in Britain?' In W. Steinmetz (ed.), *Private Law and Social Inequality in the Industrial Age*, Oxford, 265–312, 2000.

Stenton, M. *Who's Who of British Members of Parliament, vol. 1: 1832–1885*, Hassocks, 1976.

Stinchcombe, A. 'Social structure and the founding of organizations'. In his *Stratification and Organisation*, Cambridge, 196–220, 1986.

Stock Exchange, *Report of the Sub-Committee of the Stock Exchange Relative to the Late Fraud*, London, 1814.

Storrar, A. C. and Pratt, K. C. 'Accountability vs privacy, 1844–1907: the coming of the private company', *Accounting, Business and Financial History* **10**, 259–91, 2000.

Sugarman, D. and Rubin, G. R. 'Towards a new history of law and material society in England, 1750–1914'. In G. R. Rubin and D. Sugarman (eds.), *Law, Economy and society, 1750–1914: Essays in the History of English Law*, Abingdon, 1–123, 1984.

Sugarman, D. 'A hatred of disorder: legal science, liberalism and imperialism'. In P. Fitzpatrick (ed.), *Dangerous Supplements: Resistance and Renewal in Jurisprudence*, London, 34–67, 1991.

'Simple images and complex realities: English lawyers and their relationship to business and politics, 1750–1950', *Law and History Review*, **11**, 257–301, 1993.

'Who colonised whom? Historical reflections on the intersection between law, lawyers and accountants in England'. In Y. Dezalay and D. Sugarman (eds.), *Professional Competition and Professional Power: Lawyers, Accountants and the Social Construction of Markets*, London, 226–37, 1995.

Supple, B. *The Royal Exchange Assurance: A History of British Insurance 1720–1970*, Cambridge, 1970.

Swiney, W. *A Letter to the Rt. Hon. Benjamin D'Israeli Respecting Certain Life Assurance Companies*, London, 1852.

Taussig, F. W. *Wages and Capital: An Examination of the Wages Fund Doctrine*, London, 1896.

Taylor, J. 'Private property, public interest, and the role of the state in nineteenth-century Britain: the case of the lighthouses', *Historical Journal*, **44**, 749–71, 2001.

'"Wealth makes worship": attitudes to joint stock enterprise in British law, politics and culture, c. 1800–c. 1870', University of Kent PhD thesis, 2002.

Creating Capitalism: Joint-Stock Enterprise in British Politics and Culture, 1800–1870, Woodbridge, 2006.

'Company fraud in Victorian Britain: the Royal British Bank scandal of 1856'. *English Historical Review*, **122**, 700–24, 2007.

Terloc, T. L. *Life Assurance: As It Is, and As It Should Be*, Birmingham, 1887.

Thackeray, 'The history of Samuel Titmarsh and the Great Hoggarty Diamond', *Fraser's Magazine*, September–December, 1841.

The Joint-Stock Companies Directory, 1866, London, 1866.

Thomas, 10th Earl of Dundonald, *Autobiography of a Seaman*, London, 1860.

Thomas, 11th earl of Dundonald and H. R. Fox Bourne, *Life of Thomas, 10th Earl of Dundonald, Completing the Autobiography of a Seaman*, 2 vols., London, 1869.

Thompson, E. P. 'Time, work-discipline and industrial capitalism', *Past and Present*, **38**, 56–97, 1967.

Whigs and Hunters, London, 1975.

'The moral economy reviewed'. In his *Customs in Common*, London, 259–351, 1993.

Thompson, P. and Delano A. *Maxwell: A Portrait of Power*, London, 1991.

Thornton, W. *On Labour: Its Wrongful Claims and Rightful Dues, Its Actual Present and Possible Future*, London, 1869.

Todd, G. 'Some aspects of joint stock companies, 1844–1900', *Economic History Review*, **4**, 46–71, 1932.

Trainor, R. H. *Black Country Elites: The Exercise of Authority in an Industrial Area, 1830–1900*, Oxford, 1993.

Trebilcock, C. *Phoenix Assurance and the Development of British Insurance, vol. 1: 1782–1870*, Cambridge, 1985.

Treble, J. H. 'The record of the Standard Life Assurance Company in the life assurance market of the United Kingdom, 1850–64'. In O. M. Westall (ed.), *The Historian and the Business of Insurance*, Manchester, 1984.

Tressell, R. *The Ragged Trousered Philanthropists*, London, 1965 [1914].

Trollope, A. *The Way We Live Now*, London, 1994 [1875].

Turkel, G. 'Michel Foucault: Law, power, knowledge', *Journal of Law and Society*, **17**, 170–93, 1990.

Valenze, D. *The First Industrial Woman*, Oxford, 1995.

van Helton, J. J. 'Mining, share manias and speculation: British investment in overseas mining, 1880–1913'. In J. J. van Helton and Y. Cassis (eds.), *Capitalism in a Mature Economy*, Aldershot, 159–85, 1990.

Verdon, N. *Rural Women Workers in Nineteenth-Century England: Gender, Work and Wages*, Woodbridge, 2002.

Vint, J. *Capital and Wages: A Lakatosian History of the Wages Fund Doctrine*, Aldershot, 1994.

Walker, J. D. and Watson. *Investors' and Shareholders' Guide*, Edinburgh, 1894.

Walker, S. P. 'Laissez-faire, collectivism and companies legislation in nineteenth century Britain', *British Accounting Review*, **28**, 305–24, 1996.

Webb, S. and B. *History of Trade Unionism*, London, 1898.

Weintraub, S. *Disraeli: A Biography*, London, 1993.

Weiss, B. *The Hell of the English*, Lewisburg, 1986.

Wermel, M. T. *The Evolution of Classical Wage Theory*, New York, 1939.

Whately, R. *Introductory Lectures on Political Economy*, London, 1832.

Williamson, J. G. 'The structure of pay in Britain, 1710–1911', *Research in Economic History*, **7**, 1982.

Did British Capitalism Breed Inequality?, London, 1985.

Williamson, O. *The Economic Institutions of Capitalism*, London, 1987.

Wilson, A. J. *Plain Advice About Life Insurance*, London, 1898.

Wilson, J. F. *British Business History, 1720–1994*, Manchester, 1995.

Winch, D. *Adam Smith's Politics*, Cambridge, 1978.

Wohl, A. S. *Endangered Lives*, London, 1983.

Woods, D. C. 'The operation of the Master and Servant Acts in the Black Country, 1858–1875', *Midland History*, 7, 93–115, 1982.

Woodward, D. 'The determination of wage rates in the early modern north of England', *Economic History Review*, 47, 22–43, 1994.

Wright, T. *Our New Masters*, London, 1873.

Index